Mark Twain

# The 1,000,000 pounds bank-note and other new stories

Mark Twain

**The 1,000,000 pounds bank-note and other new stories**

ISBN/EAN: 9783337111038

Printed in Europe, USA, Canada, Australia, Japan

Cover: Foto ©Suzi / pixelio.de

More available books at **www.hansebooks.com**

# THE
# £1,000,000 BANK-NOTE

*AND OTHER NEW STORIES*

BY

MARK TWAIN

London
CHATTO & WINDUS, PICCADILLY
1893

# CONTENTS

WHEN I was twenty-seven years old, I was a mining-broker's clerk in San Francisco, and an expert in all the details of stock traffic. I was alone in the world, and had nothing to depend upon but my wits and a clean reputation; but these were setting my feet in the road to eventual fortune, and I was content with the prospect.

My time was my own after the afternoon board, Saturdays, and I was accustomed to put it in on a little sail-boat on the bay. One day I ventured too far, and was carried out to sea. Just at nightfall, when hope was about gone, I was picked up by a small brig which was bound for London. It was a long and stormy voyage, and they made me work my passage without pay, as a common sailor. When I stepped ashore in London my clothes were ragged and shabby, and I had only a dollar in my pocket. This money fed and

B

sheltered me twenty-four hours.  During the next twenty-four I went without food and shelter.

About ten o'clock on the following morning, seedy and hungry, I was dragging myself along Portland Place, when a child that was passing, towed by a nursemaid, tossed a luscious big pear— minus one bite—into the gutter.  I stopped, of course, and fastened my desiring eye on that muddy treasure.  My mouth watered for it, my stomach craved it, my whole being begged for it.  But every time I made a move to get it some passing eye detected my purpose, and of course I straightened up, then, and looked indifferent, and pretended that I hadn't been thinking about the pear at all.  This same thing kept happening and happening, and I couldn't get the pear.  I was just getting desperate enough to brave all the shame, and to seize it, when a window behind me was raised, and a gentleman spoke out of it, saying :

' Step in here, please.'

I was admitted by a gorgeous flunkey, and shown into a sumptuous room where a couple of elderly gentlemen were sitting.  They sent away the servant, and made me sit down.  They had just finished their breakfast, and the sight of the remains of it almost overpowered me. I could hardly keep my wits together in the presence of that food, but as I was not asked to sample it, I had to bear my trouble as best I could.

Now, something had been happening there a little before, which I did not know anything about until a good many days afterwards, but I will tell you about it now. Those two old brothers had been having a pretty hot argument a couple of days before, and had ended by agreeing to decide it by a bet, which is the English way of settling everything.

You will remember that the Bank of England once issued two notes of a million pounds each, to be used for a special purpose connected with some public transaction with a foreign country. For some reason or other only one of these had been used and cancelled; the other still lay in the vaults of the Bank. Well, the brothers, chatting along, happened to get to wondering what might be the fate of a perfectly honest and intelligent stranger who should be turned adrift in London without a friend, and with no money but that million-pound bank-note, and no way to account for his being in possession of it. Brother A said he would starve to death; Brother B said he wouldn't. Brother A said he couldn't offer it at a bank or anywhere else, because he would be arrested on the spot. So they went on disputing till Brother B said he would bet twenty thousand pounds that the man would live thirty days, *any way*, on that million, and keep out of jail, too. Brother A took him up. Brother B went down to the Bank and bought that note. Just like an Englishman, you see; pluck to the backbone. Then he dictated a letter, which one of his clerks wrote out in a beautiful round hand, and then the two brothers sat at the window a whole day watching for the right man to give it to.

They saw many honest faces go by that were not intelligent enough; many that were intelligent but not honest enough; many that were both, but the possessors were not poor enough, or, if poor enough, were not strangers. There was always a defect, until I came along; but they agreed that I filled the bill all around; so they elected me unanimously, and there I was, now, waiting to know why I was called in. They began to ask me questions about myself, and pretty soon they had my story. Finally they told me I would answer their purpose. I said I was sincerely glad, and asked what it was. Then one of them handed me an envelope, and said I would find the explanation inside. I was going to open it, but he said no; take it to my lodgings, and look it over carefully, and not be hasty or rash. I was puzzled, and wanted to discuss the matter a little further, but they didn't; so I took my leave, feeling hurt and insulted to be made the butt of what was apparently some kind of a practical joke, and yet obliged to put up with it, not being in circumstances to resent affronts from rich and strong folk.

I would have picked up the pear, now, and eaten it before all the world, but it was gone; so I had lost that by this unlucky business, and the thought of it did not soften my feeling towards those men. As soon as I was out of sight of that house I opened my envelope, and saw that it contained money! My opinion of those people changed, I can tell you! I lost not a moment, but shoved note and money into my vest-pocket, and broke for the nearest cheap eating-house. Well, how I did eat! When at last I couldn't hold any more, I took out my money and unfolded it, took one glimpse and nearly fainted. Five millions of dollars! Why, it made my head swim.

I must have sat there stunned and blinking at the note as much as a minute before I came rightly to myself again. The first thing I noticed, then, was the landlord. His eye was on the note, and he was petrified. He was worshipping, with all his body and soul, but he looked as if he couldn't stir hand or foot. I took my cue in a moment, and did the only rational thing there was to do. I reached the note towards him, and said carelessly:

'Give me the change, please.'

Then he was restored to his normal condition, and made a thousand apologies for not being able to break the bill, and I couldn't get him to touch it. He wanted to look at it, and keep on looking at it; he couldn't seem to get enough of it to quench the thirst of his eye, but he shrank from touching it as if it had been something too sacred for poor common clay to handle. I said:

'I am sorry if it is an inconvenience, but I must insist. Please change it; I haven't anything else.'

But he said that wasn't any matter; he was quite willing to let the trifle stand over till another time. I said I might not be in his neighbourhood again for a good while; but he said it was of no consequence, he could wait, and, moreover, I could have anything I wanted, any time I chose, and let the account run as long as I pleased. He said he hoped he wasn't afraid to trust as rich a gentleman as I was, merely because I was of a merry disposition, and chose to play larks on the public in the matter of dress.  By this time another customer was entering, and the landlord hinted to me to put the monster out of sight;  then he bowed me all the way to the door, and I started straight for that house and those brothers, to correct the mistake which had been made before the police should hunt me up, and help me do it.  I was pretty nervous, in fact pretty badly frightened, though, of course, I was no way in fault; but I knew men well enough to know that when they find they've given a tramp a million-pound bill when they thought it was a one-pounder, they are in a frantic rage against *him* instead of quarrelling with their own near-sightedness, as they ought.  As I approached the house my excitement began to abate, for all was quiet there, which made me feel pretty sure the blunder was not discovered yet.  I rang.  The same servant appeared.  I asked for those gentlemen.

'They are gone.'  This in the lofty, cold way of that fellow's tribe.

'Gone?  Gone where?'

'On a journey.'

'But whereabouts?'

'To the Continent, I think.'

'The Continent?'

'Yes, sir.'

'Which way—by what route?'

'I can't say, sir.'

'When will they be back?'

'In a month, they said.'

'A month! Oh, this is awful! Give me *some* sort of idea of how to get a word to them. It's of the last importance.'

'I can't, indeed. I've no idea where they've gone, sir.'

'Then I must see some member of the family.'

'Family's away too; been abroad months—in Egypt and India, I think.'

'Man, there's been an immense mistake made. They'll be back before night. Will you tell them I've been here, and that I will keep coming till it's all made right, and they needn't be afraid?'

'I'll tell them, if they come back, but I am not expecting them. They said you would be here in an hour to make inquiries, but I must tell you it's all right, they'll be here on time and expect you.'

So I had to give it up and go away. What a riddle it all was! I was like to lose my mind. They would be here 'on time.' What could that mean? Oh, the letter would explain, maybe. I had forgotten the letter; I got it out and read it. This is what it said:

'You are an intelligent and honest man, as one may see by your face. We conceive you to be poor and a stranger. Inclosed you will find a sum of money. It is lent to you for thirty days, without interest. Report at this house at the end of that time. I have a bet on you. If I win it you shall have any situation that is in my gift—any, that is, that you shall be able to prove yourself familiar with and competent to fill.'

No signature, no address, no date.

Well, here was a coil to be in! You are posted on what had preceded all this, but I was not. It was just a deep, dark puzzle to me. I hadn't the least idea what the game was, nor whether harm was meant me or a kindness. I went into a park, and sat down to try to think it out, and to consider what I had best do.

At the end of an hour, my reasonings had crystallised into this verdict.

Maybe those men mean me well, maybe they mean me ill; no way to decide that—let it go. They've got a game, or a scheme, or an experiment of some kind on hand; no way to determine what

it is—let it go. There's a bet on me; no way to
find out what it is—let it go. That disposes of the
indeterminable quantities; the remainder of the
matter is tangible, solid, and may be classed and
labelled with certainty. If I ask the Bank of
England to place this bill to the credit of the man
it belongs to, they'll do it, for they know him,
although I don't; but they will ask me how I
came in possession of it, and if I tell the truth,
they'll put me in the asylum, naturally, and a lie
will land me in jail. The same result would follow
if I tried to bank the bill anywhere or to borrow
money on it. I have got to carry this immense
burden around until those men come back, whether
I want to or not. It is useless to me, as useless as
a handful of ashes, and yet I must take care of it,
and watch over it, while I beg my living. I
couldn't *give* it away, if I should try, for neither
honest citizen nor highwayman would accept it or
meddle with it for anything. Those brothers are
safe. Even if I lose their bill, or burn it, they are
still safe, because they can stop payment, and the
Bank will make them whole; but meantime, I've
got to do a month's suffering without wages or
profit—unless I help win that bet, whatever it may
be, and get that situation that I am promised. I

*should* like to get that; men of their sort have situations in their gift that are worth having.

I got to thinking a good deal about that situation. My hopes began to rise high. Without doubt the salary would be large. It would begin in a month; after that I should be all right. Pretty soon I was feeling first-rate. By this time I was tramping the streets again. The sight of a tailor-shop gave me a sharp longing to shed my rags, and to clothe myself decently once more. Could I afford it? No; I had nothing in the world but a million pounds. So I forced myself to go on by. But soon I was drifting back again. The temptation persecuted me cruelly. I must have passed that shop back and forth six times during that manful struggle. At last I gave in; I had to. I asked if they had a misfit suit that had been thrown on their hands. The fellow I spoke to nodded his head towards another fellow, and gave me no answer. I went to the indicated fellow, and he indicated another fellow with *his* head, and no words. I went to him, and he said:

' 'Tend to you presently.'

I waited till he was done with what he was at, then he took me into a back room, and overhauled a pile of rejected suits, and selected the rattiest one for me.  I put it on.  It didn't fit, and wasn't in any way attractive, but it was new, and I was anxious to have it; so I didn't find any fault, but said with some diffidence :

'It would be an accommodation to me if you could wait some days for the money.  I haven't any small change about me.'

The fellow worked up a most sarcastic expression of countenance, and said :

'Oh, you haven't?  Well, of course, I didn't expect it.  I'd only expect gentlemen like you to carry large change.'

I was nettled, and said :

'My friend, you shouldn't judge a stranger always by the clothes he wears.  I am quite able to pay for this suit; I simply didn't wish to put you to the trouble of changing a large note.'

He modified his style a little at that, and said, though still with something of an air :

' I didn't mean any particular harm, but as long as rebukes are going, I might say it wasn't quite your affair to jump to the conclusion that we couldn't change any note that you might happen to be carrying around.  On the contrary, we *can*.'

I handed the note to him, and said :

'Oh, very well ; I apologise.'

He received it with a smile, one of those large smiles which goes all around over, and has folds in it, and wrinkles, and spirals, and looks like the place where you have thrown a brick in a pond; and then in the act of his taking a glimpse of the bill this smile froze solid, and turned yellow, and looked like those wavy, wormy spreads of lava which you find hardened on little levels on the side of Vesuvius. I never before saw a smile caught like that, and perpetuated. The man stood there holding the bill, and looking like that, and the proprietor hustled up to see what was the matter, and said briskly:

'Well, what's up? what's the trouble? what's wanting?'

I said, 'There isn't any trouble. I'm waiting for my change.'

'Come, come; get him his change, Tod; get him his change.'

Tod retorted: 'Get him his change! It's easy to say, sir; but look at the bill yourself.'

The proprietor took a look, gave a low, eloquent whistle, then made a dive for the pile of rejected clothing, and began to snatch it this way and that, talking all the time excitedly, and as if to himself:

'Sell an eccentric millionaire such an unspeakable suit as that! Tod's a fool—a born fool. Always doing something like this. Drives every millionaire away from this place, because he can't tell a millionaire from a tramp, and never could. Ah, here's the thing I'm after. Please get those things off, sir, and throw them in the fire. Do me the favour to put on this shirt and this suit; it's just the thing, the very thing—plain, rich, modest, and just ducally nobby; made to order for a foreign prince—you may know him, sir, his Serene Highness the Hospodar of Halifax; had to leave it with us and take a mourning-suit because his mother was going to die—which she didn't. But that's all right; we can't always have things the way we— that is, the way they—there! trousers all right, they fit you to a charm, sir; now the waistcoat: aha, right again! now the coat—lord! look at that, now! Perfect, the whole thing! I never saw such a triumph in all my experience.'

I expressed my satisfaction.

' Quite right, sir, quite right; it'll do for a makeshift, I'm bound to say. But wait till you see what we'll get up for you on your own measure. Come, Tod, book and pen; get at it. Length of leg, 32' —and so on. Before I could get in a word he had measured me, and was giving orders for dress-suits, morning suits, shirts, and all sorts of things. When I got a chance I said :

'But, my dear sir, I *can't* give these orders, unless you can wait indefinitely, or change the bill.'

'Indefinitely! It's a weak word, sir, a weak word. Eternally—*that's* the word, sir. Tod, rush these things through, and send them to the gentleman's address without any waste of time. Let the minor customers wait. Set down the gentleman's address and——'

'I'm changing my quarters. I will drop in and leave the new address.'

'Quite right, sir, quite right. One moment—let me show you out, sir. There—good day, sir, good day.'

Well, don't you see what was bound to happen? I drifted naturally into buying whatever I wanted, and asking for change. Within a week I was sumptuously equipped with all needful comforts and luxuries, and was housed in an expensive private hotel in Hanover Square. I took my dinners there, but for breakfast I stuck by Harris's humble feeding-house, where I had got my first meal on my million-pound bill. I was the making of Harris. The fact had gone all abroad that the foreign crank who carried million-pound bills in his vest-pocket was the patron saint of the place. That was enough. From being a poor, struggling, little hand-to-mouth enterprise, it had become celebrated, and overcrowded with customers. Harris was so grateful that he forced loans upon me, and would not be denied; and so, pauper as I was, I had money to spend, and was living like the rich and the great. I judged that there was going to be a crash by and by, but I was in, now, and must swim across or drown. You see there was just that element of impending disaster to give a serious side, a sober side, yes, a tragic side, to a state of things which would otherwise have been purely ridiculous. In the night, in the dark, the tragedy part was always to the front, and always warning, always threatening; and so I moaned and tossed, and sleep was hard to find. But in the cheerful daylight the tragedy element faded out and disappeared, and I walked on air, and was happy to giddiness, to intoxication, you may say.

And it was natural; for I had become one of the notorieties of the metropolis of the world, and it turned my head, not just a little, but a good deal. You could not take up a newspaper, English, Scotch, or Irish, without finding in it one or more

references to the 'vest-pocket million-pounder' and
his latest doings and sayings.  At first, in these
mentions, I was at the bottom of the personal
gossip column ; next, I was listed above the
knights, next above the baronets, next above the
barons, and so on, and so on, climbing steadily, as
my notoriety augmented, until I reached the
highest altitude possible, and there I remained,
taking precedence of all dukes not royal, and of all
ecclesiastics except the Primate of all England.
But, mind, this was not fame ; as yet I had achieved
only notoriety.  Then came the climaxing stroke—
the accolade, so to speak—which in a single instance
transmuted the perishable dross of notoriety into
the enduring gold of fame : 'Punch' caricatured
me !  Yes, I was a made man, now : my place was
established.  I might be joked about still, but
reverently, not hilariously, not rudely ; I could be
smiled at, but not laughed at.  The time for that
had gone by.  'Punch' pictured me all a-flutter
with rags, dickering with a beefeater for the Tower
of London.  Well, you can imagine how it was
with a young fellow who had never been taken
notice of before, and now all of a sudden couldn't
say a thing that wasn't taken up and repeated
everywhere ; couldn't stir abroad without con-

stantly overhearing the remark flying from lip to lip, 'There he goes; that's him!' couldn't take his breakfast without a crowd to look on; couldn't appear in an opera-box without concentrating there the fire of a thousand lorgnettes. Why, I just swam in glory all day long—that is the amount of it.

You know, I even kept my old suit of rags, and every now and then appeared in them, so as to have the old pleasure of buying trifles, and being insulted, and then shooting the scoffer dead with the million-pound bill. But I couldn't keep that up. The illustrated papers made the outfit so familiar that when I went out in it I was at once recognised and followed by a crowd, and if I attempted a purchase the man would offer me his whole shop on credit before I could pull my note on him.

About the tenth day of my fame I went to fulfil my duty to my flag by paying my respects to the American minister. He received me with the enthusiasm proper in my case, upbraided me for being so tardy in my duty, and said that there was only one way to get his forgiveness, and that was to take the seat at his dinner-party that night made vacant by the illness of one of his guests. I said I

would, and we got to talking.  It turned out that
he and my father had been schoolmates in boyhood, Yale students together later, and always
warm friends up to my father's death.  So then he
required me to put in at his house all the odd time
I might have to spare, and I was very willing, of
course.

In fact I was more than willing; I was glad.
When the crash should come, he might somehow
be able to save me from total destruction; I didn't
know how, but he might think of a way, maybe.  I
couldn't venture to unbosom myself to him at this
late date, a thing which I would have been quick to
do in the beginning of this awful career of mine in
London.  No, I couldn't venture it now; I was in
too deep; that is, too deep for me to be risking
revelations to so new a friend, though not clear beyond my depth, as *I* looked at it.  Because, you
see, with all my borrowing, I was carefully keeping
within my means—I mean within my salary.  Of
course I couldn't *know* what my salary was going
to be, but I had a good enough basis for an estimate in the fact that, if I won the bet, I was to have
*choice* of any situation in that rich old gentleman's
gift provided I was competent—and I should certainly prove competent; I hadn't any doubt about

that.   And as to the bet, I wasn't worrying about that; I had always been lucky.   Now, my estimate of the salary was six hundred to a thousand a year; say, six hundred for the first year, and so on up year by year, till I struck the upper figure by proved merit.   At present I was only in debt for my first year's salary.   Everybody had been trying to lend me money, but I had fought off the most of them on one pretext or another; so this indebtedness represented only £300 borrowed money, the other £300 represented my keep and my purchases. I believed my second year's salary would carry me through the rest of the month if I went on being cautious and economical, and I intended to look sharply out for that.   My month ended, my employer back from his journey, I should be all right once more, for I should at once divide the two years' salary among my creditors by assignment, and get right down to my work.

It was a lovely dinner party of fourteen.   The Duke and Duchess of Shoreditch, and their daughter the Lady Anne-Grace-Eleanor-Celeste-and-so-forth-and-so-forth-de-Bohun, the Earl and Countess of Newgate, Viscount Cheapside, Lord and Lady Blatherskite, some untitled people of both sexes, the minister and his wife and daughter, and his daughter's visiting friend, an English girl of twenty-two, named Portia Langham, whom I fell in love with in two minutes, and she with me—I could see it without glasses. There was still another guest, an American—but I am a little ahead of my story. While the people were still in the drawing-room, whetting up for dinner, and coldly inspecting the late comers, the servant announced:

'Mr. Lloyd Hastings.'

The moment the usual civilities were over, Hastings caught sight of me, and came straight with cordially outstretched hand; then stopped short when about to shake, and said with an embarrassed look:

'I beg your pardon, sir, I thought I knew you.'

'Why, you do know me, old fellow.'

'No!   Are *you* the —the—— ?'

'Vest-pocket monster?  I am, indeed.  Don't be afraid to call me by my nickname; I'm used to it.'

'Well, well, well, this is a surprise. Once or twice I've seen your own name coupled with the nickname, but it never occurred to me that *you* could be the Henry Adams referred to.  Why, it isn't six months since you were clerking away for Blake Hopkins in Frisco on a salary, and sitting up nights on an extra allowance, helping me arrange and verify the

Gould and Curry Extension papers and statistics.
The idea of your being in London, and a vast millionaire, and a colossal celebrity !  Why, it's the
Arabian Nights come again.  Man, I can't take it
in at all ; can't realise it ; give me time to settle the
whirl in my head.'

'The fact is, Lloyd, you are no worse off than I
am.  I can't realise it myself.'

'Dear me, it *is* stunning, now, isn't it ?  Why,
it's just three months to-day since we went to the
Miners' restaurant——'

'No ; the What Cheer.'

'Right, it *was* the What Cheer ; went there at
two in the morning, and had a chop and coffee after
a hard six hours' grind over those Extension papers,
and I tried to persuade you to come to London with
me, and offered to get leave of absence for you and
pay all your expenses, and give you something over
if I succeeded in making the sale ; and you would
not listen to me, said I wouldn't succeed, and you
couldn't afford to lose the run of business and be
no end of time getting the hang of things again
when you got back home.  And yet here you are.
How odd it all is !  How did you happen to come,
and whatever *did* give you this incredible start ? '

'Oh, just an accident.  It's a long story—a

romance, a body may say.  I'll tell you all about it, but not now.

'When?'

'The end of this month.'

'That's more than a fortnight yet.  It's too much of a strain on a person's curiosity.  Make it a week.'

'I can't.  You'll know why, by and by.  But how's the trade getting along?'

His cheerfulness vanished like a breath, and he said with a sigh:

'You were a true prophet, Hal, a true prophet. I wish I hadn't come.  I don't want to talk about it.'

'But you must.  You must come and stop with me to-night, when we leave here, and tell me all about it.'

'Oh, may I?  Are you in earnest?' and the water showed in his eyes.

'Yes; I want to hear the whole story, every word.'

'I'm so grateful!  Just to find a human interest once more, in some voice and in some eye, in me and affairs of mine, after what I've been through here—lord!  I could go down on my knees for it!'

He gripped my hand hard, and braced up, and
was all right and lively after that for the dinner—
which didn't come off.  No; the usual thing happened, the thing that is always happening under
that vicious and aggravating English system—the
matter of precedence couldn't be settled, and so
there was no dinner.  Englishmen always eat
dinner before they go out to dinner, because *they*
know the risks they are running; but nobody ever
warns the stranger, and so he walks placidly into
the trap.  Of course nobody was hurt this time,
because we had all been to dinner, none of us being
novices except Hastings, and he having been informed by the minister at the time that he invited
him that in deference to the English custom he
had not provided any dinner.  Everybody took a
lady and processioned down to the dining-room,
because it is usual to go through the motions; but
there the dispute began.  The Duke of Shoreditch
wanted to take precedence, and sit at the head of
the table, holding that he outranked a minister
who represented merely a nation and not a monarch; but I stood for my rights, and refused to
yield.  In the gossip column I ranked all dukes
not royal, and said so, and claimed precedence of
this one.  It couldn't be settled, of course, struggle

as we might and did, he finally (and injudiciously) trying to play birth and antiquity, and I 'seeing' his Conqueror and 'raising' him with Adam, whose direct posterity I was, as shown by my name, while *he* was of a collateral branch, as shown by *his*, and by his recent Norman origin; so we all processioned back to the drawing-room again and had a perpendicular lunch—plate of sardines and a strawberry, and you group yourself and stand up and eat it. Here the religion of precedence is not so strenuous; the two persons of highest rank chuck up a shilling, the one that wins has first go at his strawberry, and the loser gets the shilling. The next two chuck up, then the next two, and so on. After refreshment, tables were brought, and we all played cribbage, sixpence a game. The English never play any game for amusement. If they can't make something or lose something—they don't care which—they won't play.

We had a lovely time; certainly two of us had, Miss Langham and I. I was so bewitched with her that I couldn't count my hands if they went above a double sequence; and when I struck home I never discovered it, and started up the outside row again, and would have lost the game every

time, only the girl did the same, she being in just
my condition, you see; and consequently neither
of us ever got out, or cared to wonder why we
didn't; we only just knew we were happy, and
didn't wish to know anything else, and didn't want
to be interrupted.   And I *told* her—I did indeed—
told her I loved her; and she—well, she blushed
till her hair turned red, but she liked it; she *said*
she did.   Oh, there was never such an evening!
Every time I pegged I put on a postscript; every
time she pegged she acknowledged receipt of it,
counting the hands the same.   Why, I couldn't
even say, ' Two for his heels,' without adding, ' *My*,
how sweet you do look! '   And she would say,
' Fifteen two, fifteen four, fifteen six, and a pair
are eight, and eight are sixteen—*do* you think so ? '
peeping out aslant from under her lashes, you
know, so sweet and cunning.   Oh, it was just *too-
too* !

Well, I was perfectly honest and square with
her; told her I hadn't a cent in the world but just
the million-pound note she'd heard so much talk
about, and *it* didn't belong to me; and that started
her curiosity, and then I talked low, and told her
the whole history right from the start, and it nearly
killed her, laughing.   What in the nation she

could find to laugh about, *I* couldn't see, but there it was; every half minute some new detail would fetch her, and I would have to stop as much as a minute and a half to give her a chance to settle down again. Why, she laughed herself lame, she did indeed; I never saw anything like it. I mean I never saw a painful story—a story of a person's troubles and worries and fears—produce just *that* kind of effect before. So I loved her all the more, seeing she could be so cheerful when there wasn't anything to be cheerful about; for I might soon need that kind of wife, you know, the way things looked. Of course I told her we should have to wait a couple of years, till I could catch up on my salary; but she didn't mind that, only she hoped I would be as careful as possible in the matter of expenses, and not let them run the least risk of trenching on our third year's pay. Then she began to get a little worried, and wondered if we were making any mistake, and starting the salary on a higher figure for the first year than I would get. This was good sense, and it made me feel a little less confident than I had been feeling before; but it gave me a good business idea, and I brought it frankly out.

'Portia, dear, would you mind going with

me that day, when I confront those old gentlemen?'

She shrank a little, but said:

'N-o; if my being with you would help hearten
you. But—would it be quite proper, do you
think?'

'No, I don't know that it would; in fact, I'm
afraid it wouldn't; but, you see, there's so *much*
dependent upon it that——'

'Then I'll go anyway, proper or improper,' she
said, with a beautiful and generous enthusiasm.
'Oh, I shall be so happy to think I'm helping.'

'Helping, dear? Why, you'll be doing it all.
You're so beautiful, and so lovely, and so winning,
that with you there I can pile our salary up till I
break those good old fellows, and they'll never
have the heart to struggle.'

Sho! you should have seen the rich blood
mount, and her happy eyes shine!

'You wicked flatterer! There isn't a word of
truth in what you say, but still I'll go with you.
Maybe it will teach you not to expect other people
to look with your eyes.'

Were my doubts dissipated? Was my confidence restored? You may judge by this fact:
privately I raised my salary to twelve hundred the

first year on the spot.  But I didn't tell her; I
saved it for a surprise.

All the way home I was in the clouds, Hastings
talking, I not hearing a word.  When he and I
entered my parlour he brought me to myself with
his fervent appreciations of my manifold comforts
and luxuries.

'Let me just stand here a little and look my
fill!  Dear me, it's a palace; it's just a palace!
And in it everything a body *could* desire, including cozy coal fire and supper standing ready.
Henry, it doesn't merely make me realise how rich
you are; it makes me realise to the bone, to the
marrow, how poor I am—how poor I am—and how
miserable, how defeated, routed, annihilated!'

Plague take it! this language gave me the cold
shudders.  It scared me broad awake, and made
me comprehend that I was standing on a half-inch
crust, with a crater underneath.  *I* didn't know I
had been dreaming—that is, I hadn't been allowing
myself to know it for a while back; but *now*—oh,
dear!  Deep in debt, not a cent in the world, a
lovely girl's happiness or woe in my hands, and
nothing in front of me but a salary which might
never—oh, *would* never—materialise!  Oh, oh, oh,
I am ruined past hope; nothing can save me!

'Henry, the mere unconsidered drippings of your daily income would——'

'Oh, my daily income!  Here, down with this hot Scotch, and cheer up your soul.  Here's with you!  Or, no—you're hungry; sit down and——'

'Not a bite for me; I'm past it.  I can't eat, these days; but I'll drink with you till I drop.  Come!'

'Barrel for barrel, I'm with you!  Ready!  Here we go!  Now, then, Lloyd, unreel your story while I brew.'

'Unreel it?  What, again?'

'Again?  What do you mean by that?'

'Why, I mean do you want to hear it *over* again?'

'Do I want to hear it *over* again?  This *is* a puzzler.  Wait; dont take any more of that liquid.  You don't need it.'

'Look here, Henry, you alarm me.  Didn't I tell you the whole story on the way here?'

'You?'

'Yes, I.'

'I'll be hanged if I heard a word of it.'

'Henry, this is a serious thing.  It troubles me.  What did you take up yonder at the minister's?'

Then it all flashed on me, and I owned up, like a man.

'I took the dearest girl in this world—prisoner !'

So then he came with a rush, and we shook, and shook, and shook till our hands ached; and he didn't blame me for not having heard a word of a story which had lasted while we walked three miles. He just sat down then, like the patient, good fellow he was, and told it all over again. Synopsised, it amounted to this : He had come to England with what he thought was a grand opportunity; he had an 'option' to sell the Gould and Curry Extension for the 'locators' of it, and keep all he could get over a million dollars. He had worked hard, had pulled every wire he knew of, had left no honest expedient untried, had spent nearly all the money he had in the world, had not been able to get a solitary capitalist to listen to him, and his option would run out at the end of the month. In a word, he was ruined. Then he jumped up and cried out :

'Henry, you can save me ! You can save me, and you're the only man in the universe that can. Will you do it ? *Won't* you do it ?'

'Tell me how. Speak out, my boy.'

'Give me a million and my passage home for my 'option'!  Don't, *don't* refuse!'

I was in a kind of agony.  I was right on the point of coming out with the words, 'Lloyd, I'm a pauper myself—absolutely penniless, and in *debt!*' But a white-hot idea came flaming through my head, and I gripped my jaws together, and calmed myself down till I was as cold as a capitalist.  Then I said, in a commercial and self-possessed way:

'I will save you, Lloyd——'

'Then I'm already saved!  God be merciful to you for ever!  If ever I——'

'Let me finish, Lloyd.  I will save you, but not in that way; for that would not be fair to you, after your hard work, and the risks you've run. I don't need to buy mines; I can keep my capital moving, in a commercial centre like London, without that; it's what I'm at, all the time; but here is what I'll do.  I know all about that mine, of course; I know its immense value, and can swear to it if anybody wishes it.  You shall sell out inside of the fortnight for three millions cash, using my name freely, and we'll divide, share and share alike.'

Do you know, he would have danced the furniture to kindling-wood in his insane joy, and broken everything on the place, if I hadn't tripped him up and tied him.

Then he lay there, perfectly happy, saying:

'I may use your name! Your name—think of it! Man, they'll flock in droves, these rich Londoners; they'll *fight* for that stock! I'm a made man, I'm a made man for ever, and I'll never forget you as long as I live!'

In less than twenty-four hours London was abuzz! I hadn't anything to do, day after day, but sit at home, and say to all comers:

'Yes; I told him to refer to me. I know the man and I know the mine. His character is above reproach, and the mine is worth far more than he asks for it.'

Meantime I spent all my evenings at the minister's with Portia. I didn't say a word to her about the mine; I saved it for a surprise. We talked salary; never anything but salary and love; sometimes love, sometimes salary, sometimes love and salary together. And my! the interest the minister's wife and daughter took in our little affair, and the endless ingenuities they invented to save us from interruption, and to keep the minister in the dark and unsuspicious—well, it was just lovely of them!

D

When the month was up, at last, I had a million dollars to my credit in the London and County Bank, and Hastings was fixed in the same way.  Dressed at my level best, I drove by the house in Portland Place, judged by the look of things that my birds were home again, went on towards the minister's and got my precious, and we started back, talking salary with all our might. She was so excited and anxious that it made her just intolerably beautiful.  I said :

'Dearie, the way you're looking it's a crime to strike for a salary a single penny under three thousand a year.'

'Henry, Henry, you'll ruin us ! '

'Don't you be afraid.  Just keep up those looks, and trust to me.  It'll all come out right.'

So, as it turned out, I had to keep bolstering up *her* courage all the way.  She kept pleading with me, and saying :

'Oh, please remember that if we ask for too much we may get no salary at all; and then what will become of us, with no way in the world to earn our living ? '

We were ushered in by that same servant, and there they were, the two old gentlemen.  Of course

they were surprised to see that wonderful creature
with me, but I said:

'It's all right, gentlemen; she is my future
stay and helpmate.'

And I introduced them to her, and called them
by name. It didn't surprise them; they knew I
would know enough to consult the directory. They
seated us, and were very polite to me, and very
solicitous to relieve her from embarrassment, and
put her as much at her ease as they could. Then
I said:

'Gentlemen, I am ready to report.'

'We are glad to hear it,' said *my* man, 'for now
we can decide the bet which my brother Abel and
I made. If you have won for me, you shall have
any situation in my gift. Have you the million-
pound note?'

'Here it is, sir,' and I handed it to him.

'I've won!' he shouted, and slapped Abel on
the back. '*Now* what do you say, brother?'

'I say he *did* survive, and I've lost twenty
thousand pounds. I never would have believed
it.'

'I've a further report to make,' I said, 'and a
pretty long one. I want you to let me come soon,
and detail my whole month's history; and I

promise you it's worth hearing.  Meantime, take
a look at that.'

'What, man!  Certificate of deposit for
£200,000?  Is it yours?'

'Mine!  I earned it by thirty days' judicious
use of that little loan you let me have.  And the
only use I made of it was to buy trifles and offer
the bill in change.'

'Come, this is astonishing!  It's incredible,
man!'

'Never mind, I'll prove it.  Don't take my
word unsupported.'

But now Portia's turn was come to be surprised.
Her eyes were spread wide, and she said:

'Henry, is that really your money?  Have you
been fibbing to me?'

'I have indeed, dearie.  But you'll forgive me,
*I* know.'

She put up an arch pout, and said:

'Don't you be so sure.  You are a naughty thing
to deceive me so!'

'Oh, you'll get over it, sweetheart, you'll get
over it; it was only fun, you know.  Come, let's
be going.'

'But wait, wait!  The situation, you know.  I
want to give you the situation,' said my man.

' Well,' I said, ' I'm just as grateful as I can be, but really I don't want one.'

' But you can have the very choicest one in my gift.'

' Thanks again, with all my heart; but I don't even want *that* one.'

' Henry, I'm ashamed of you. You don't half thank the good gentleman. May I do it for you? '

' Indeed you shall, dear, if you can improve it. Let us see you try.'

She walked to my man, got up in his lap, put her arm round his neck, and kissed him right on the mouth. Then the two old gentlemen shouted with laughter, but I was dumfounded, just petrified, as you may say. Portia said :

' Papa, he has said you haven't a situation in your gift that he'd take; and I feel just as hurt as——'

' My darling! is that your papa? '

' Yes ; he's my step-papa, and the dearest one that ever was. You understand now, don't you, why I was able to laugh when you told me at the minister's, not knowing my relationships, what trouble and worry papa's and Uncle Abel's scheme was giving you? '

Of course I spoke right up, now, without any fooling, and went straight to the point.

'Oh, my dearest dear sir, I want to take back what I said.  You *have* got a situation open that I want.'

'Name it.'

'Son-in-law.'

'Well, well, well!  But you know, if you haven't ever served in that capacity, you of course can't furnish recommendations of a sort to satisfy the conditions of the contract, and so——'

'Try me—oh, do, I beg of you!  Only just try me thirty or forty years, and if——'

'Oh, well, all right; it's but a little thing to ask.  Take her along.'

Happy, we too?  There are not words enough in the unabridged to describe it.  And when London got the whole history, a day or two later, of my month's adventures with that bank-note, and how they ended, did London talk, and have a good time?  Yes.

My Portia's papa took that friendly and hospitable bill back to the Bank of England and cashed it; then the Bank cancelled it and made him a present of it, and he gave it to us at our wedding, and it has always hung in its frame in the sacredest

place in our home, ever since.  For it gave me my
Portia.  But for it I could not have remained in
London, would not have appeared at the minister's,
never should have met her.  And so I always say,
'Yes, it's a million-pounder, as you see; but it
never made but one purchase in its life, and *then*
got the article for only about a tenth part of its
value.'

# MENTAL TELEGRAPHY

## A MANUSCRIPT WITH A HISTORY

NOTE TO THE EDITOR.—By glancing over the enclosed bundle of rusty old manuscript, you will perceive that I once made a great discovery: the discovery that certain sorts of things which, from the beginning of the world, had always been regarded as merely 'curious coincidences'—that is to say, accidents—were no more accidental than is the sending and receiving of a telegram an accident. I made this discovery sixteen or seventeen years ago, and gave it a name—'Mental Telegraphy.' It is the same thing around the outer edges of which the Psychical Society of England began to grope (and play with) four or five years ago, and which they named 'Telepathy.' Within the last two or three years they have penetrated towards the heart of the matter, however, and have found out that mind can act upon mind in a quite detailed and elaborate way over vast stretches of land and water. And they have succeeded in doing, by their great credit and influence, what I could never have done—they have convinced the world that mental telegraphy is not a jest, but a fact, and that it is a thing not rare, but exceedingly common. They have done our age a service—and a very great service, I think.

In this old manuscript you will find mention of an extraordinary experience of mine in the mental telegraphic line, of date about the year 1874 or 1875—the one concerning the

Great Bonanza book.   It was this experience that called my attention to the matter under consideration.   I began to keep a record, after that, of such experiences of mine as seemed explicable by the theory that minds telegraph thoughts to each other.   In 1878 I went to Germany and began to write the book called *A Tramp Abroad*.   The bulk of this old batch of manuscript was written at that time and for that book. But I removed it when I came to revise the volume for the press; for I feared that the public would treat the thing as a joke and throw it aside, whereas I was in earnest.

At home, eight or ten years ago, I tried to creep in under shelter of an authority grave enough to protect the article from ridicule—the *North American Review*.   But Mr. Metcalf was too wary for me.   He said that to treat these mere 'coincidences' seriously was a thing which the *Review* couldn't dare to do; that I must put either my name or my *nom de plume* to the article, and thus save the *Review* from harm.   But I couldn't consent to that; it would be the surest possible way to defeat my desire that the public should receive the thing seriously, and be willing to stop and give it some fair degree of attention.   So I pigeon-holed the MS., because I could not get it published anonymously.

Now see how the world has moved since then.   These small experiences of mine, which were too formidable at that time for admission to a grave magazine—if the magazine must allow them to appear as something above and beyond 'accidents' and 'coincidences'—are trifling and commonplace now, since the flood of light recently cast upon mental telegraphy by the intelligent labours of the Psychical Society. But I think they are worth publishing, just to show what harmless and ordinary matters were considered dangerous and incredible eight or ten years ago.

As I have said, the bulk of this old manuscript was written in 1878; a later part was written from time to time, two, three, and four years afterwards.   The 'Postscript' I add to-day.

MAY, '78.—Another of those apparently trifling things has happened to me which puzzle and perplex all men every now and then, keep them thinking an hour or two, and leave their minds barren of explanation or solution at last. Here it is—and it looks inconsequential enough, I am obliged to say. A few days ago I said: 'It must be that Frank Millet doesn't know we are in Germany, or he would have written long before this. I have been on the point of dropping him a line at least a dozen times during the past six weeks, but I always decided to wait a day or two longer, and see if we shouldn't hear from him. But now I *will* write.' And so I did. I directed the letter to Paris, and thought, '*Now* we shall hear from him before this letter is fifty miles from Heidelberg—it always happens so.'

True enough; but *why* should it? That is the puzzling part of it. We are always talking about letters 'crossing' each other, for that is one of the very commonest accidents of this life. We call it 'accident,' but perhaps we misname it. We have the instinct a dozen times a year that the letter we are writing is going to 'cross' the other person's letter; and if the reader will rack his memory a little he will recall the fact that this presentiment had strength enough to it to make him cut his letter down to a decided briefness, because it would be a waste of time to write a letter which was going to 'cross,' and hence be a useless letter. I think that in my experience this instinct has generally come to me in cases where I had put off my letter a good while in the hope that the other person would write.

Yes, as I was saying, I had waited five or six weeks; then I wrote but three lines, because I felt and seemed to know that a letter from Millet would cross mine. And so it did. He wrote the same day that I wrote. The letters crossed each other. His letter went to Berlin, care of the American minister, who sent it to me. In this letter Millet said he had been trying for six weeks to stumble upon somebody who knew my German address, and at last the idea had occurred to him that a letter sent to the care of the embassy at Berlin might possibly find me.

Maybe it was an 'accident' that he finally determined to write me at the same moment that I finally determined to write him, but I think not.

With me the most irritating thing has been to wait a tedious time in a purely business matter, hoping that the other party will do the writing, and then sit down and do it myself, perfectly satisfied that that other man is sitting down at the same moment to write a letter which will 'cross' mine. And yet one must go on writing, just the same ; because if you get up from your table and postpone, that other man will do the same thing, exactly as if you two were harnessed together like the Siamese twins, and must duplicate each other's movements.

Several months before I left home a New York firm did some work about the house for me, and did not make a success of it, as it seemed to me. When the bill came, I wrote and said I wanted the work perfected before I paid. They replied that they were very busy, but that as soon as they could spare the proper man the thing should be done. I waited more than two months, enduring as patiently as possible the companionship of bells which would fire away of their own accord sometimes when nobody was touching them, and at other times wouldn't ring though you struck the button with a sledge-hammer. Many a time I got ready to write and then postponed it ; but at last I sat down one evening and poured out my grief to the extent of a page or so, and then cut my letter suddenly short, because a strong instinct told me that the firm had begun to move in the matter. When I came down to breakfast next morning the postman had not yet taken my letter away, but the electrical man had been there, done his work, and was gone again! He had received his orders the previous evening from his employers, and had come up by the night train.

If that was an 'accident,' it took about three months to get it up in good shape.

One evening last summer I arrived in Washington, registered at the Arlington Hotel, and went to my room. I read and smoked until ten o'clock; then, finding I was not yet sleepy, I thought I would take a breath of fresh air. So I went forth in the rain, and tramped through one street after another in an aimless and enjoyable way. I knew that Mr. O——, a friend of mine, was in town, and I wished I might run across him; but I did not propose to hunt for him at midnight, especially as I did not know where he was stopping. Towards twelve o'clock the streets had become so deserted that I felt lonesome; so I stepped into a cigar shop far up the Avenue, and remained there fifteen minutes listening to some bummers discussing national politics. Suddenly the spirit of prophecy came upon me, and I said to myself, ' Now I will go out at this door, turn to the left, walk ten steps, and meet Mr. O—— face to face.' I did it, too! I could not see his face, because he had an umbrella before it, and it was pretty dark, anyhow, but he interrupted the man he was walking and talking with, and I recognised his voice and stopped him.

That I should step out there and stumble upon Mr. O—— was nothing, but that I should know beforehand that I was going to do it was a good deal. It is a very curious thing when you come to look at it. I stood far within the cigar shop when I delivered my prophecy; I walked about five steps to the door, opened it, closed it after me, walked down a flight of three steps to the sidewalk, then turned to the left and walked four or five more, and found my man. I repeat that in itself the thing was nothing; but to know it would happen so *beforehand*, wasn't that really curious?

I have criticised absent people so often, and then discovered, to my humiliation, that I was talking with their relatives, that I have grown superstitious about that sort of thing and dropped it. How like an idiot one feels after a blunder like that!

We are always mentioning people, and in that very instant they appear before us. We laugh, and say, 'Speak of the devil,' and so forth, and there we drop it, considering it an 'accident.' It is a cheap and convenient way of disposing of a grave

and very puzzling mystery.  The fact is, it does
seem to happen too often to be an accident.

Now I come to the oddest thing that ever happened to me.  Two or three years ago I was lying
in bed, idly musing, one morning—it was the 2nd
of March—when suddenly a red-hot new idea came
whistling down into my camp, and exploded with
such comprehensive effectiveness as to sweep the
vicinity clean of rubbishy reflections, and fill the air
with their dust and flying fragments.  This idea,
stated in simple phrase, was that the time was ripe
and the market ready for a certain book; a book
which ought to be written at once; a book which
must command attention and be of peculiar interest
—to wit, a book about the Nevada silver mines.
The ' Great Bonanza ' was a new wonder then, and
everybody was talking about it.  It seemed to me
that the person best qualified to write this book was
Mr. William H. Wright, a journalist of Virginia,
Nevada, by whose side I had scribbled many months
when I was a reporter there ten or twelve years before.  He might be alive still; he might be dead;
I could not tell; but I would write him, anyway.
I began by merely and modestly suggesting that he
make such a book; but my interest grew as I went
on, and I ventured to map out what I thought ought

to be the plan of the work, he being an old friend,
and not given to taking good intentions for ill. I
even dealt with details, and suggested the order and
sequence which they should follow. I was about to
put the manuscript in an envelope, when the thought
occurred to me that if this book should be written
at my suggestion, and then no publisher happened
to want it, I should feel uncomfortable; so I concluded to keep my letter back until I should have
secured a publisher. I pigeon-holed my document,
and dropped a note to my own publisher, asking
him to name a day for a business consultation. He
was out of town on a far journey. My note remained unanswered, and at the end of three or four
days the whole matter had passed out of my mind.
On the 9th of March the postman brought three or
four letters, and among them a thick one whose
superscription was in a hand which seemed dimly
familiar to me. I could not ' place' it at first, but
presently I succeeded. Then I said to a visiting
relative who was present :

'Now I will do a miracle. I will tell you
everything this letter contains—date, signature, and
all—without breaking the seal. It is from a
Mr. Wright, of Virginia, Nevada, and is dated
March 2,—seven days ago. Mr. Wright proposes

to make a book about the silver mines and the Great Bonanza, and asks what I, as a friend, think of the idea. He says his subjects are to be so-and-so, their order and sequence so-and-so, and he will close with a history of the chief feature of the book, the Great Bonanza.'

I opened the letter, and showed that I had stated the date and the contents correctly. Mr. Wright's letter simply contained what my own letter, written on the same date, contained, and mine still lay in its pigeon-hole, where it had been lying during the seven days since it was written.

There was no clairvoyance about this, if I rightly comprehend what clairvoyance is. I think the clairvoyant professes to actually *see* concealed writing, and read it off word for word. This was not my case. I only seemed to know, and to know absolutely the contents of the letter in detail and due order, but I had to *word* them myself. I translated them, so to speak, out of Wright's language into my own.

Wright's letter and the one which I had written to him but never sent were in substance the same.

Necessarily this could not come by accident; such elaborate accidents cannot happen. Chance might have duplicated one or two of the details, but

she would have broken down on the rest. I could
not doubt—there was no tenable reason for doubting—that Mr. Wright's mind and mine had been
in close and crystal-clear communication with each
other across three thousand miles of mountain and
desert on the morning of March 2. I did not
consider that both minds *originated* that succession of ideas, but that one mind originated them,
and simply telegraphed them to the other. I was
curious to know which brain was the telegrapher
and which the receiver, so I wrote and asked for
particulars. Mr. Wright's reply showed that his
mind had done the originating and telegraphing
and mine the receiving. Mark that significant
thing, now; consider for a moment how many a
splendid 'original' idea has been unconsciously
stolen from a man three thousand miles away! If
one should question that this is so, let him look
into the Cyclopædia, and con once more that curious
thing in the history of inventions which has puzzled
everyone so much—that is, the frequency with
which the same machine or other contrivance has
been invented at the same time by several persons
in different quarters of the globe. The world was
without an electric telegraph for several thousand
years; then Professor Henry, the American, Wheat-

stone in England, Morse on the sea, and a German in Munich, all invented it at the same time. The discovery of certain ways of applying steam was made in two or three countries in the same year. Is it not possible that inventors are constantly and unwittingly stealing each other's ideas whilst they stand thousands of miles asunder ?

Last spring a literary friend of mine,[1] who lived a hundred miles away, paid me a visit, and in the course of our talk he said he had made a discovery—conceived an entirely new idea—one which certainly had never been used in literature. He told me what it was. I handed him a manuscript, and said he would find substantially the same idea in that—a manuscript which I had written a week before. The idea had been in my mind since the previous November ; it had only entered his while I was putting it on paper, a week gone by. He had not yet written his ; so he left it unwritten, and gracefully made over all his right and title in the idea to me.

The following statement, which I have clipped from a newspaper, is true. I had the facts from Mr. Howells's lips when the episode was new :

' A remarkable story of a literary coincidence is

<hr>

[1] W. D. Howells.

told of Mr. Howells's "Atlantic Monthly" serial, "Dr. Breen's Practice." A lady of Rochester, New York, contributed to the magazine, after "Dr. Breen's Practice" was in type, a short story which so much resembled Mr. Howells's that he felt it necessary to call upon her and explain the situation of affairs in order that no charge of plagiarism might be preferred against him. He showed her the proof-sheets of his story, and satisfied her that the similarity between her work and his was one of those strange coincidences which have from time to time occurred in the literary world.'

I had read portions of Mr. Howells's story, both in manuscript and in proof, before the lady offered her contribution to the magazine.

Here is another case. I clip it from a newspaper:

'The republication of Miss Alcott's novel "Moods" recalls to a writer in the Boston *Post* a singular coincidence which was brought to light before the book was first published: "Miss Anna M. Crane, of Baltimore, published 'Emily Chester,' a novel which was pronounced a very striking and strong story. A comparison of this book with 'Moods' showed that the two writers, though entire strangers to each other, and living hundreds of miles apart, had both chosen the same subject for their novels, had followed almost the same line of treatment up to a certain point, where the parallel ceased, and the dénouements were entirely opposite.  And even more curious, the leading characters in both books had identically the same names, so that the names in Miss Alcott's novel had to be changed.  Then the book was published by Loring." '

Four or five times within my recollection there has been a lively newspaper war in this country over poems whose authorship was claimed by two or three different people at the same time.  There was a war of this kind over 'Nothing to Wear,' 'Beautiful Snow,' 'Rock Me to Sleep, Mother,' and also over one of Mr. Will Carleton's early ballads, I think.  These were all blameless cases of unintentional and unwitting mental telegraphy, I judge.

A word more as to Mr. Wright.  He had had his book in his mind some time; consequently he, and not I, had originated the idea of it.  The subject was entirely foreign to my thoughts; I was wholly absorbed in other things.  Yet this friend, whom I had not seen and had hardly thought of for eleven years, was able to shoot his thoughts at me across three thousand miles of country, and fill my head with them, to the exclusion of every other interest, **in** a single moment. He had begun his letter after finishing his work on the morning paper —a little after three o'clock, he said. When it was three in the morning in Nevada it was about six in Hartford, where I lay awake thinking about nothing in particular; and just about that time his ideas came pouring into my head from across the continent, and I got up and put them on paper, under the impression that they were my own original thoughts.

I have never seen any mesmeric or clairvoyant performances or spiritual manifestations which were in the least degree convincing—a fact which is not of consequence, since my opportunities have been meagre; but I am forced to believe that one human mind (still inhabiting the flesh) can communicate with another, over any sort of a distance, and without any *artificial* preparation of 'sympathetic conditions' to act as a transmitting agent. I suppose that when the sympathetic conditions happen to exist the two minds communicate with each other, and that otherwise they don't; and I suppose that if the sympathetic conditions could be kept up right along, the two minds would continue to correspond without limit as to time.

Now there is that curious thing which happens to everybody : suddenly a succession of thoughts or sensations flock in upon you, which startles you with the weird idea that you have ages ago experienced just this succession of thoughts or sensations in a previous existence.  The previous existence is possible, no doubt, but I am persuaded that the solution of this hoary mystery lies not there, but in the fact that some far-off stranger has been telegraphing his thoughts and sensations into your consciousness, and that he stopped because some counter-current or other obstruction intruded and broke the line of communication.  Perhaps they seem repetitions to you because they *are* repetitions got at second hand from the other man.  Possibly Mr. Brown, the ' mind-reader,' reads other people's minds, possibly he does not; but I know of a surety that I have read another man's mind, and therefore I do not see why Mr. Brown shouldn't do the like also.

I wrote the foregoing about three years ago, in Heidelberg, and laid the manuscript aside, purposing to add to it instances of mind-telegraphing from time to time as they should fall under my experience.  Meantime the ' crossing ' of letters has been so frequent as to become monotonous.  However, I have managed to get something useful out of this hint; for now, when I get tired of waiting upon a man whom I very much wish to hear from, I sit down and *compel* him to write, whether he wants to or not; that is to say, I sit down and write him, and then tear my letter up, satisfied that my act has forced him to write me at the same moment. I do not need to mail my letter—the writing it is the only essential thing.

Of course I have grown superstitious about this letter-crossing business—this was natural. We stayed awhile in Venice after leaving Heidelberg. One day I was going down the Grand Canal in a gondola, when I heard a shout behind me, and looked around to see what the matter was; a gondola was rapidly following, and the gondolier was making signs to me to stop. I did so, and the pursuing boat ranged up alongside. There was an American lady in it—a resident of Venice. She was in a good deal of distress. She said:

'There's a New York gentleman and his wife at the Hotel Britannia who arrived a week ago, expecting to find news of their son, whom they have heard nothing about during eight months. There was no news. The lady is down sick with despair; the gentleman can't sleep or eat. Their son arrived at San Francisco eight months ago, and announced the fact in a letter to his parents the same day. That is the last trace of him. The parents have been in Europe ever since; but their trip has been spoiled, for they have occupied their time simply in drifting restlessly from place to place, and writing letters everywhere and to everybody, begging for news of their son; but the mystery remains as dense as ever. Now the gentleman wants to stop writing and go to cabling. He wants to cable San Francisco. He has never done it before, because he is afraid of—of he doesn't know what—death of his son, no doubt. But he wants somebody to *advise* him to cable—wants me to do it. Now I simply can't; for if no news came that mother yonder would die. So I have chased you up in order to get you to support me in urging him to be patient, and put the thing off a week or two longer; it may be the saving of this lady. Come along; let's not lose any time.'

So I went along, but I had a programme of my own. When I was introduced to the gentleman I said : 'I have some superstitions, but they are worthy of respect. If you will cable San Francisco immediately, you will hear news of your son inside of twenty-four hours. I don't know that you will get the news from San Francisco, but you will get it from somewhere. The only necessary thing is to *cable*—that is all. The news will come within twenty-four hours. Cable Pekin, if you prefer; there is no choice in this matter. This delay is all occasioned by your not cabling long ago, when you were first moved to do it.'

It seems absurd that this gentleman should have been cheered up by this nonsense, but he was; he brightened up at once, and sent his cablegram; and next day, at noon, when a long letter arrived from his lost son, the man was as grateful to me as if I had really had something to do with the hurrying up of that letter. The son had shipped from San Francisco in a sailing vessel, and his letter was written from the first port he touched at, months afterwards.

This incident argues nothing, and is valueless. I insert it only to show how strong is the superstition which 'letter-crossing' has bred in me. I was so sure that a cablegram sent to any place, no matter where, would defeat itself by 'crossing' the incoming news, that my confidence was able to raise up a hopeless man, and make him cheery and hopeful.

But here are two or three incidents which come

strictly under the head of mind-telegraphing.  One
Monday morning, about a year ago, the mail came
in, and I picked up one of the letters, and said to
a friend : ' Without opening this letter I will tell
you what it says.  It is from Mrs. ——, and she says
she was in New York last Saturday, and was purposing to run up here in the afternoon train and
surprise us, but at the last moment changed her
mind and returned westward to her home.'

I was right ; my details were exactly correct.
Yet we had had no suspicion that Mrs. —— was
coming to New York, or that she had even a remote
intention of visiting us.

I smoke a good deal—that is to say, all the
time—so, during seven years, I have tried to keep
a box of matches handy, behind a picture on the
mantelpiece ; but I have had to take it out in
trying, because George (coloured), who makes the
fires and lights the gas, always uses my matches
and never replaces them.  Commands and per-
suasions have gone for nothing with him all these
seven years.  One day last summer, when our
family had been away from home several months,
I said to a member of the household :

' Now, with all this long holiday, and nothing
in the way, to interrupt——'

'I can finish the sentence for you,' said the member of the household.

'Do it, then,' said I.

'George ought to be able, by practising, to learn to let those matches alone.'

It was correctly done. That was what I was going to say. Yet until that moment George and the matches had not been in my mind for three months, and it is plain that the part of the sentence which I uttered offers not the least cue or suggestion of what I was purposing to follow it with.

My mother [1] is descended from the younger of two English brothers named Lambton, who settled in this country a few generations ago. The tradition goes that the elder of the two eventually fell heir to a certain estate in England (now an earldom), and died right away. This has always been the way with our family. They always die when they could make anything by not doing it. The two Lambtons left plenty of Lambtons behind them ; and when at last, about fifty years ago, the English baronetcy was exalted to an earldom, the great tribe of American Lambtons began to bestir themselves—that is, those descended from the elder branch. Ever since that day one or another

---

[1] She was still living when this was written.

of these has been fretting his life uselessly away with schemes to get at his 'rights.' The present 'rightful earl'—I mean the American one—used to write me occasionally, and try to interest me in his projected raids upon the title and estates by offering me a share in the latter portion of the spoil; but I have always managed to resist his temptations.

Well, one day last summer I was lying under a tree, thinking about nothing in particular, when an absurd idea flashed into my head, and I said to a member of the household, ' Suppose I should live to be ninety-two, and dumb and blind and toothless, and just as I was gasping out what was left of me on my death-bed——'

' Wait, I will finish the sentence,' said the member of the household.

' Go on,' said I.

' Somebody should rush in with a document, and say, " All the other heirs are dead, and you are the Earl of Durham ! " '

That is truly what I was going to say. Yet until that moment the subject had not entered my mind or been referred to in my hearing for months before. A few years ago this thing would have astounded me, but the like could not much surprise me now, though it happened every week; for I think I *know* now that mind can communicate accurately with mind without the aid of the slow and clumsy vehicle of speech.

This age does seem to have exhausted invention nearly; still, it has one important contract on its hands yet—the invention of the *phrenophone*; that is to say, a method whereby the communicating of mind with mind may be brought under command and reduced to certainty and system. The telegraph and the telephone are going to become too slow and wordy for our needs. We must have the *thought* itself shot into our minds from a distance; then, if we need to put it into words, we can do that tedious work at our leisure. Doubtless the something which conveys our thoughts through the air from brain to brain is a finer and subtler form of electricity, and all we need do is to find out how to capture it and how to force it to do its work, as we have had to do in the case of the electric currents. Before the day of telegraphs neither one of these marvels would have seemed any easier to achieve than the other.

While I am writing this, doubtless somebody on the other side of the globe is writing it too. The question is, am I inspiring him or is he inspiring me? I cannot answer that; but that these thoughts have been passing through somebody else's mind all the time I have been setting them down I have no sort of doubt.

I will close this paper with a remark which I found some time ago in Boswell's ' Johnson ' :

' Voltaire's " Candide " is wonderfully similar in its plan and conduct to Johnson's " Rasselas "; insomuch that I have heard Johnson say that if they had not been published so closely one after the other that there was not time for imitation, *it would have been in vain to deny that the scheme of that which came latest was taken from the other.*'

The two men were widely separated from each other at the time, and the sea lay between.

POSTSCRIPT

In the ' Atlantic ' for June 1882, Mr. John Fiske refers to the often-quoted Darwin-and-Wallace ' coincidence ' :

' I alluded, just now, to the " unforeseen circumstance " which led Mr. Darwin in 1859 to break his long silence, and to write and publish the " Origin of Species." This circumstance served, no less than the extraordinary success of his book, to show how ripe the minds of men had become for entertaining such views as those which Mr.

Darwin propounded. In 1858 Mr. Wallace, who was then engaged in studying the natural history of the Malay Archipelago, sent to Mr. Darwin (as to the man most likely to understand him) a paper in which he sketched the outlines of a theory identical with that upon which Mr. Darwin had so long been at work. The same sequence of observed facts and inferences that had led Mr. Darwin to the discovery of Natural Selection and its consequences had led Mr. Wallace to the very threshold of the same discovery ; but in Mr. Wallace's mind the theory had by no means been wrought out to the same degree of completeness to which it had been wrought in the mind of Mr. Darwin. In the preface to his charming book on Natural Selection, Mr. Wallace, with rare modesty and candour, acknowledges that whatever value his speculations may have had, they have been utterly surpassed in richness and cogency of proof by those of Mr. Darwin. This is no doubt true, and Mr. Wallace has done such good work in further illustration of the theory that he can well afford to rest content with the second place in the first announcement of it.

'The coincidence, however, between Mr. Wallace's conclusions and those of Mr. Darwin was very remarkable.  But, after all, coincidences of this sort have not been uncommon in the history of scientific inquiry.  Nor is it at all surprising that they should occur now and then, when we remember that a great and pregnant discovery must always be concerned with some question which many of the foremost minds in the world are busy thinking about.  It was so with the discovery of the differential calculus, and again with the discovery of the planet Neptune.  It was so with the interpretation of the Egyptian hieroglyphics, and with the establishment of the undulatory theory of light.  It was so, to a considerable extent, with the introduction of the new chemistry, with the discovery of the mechanical equivalent of heat, and the whole doctrine of the correlation of forces.  It was so with the invention of the electric telegraph and with the discovery of spectrum analysis.  And it is not at all strange that it should have been so with the doctrine of the origin of species through natural selection.'

He thinks these 'coincidences' were apt to happen because the matters from which they sprang were matters which many of the foremost minds in the world were busy thinking about.  But perhaps *one* man in each case did the telegraphing to the others.  The aberrations which gave Leverrier the idea that there must be a planet of such and such mass and such and such an orbit hidden from sight out yonder in the remote abysses of space were not new; they had been noticed by astronomers for generations.  Then why should it happen to occur to three people, widely separated —Leverrier, Mrs. Somerville, and Adams—to suddenly go to worrying about those aberrations all at the same time, and set themselves to work to find out what caused them, and to measure and weigh an invisible planet, and calculate its orbit, and hunt it down and catch it ?—a strange project which nobody but they had ever thought of before.  If one astronomer had invented that odd and happy project fifty years before, don't you think he would have telegraphed it to several others without knowing it ?

But now I come to a puzzler.  How is it that *inanimate* objects are able to affect the mind? They seem to do that.  However, I wish to throw in a parenthesis first—just a reference to a thing everybody is familiar with—the experience of receiving a clear and particular *answer* to your telegram before your telegram has reached the sender of the answer.  That is a case where your telegram has gone straight from your brain to the man it was meant for, far out-

stripping the wire's slow electricity, and it is an
exercise of mental telegraphy which is as common
as dining.   To return to the influence of inanimate
things.  In the cases of non-professional clairvoyance
examined by the Psychical Society the clairvoyant
has usually been blindfolded, then some object
which has been touched or worn by a person is
placed in his hand ; the clairvoyant immediately describes that person, and goes on and gives a history
of some event with which the text object has been
connected.   If the inanimate object is able to affect
and inform the clairvoyant's mind, maybe it can do
the same when it is working in the interest of mental telegraphy.   Once a lady in the West wrote me
that her son was coming to New York to remain
three weeks, and would pay me a visit if invited,
and she gave me his address.   I mislaid the letter,
and forgot all about the matter till the three weeks
were about up.   Then a sudden and fiery irruption
of remorse burst up in my brain that illuminated all
the region round about, and I sat down at once and
wrote to the lady and asked for that lost address.
But, upon reflection, I judged that the stirring up
of my recollection had not been an accident, so I
added a postscript to say, never mind, I should get
a letter from her son before night.   And I did get

it; for the letter was already in the town, although not delivered yet. It had influenced me somehow. I have had so many experiences of this sort—a dozen of them at least—that I am nearly persuaded that inanimate objects do not confine their activities to helping the clairvoyant, but do every now and then give the mental telegraphist a lift.

The case of mental telegraphy which I am coming to now comes under I don't exactly know what head. I clipped it from one of our local papers six or eight years ago. I know the details to be right and true, for the story was told to me in the same form by one of the two persons concerned (a clergyman of Hartford) at the time that the curious thing happened:

'A REMARKABLE COINCIDENCE.—Strange coincidences make the most interesting of stories and most curious of studies. Nobody can quite say how they come about, but everybody appreciates the fact when they do come, and it is seldom that any more complete and curious coincidence is recorded of minor importance than the following, which is absolutely true and occurred in this city:

'At the time of the building of one of the finest residences of Hartford, which is still a very new house, a local firm supplied the wall-paper for certain rooms, contracting both to furnish and to put on the paper. It happened that they did not calculate the size of one room exactly right, and the paper of the design selected for it fell short just half a roll. They asked for delay enough to send on to the manufacturers for what was needed, and were told that there was no especial hurry. It happened that the manufacturers had none on hand, and had destroyed the blocks from which it was printed. They wrote that they had a full list of the dealers to whom they had sold that paper, and that they would write to each of these, and get from some of them a roll. It might involve a delay of a couple of weeks, but they would surely get it.

' In the course of time came a letter saying that, to their great surprise, they could not find a single roll. Such a thing was very unusual, but in this case it had so happened. Accordingly the local firm asked for further time, saying they would write to their own customers who had bought of that pattern, and would get the piece from them. But to their surprise, this effort also failed. A long time had now elapsed, and there was no use of delaying any longer. They had contracted to paper the room, and their only course was to take off that which was insufficient and put on some other of

which there was enough to go around. Accordingly,
at length a man was sent out to remove the paper.
He got his apparatus ready, and was about to begin
work, under the direction of the owner of the building, when the latter was for the moment called
away. The house was large and very interesting,
and so many people had rambled about it that
finally admission had been refused by a sign at the
door. On the occasion, however, when a gentleman
had knocked and asked for leave to look about, the
owner, being on the premises, had been sent for to
reply to the request in person. That was the call
that for the moment delayed the final preparations.
The gentleman went to the door and admitted the
stranger, saying he would show him about the
house, but first must return for a moment to that
room to finish his directions there, and he told the
curious story about the paper as they went on.
They entered the room together, and the first thing
the stranger, who lived fifty miles away, said on
looking about was, " Why, I have that very paper
on a room in my house, and I have an extra roll of
it laid away, which is at your service." In a few
days the wall was papered according to the original
contract. Had not the owner been at the house,
the stranger would not have been admitted; had

he called a day later, it would have been too late; had not the facts been almost accidentally told to him, he would probably have said nothing of the paper, and so on. The exact fitting of all the circumstances is something very remarkable, and makes one of those stories that seem hardly accidental in their nature.'

Something that happened the other day brought my hoary MS. to mind, and that is how I came to dig it out from its dusty pigeon-hole grave for publication. The thing that happened was a question. A lady asked it: 'Have you ever had a vision—when awake?' I was about to answer promptly, when the last two words of the question began to grow and spread and swell, and presently they attained to vast dimensions. She did not know that they were important; and I did not at first, but I soon saw that they were putting me on the track of the solution of a mystery which had perplexed me a good deal. You will see what I mean when I get down to it. Ever since the English Society for Psychical Research began its searching investigations of ghost stories, haunted houses, and apparitions of the living and the dead, I have read their pamphlets with avidity as fast as they arrived. Now one of their commonest inquiries of a dreamer or a vision-seer is, ' Are you sure you were awake at the time ? '  If the man can't say he is sure he was awake, a doubt falls upon his tale right there.  But if he is positive he was awake, and offers reasonable evidence to substantiate it, the fact counts largely for the credibility of his story.  It does with the Society, and it did with me until that lady asked me the above question the other day.

The question set me to considering, and brought me to the conclusion that you can be asleep—at least wholly unconscious—for a time, and not suspect that it has happened, and not have any way to prove that it *has* happened.  A memorable case was in my mind.  About a year ago I was standing on the porch one day, when I saw a man coming up the walk.  He was a stranger, and I hoped he would ring and carry his business into the house without stopping to argue with me ; he would have to pass the front door to get to me, and I hoped he wouldn't take the trouble ; to help, I tried to look like a stranger myself—it often works.  I was looking straight at that man ; he had got to within ten feet of the door and within twenty-five feet of me—and suddenly he disappeared.  It was as astounding as if a church should vanish from before your face and leave nothing behind it but a vacant lot.  I was unspeakably delighted.  I had seen an apparition at last, with my own eyes, in broad daylight.  I made up my mind to write an account of it to the Society.  I ran to where the spectre had been, to make sure he was playing fair, then I ran to the other end of the porch, scanning the open grounds as I went.  No, everything was perfect; he couldn't have escaped without my seeing him; he was an apparition, without the slightest doubt, and I would write him up before he was cold.  I ran, hot with excitement, and let myself in with a latch-key.  When I stepped into the hall my lungs collapsed and my heart stood still.  For there sat that same apparition in a chair, all alone, and as quiet and reposeful as if he had come to stay a year!  The shock kept me dumb for a moment or two, then I said, 'Did you come in at that door?'

'Yes.'

'Did *you* open it, or did you ring?'

'I rang, and the coloured man opened it.'

I said to myself: 'This is astonishing.  It takes George all of two minutes to answer the door-bell when he is in a hurry, and I have never seen him in a hurry.  How *did* this man stand two minutes at that door, within five steps of me, and I did not see him?'

I should have gone to my grave puzzling over that riddle but for that lady's chance question last week: 'Have you ever had a vision—when awake?' It stands explained now. During at least sixty seconds that day I was asleep, or at least totally unconscious, without suspecting it. In that interval the man came to my immediate vicinity, rang, stood there and waited, then entered and closed the door, and I did not see him and did not hear the door slam.

If he had slipped around the house in that interval and gone into the cellar—he had time enough—I should have written him up for the Society, and magnified him, and gloated over him, and hurrahed about him, and thirty yoke of oxen could not have pulled the belief out of me that I was of the favoured ones of the earth, and had seen a vision—while wide awake.

Now, how are you to tell when you are awake? What are you to go by? People bite their fingers to find out. Why, you can do that in a dream.

# A CURE FOR THE BLUES

BY courtesy of Mr. Cable I came into possession of a singular book eight or ten years ago. It is likely that mine is now the only copy in existence. Its title-page, unabbreviated, reads as follows :

' The Enemy Conquered ; or, Love Triumphant. By G. Ragsdale McClintock,[1] author of " An Address," etc., delivered at Sunflower Hill, South Carolina, and member of the Yale Law School, New Haven : published by T. H. Pease, 83 Chapel Street, 1845.'

No one can take up this book, and lay it down again unread. Whoever reads one line of it is caught, is chained ; he has become the contented slave of its fascinations ; and he will read and read, devour and devour, and will not let it go out of his hand till it is finished to the last line, though the house be on fire over his head. And after a

---

[1] The name here given is a substitute for the one actually attached to the pamphlet.

first reading, he will not throw it aside, but will
keep it by him, with his Shakspeare and his
Homer, and will take it up many and many a
time, when the world is dark, and his spirits are
low, and be straightway cheered and refreshed.
Yet this work has been allowed to lie wholly
neglected, unmentioned, and apparently unre-
gretted, for nearly half a century.

The reader must not imagine that he is to find
in it wisdom, brilliancy, fertility of invention,
ingenuity of construction, excellence of form,
purity of style, perfection of imagery, truth to
nature, clearness of statement, humanly possible
situations, humanly possible people, fluent narrative, connected sequence of events—or philosophy,
or logic, or sense.  No ; the rich, deep, beguiling
charm of the book lies in the total and miraculous
*absence* from it of all these qualities—a charm
which is completed and perfected by the evident
fact that the author, whose naïve innocence easily
and surely wins our regard, and almost our worship, does not know that they are absent, does not
even suspect that they are absent.  When read by
the light of these helps to an understanding of the
situation, the book is delicious—profoundly and
satisfyingly delicious.

1 call it a book because the author calls it a book; I call it a work because he calls it a work; but in truth it is merely a duodecimo pamphlet of thirty-one pages. It was written for fame and money, as the author very frankly—yes, and very hopefully, too, poor fellow—says in his preface. The money never came; no penny of it ever came; and how long, how pathetically long, the fame has been deferred—forty-seven years! He was young then, it would have been so much to him then; but will he care for it now?

As time is measured in America, McClintock's epoch is antiquity. In his long-vanished day the Southern author had a passion for 'eloquence'; it was his pet, his darling. He would be eloquent, or perish. And he recognised only one kind of eloquence, the lurid, the tempestuous, the volcanic. He liked words; big words, fine words, grand words, rumbling, thundering, reverberating words —with sense attaching if it could be got in without marring the sound, but not otherwise. He loved to stand up before a dazed world, and pour forth flame, and smoke, and lava, and pumice-stone, into the skies, and work his subterranean thunders, and shake himself with earthquakes, and stench himself with sulphur fumes. If he consumed his own fields and vineyards, that was a pity, yes; but he would have his eruption at any cost. Mr. McClintock's eloquence—and he is always eloquent, his crater is always spouting—is of the pattern common to his day, but he departs from the custom of the time in one respect: his brethren allowed sense to intrude when it did not mar the sound, but he does not allow it to intrude at all. For example, consider this figure, which he uses in the village 'Address' referred to with such candid complacency in the title-page above quoted—'like the topmast topaz of an ancient tower.' Please read it again; contemplate it; measure it; walk around it; climb up it; try to get at an approximate realisation of the size of it. Is the fellow to that to be found in literature, ancient or modern, foreign or domestic, living or dead, drunk or sober? One notices how fine and grand it sounds. We know that if it was loftily uttered, it got a noble burst of applause from the villagers; yet there isn't a ray of sense in it, or meaning to it.

McClintock finished his education at Yale in 1843, and came to Hartford on a visit that same year. I have talked with men who at that time talked with him, and felt of him, and knew he was real. One needs to remember that fact, and to keep fast hold of it; it is the only way to keep McClintock's book from undermining one's faith in McClintock's actuality.

As to the book. The first four pages are devoted to an inflamed eulogy of Woman—simply Woman in general, or perhaps as an Institution—wherein, among other compliments to her details, he pays a unique one to her voice. He says it 'fills the breast with fond alarms, echoed by every rill.' It sounds well enough, but it is not true. After the eulogy he takes up his real work, and the novel begins. It begins in the woods, near the village of Sunflower Hill.

'Brightening clouds seemed to rise from the mist of the fair Chattahoochee, to spread their beauty over the thick forest, to guide the hero whose bosom beats with aspirations to conquer the enemy that would tarnish his name and to win back the admiration of his long-tried friend.'

It seems a general remark, but it is not general; the hero mentioned is the to-be hero of the book; and in this abrupt fashion, and without name or description, he is shovelled into the tale. 'With aspirations to conquer the enemy that would tarnish his name' is merely a phrase flung in for the sake of the sound—let it not mislead the reader. No one is trying to tarnish this person; no one has thought of it. The rest of the sentence is also merely a phrase; the man has no friend as yet, and of course has had no chance to try him, or win back his admiration, or disturb him in any other way.

The hero climbs up over 'Sawney's Mountain,' and down the other side, making for an old Indian 'castle'—which becomes 'the red man's hut' in the next sentence; and when he gets there at last, he 'surveys with wonder and astonishment' the invisible structure, 'which time had buried in the dust; and thought to himself his happiness was not yet complete.' One doesn't know why it wasn't, nor how near it came to being complete, nor what was still wanting to round it up and make it so. Maybe it was the Indian; but the book does not say. At this point we have an episode:

'Beside the shore of the brook sat a young man, about eighteen or twenty, who seemed to be reading some favourite book, and who had a remarkably noble countenance—eyes which betrayed more than a common mind. This, of course, made the youth a welcome guest, and gained him friends in whatever condition of life he might be placed. The traveller observed that he was a well-built figure which showed strength and grace in every movement. He accordingly addressed him in quite a gentlemanly manner, and inquired of him the way to the village. After he had received the desired information, and was about taking his leave, the youth said, "Are you not Major Elfonzo, the great musician [1]—the champion of a noble cause—the modern Achilles, who gained so many victories in the Florida War?" "I bear that name," said the Major, "and those titles, trusting at the same time that the ministers of grace will carry me triumphantly through all my laudable undertakings, and if," continued the Major, "you, sir, are the patroniser of noble deeds, I should like to make you my confidant, and learn your address." The youth looked somewhat amazed, bowed low, mused for a moment, and began: "My name is Roswell. I have been recently admitted to the bar, and can only give a faint outline of my future success in that honourable profession; but I trust, sir, like the Eagle, I shall look down from lofty rocks upon the dwellings of man, and shall ever be ready to

[1] Further on it will be seen that he is a country expert on the fiddle, and has a three-township fame.

give you any assistance in my official capacity, and whatever this muscular arm of mine can do, whenever it shall be called from its buried greatness." The Major grasped him by the hand, and exclaimed: "O! thou exalted spirit of inspiration— thou flame of burning prosperity, may the Heaven-directed blaze be the glare of thy soul, and battle down every rampart that seems to impede your progress!"'

There is a strange sort of originality about McClintock; he imitates other people's styles, but nobody can imitate his, not even an idiot. Other people can be windy, but McClintock blows a gale; other people can blubber sentiment, but McClintock spews it; other people can mishandle metaphors, but only McClintock knows how to make a business of it. McClintock is always McClintock, he is always consistent, his style is always his own style. He does not make the mistake of being relevant on one page and irrelevant on another; he is irrelevant on all of them. He does not make the mistake of being lucid in one place and obscure in another; he is obscure all the time. He does not make the mistake of slipping in a name here and there that is out of character with his work; he always uses names that exactly and fantastically fit his lunatics. In the matter of undeviating consistency he stands alone in authorship. It is this that makes his style unique, and entitles it to a name of its own—McClintockian. It is this that protects it from being mistaken for anybody else's.

Uncredited quotations from other writers often leave a reader in doubt as to their authorship, but McClintock is safe from that accident; an uncredited quotation from him would always be recognisable. When a boy nineteen years old, who had just been admitted to the bar, says, 'I trust, sir, like the Eagle, I shall look down from lofty rocks upon the dwellings of man,' we know who is speaking through that boy; we should recognise that note anywhere. There be myriads of instruments in this world's literary orchestra, and a multitudinous confusion of sounds that they make, wherein fiddles are drowned, and guitars smothered, and one sort of drum mistaken for another sort; but whensoever the brazen note of the McClintockian trombone breaks through that fog of music, that note is recognisable, and about it there can be no blur of doubt.

The novel now arrives at the point where the Major goes home to see his father. When McClin-

tock wrote this interview, he probably believed it
was pathetic.

'The road which led to the town presented
many attractions. Elfonzo had bid farewell to the
youth of deep feeling, and was now wending his
way to the dreaming spot of his fondness. The
south winds whistled through the woods, as the
waters dashed against the banks, as rapid fire in
the pent furnace roars. This brought him to remember while alone that he quietly left behind the
hospitality of a father's house, and gladly entered
the world, with higher hopes than are often realised.
But as he journeyed onward he was mindful of
the advice of his father, who had often looked
sadly on the ground, when tears of cruelly deceived
hope moistened his eyes. Elfonzo had been somewhat of a dutiful son, yet fond of the amusements
of life—had been in distant lands, had enjoyed the
pleasure of the world, and had frequently returned
to the scenes of his boyhood almost destitute of
many of the comforts of life. In this condition
he would frequently say to his father, "Have I
offended you, that you look upon me as a stranger,
and frown upon me with stinging looks? Will
you not favour me with the sound of your voice?
If I have trampled upon your veneration, or have

spread a humid veil of darkness around your expectations, send me back into the world, where no
heart beats for me—where the foot of man has
never yet trod; but give me at least one kind
word—allow me to come into the presence sometimes of thy winter-worn locks." "Forbid it,
Heaven, that I should be angry with thee,"
answered the father, "my son, and yet I send thee
back to the children of the world—to the cold
charity of the combat, and to a land of victory. I
read another destiny in thy countenance—I learn
thy inclinations from the flame that has already
kindled in my soul a strange sensation. It will seek
thee, my dear Elfonzo, it will find thee—thou canst
not escape that lighted torch, which shall blot out
from the remembrance of men a long train of
prophecies which they have foretold against thee.
I once thought not so. Once, I was blind; but
now the path of life is plain before me, and my
sight is clear; yet, Elfonzo, return to thy worldly
occupation—take again in thy hand that chord of
sweet sounds—struggle with the civilised world,
and with your own heart; fly swiftly to the enchanted ground—let the night-owl send forth its
screams from the stubborn oak—let the sea sport
upon the beach, and the stars sing together; but

learn of these, Elfonzo, thy doom, and thy hiding-
place.  Our most innocent as well as our most
lawful desires must often be denied us, that we
may learn to sacrifice them to a Higher will."

'Remembering such admonitions with gratitude,
Elfonzo was immediately urged by the recollection
of his father's family to keep moving.'

McClintock has a fine gift in the matter of surprises ; but as a rule they are not pleasant ones,
they jar upon the feelings.  His closing sentence
in the last quotation is of that sort.  It brings one
down out of the tinted clouds in too sudden and
collapsed a fashion.  It incenses one against the
author for a moment.  It makes the reader want
to take him by his winter-worn locks, and trample
on his veneration, and deliver him over to the cold
charity of combat, and blot him out with his own
lighted torch.  But the feeling does not last.  The
master takes again in his hand that concord of
sweet sounds of his, and one is reconciled, pacified.

'His steps became quicker and quicker—he
hastened through the piny woods, dark as the
forest was, and with joy he very soon reached the
little village of repose, in whose bosom rested the
boldest chivalry.  His close attention to every
important object—his modest questions about

whatever was new to him—his reverence for wise old age, and his ardent desire to learn many of the fine arts, soon brought him into respectable notice.

'One mild winter day, as he walked along the streets towards the Academy, which stood upon a small eminence, surrounded by native growth— some venerable in its appearance, others young and prosperous—all seemed inviting, and seemed to be the very place for learning as well as for genius to spend its research beneath its spreading shades. He entered its classic walls in the usual mode of Southern manners.'

The artfulness of this man! None knows so well as he how to pique the curiosity of the reader —and how to disappoint it. He raises the hope, here, that he is going to tell all about how one enters a classic wall in the usual mode of Southern manners; but does he? No; he smiles in his sleeve, and turns aside to other matters.

'The principal of the Institution begged him to be seated, and listen to the recitations that were going on. He accordingly obeyed the request, and seemed to be much pleased. After the school was dismissed, and the young hearts regained their freedom, with the songs of the evening, laughing at the anticipated pleasures of a happy home, while others tittered at the actions of the past day, he addressed the teacher in a tone that indicated a resolution—with an undaunted mind. He said he had determined to become a student, if he could meet with his approbation. "Sir," said he, "I have spent much time in the world. I have travelled among the uncivilised inhabitants of America. I have met with friends, and combated with foes; but none of these gratify my ambition, or decide what is to be my destiny. I see the learned world have an influence with the voice of the people themselves. The despoilers of the remotest kingdoms of the earth refer their differences to this class of persons. This the illiterate and inexperienced little dream of; and now, if you will receive me as I am, with these deficiencies— with all my misguided opinions, I will give you my honour, sir, that I will never disgrace the Institution or those who have placed you in this honourable station." The instructor, who had met with many disappointments, knew how to feel for a stranger who had been thus turned upon the charities of an unfeeling community. He looked at him earnestly, and said: "Be of good cheer— look forward, sir, to the high destination you may attain. Remember, the more elevated the mark at which you aim, the more sure, the more glorious, the more magnificent the prize." From wonder to wonder, his encouragement led the impatient listener. A strange nature bloomed before him—giant streams promised him success— gardens of hidden treasures opened to his view. All this, so vividly described, seemed to gain a new witchery from his glowing fancy.'

It seems to me that this situation is new in romance. I feel sure it has not been attempted before. Military celebrities have been disguised and set at lowly occupations for dramatic effect, but I think McClintock is the first to send one of them to school. Thus, in this book, you pass from wonder to wonder, through gardens of hidden treasure, where giant streams bloom before you, and behind you, and all around, and you feel as happy, and groggy, and satisfied, with your quart of mixed metaphor aboard, as you would if it had been mixed in a sample-room, and delivered from a jug.

Now we come upon some more McClintockian surprises—a sweetheart who is sprung upon us without any preparation, along with a name for her which is even a little more of a surprise than she herself is.

'In 1842 he entered the class, and made rapid progress in the English and Latin departments. Indeed, he continued advancing with such rapidity that he was like to become the first in his class, and made such unexpected progress, and was so studious, that he had almost forgotten the pictured saint of his affections. The fresh wreaths of the pine and cypress had waited anxiously to drop once more the dews of Heaven upon the heads of those who had so often poured forth the tender emotions of their souls under its boughs. He was aware of the pleasure that he had seen there. So one evening, as he was returning from his reading, he concluded he would pay a visit to this enchanting spot. Little did he think of witnessing a shadow of his former happiness, though no doubt he wished it might be so. He continued sauntering by the road-side, meditating on the past. The nearer he approached the spot, the more anxious he became. At that moment a tall female figure flitted across his path, with a bunch of roses in her hand; her countenance showed uncommon vivacity, with a resolute spirit; her ivory teeth already appeared as she smiled beautifully, promenading, while her ringlets of hair dangled unconsciously around her snowy neck.

Nothing was wanting to complete her beauty. The tinge of the rose was in full bloom upon her cheek; the charms of sensibility and tenderness were always her associates. In Ambulinia's bosom dwelt a noble soul—one that never faded—one that never was conquered.'

Ambulinia! It can hardly be matched in fiction. The full name is Ambulinia Valeer. Marriage will presently round it out and perfect it. Then it will be Mrs. Ambulinia Valeer Elfonzo. It takes the chromo.

' Her heart yielded to no feeling but the love of Elfonzo, on whom she gazed with intense delight, and to whom she felt herself more closely bound, because he sought the hand of no other. Elfonzo was roused from his apparent reverie. His books no longer were his inseparable companions—his thoughts arrayed themselves to encourage him to the field of victory. He endeavoured to speak to his supposed Ambulinia, but his speech appeared not in words. No, his effort was a stream of fire that kindled his soul into a flame of admiration and carried his senses away captive. Ambulinia had disappeared, to make him more mindful of his duty. As she walked speedily away through the piny woods she calmly echoed: " O! Elfonzo,

thou wilt now look from thy sunbeams. Thou
shalt now walk in a new path—perhaps thy way
leads through darkness; but fear not, the stars
foretell happiness." '

To McClintock that jingling jumble of fine words
meant something, no doubt, or seemed to mean
something; but it is useless for us to try to divine
what it was. Ambulinia comes—we don't know
whence nor why; she mysteriously intimates—we
don't know what; and then she goes echoing away
—we don't know whither; and down comes the
curtain. McClintock's art is subtle; McClintock's
art is deep.

' Not many days afterwards, as surrounded by
fragrant flowers, she sat one evening at twilight
to enjoy the cool breeze that whispered notes of
melody along the distant groves, the little birds
perched on every side, as if to watch the movements of their new visitor. The bells were tolling,
when Elfonzo silently stole along by the wild wood
flowers, holding in his hand his favourite instrument of music—his eye continually searching for
Ambulinia, who hardly seemed to perceive him as
she played carelessly with the songsters that hopped
from branch to branch. Nothing could be more
striking than the difference between the two.

Nature seemed to have given the more tender soul to Elfonzo, and the stronger and more courageous to Ambulinia. A deep feeling spoke from the eyes of Elfonzo—such a feeling as can only be expressed by those who are blessed as admirers, and by those who are able to return the same with sincerity of heart. He was a few years older than Ambulinia: she had turned a little into her seventeenth. He had almost grown up in the Cherokee country, with the same equal proportions as one of the natives. But little intimacy had existed between them until the year forty-one—because the youth felt that the character of such a lovely girl was too exalted to inspire any other feeling than that of quiet reverence. But as lovers will not always be insulted, at all times and under all circumstances, by the frowns and cold looks of crabbed old age, which should continually reflect dignity upon those around, and treat the unfortunate as well as the fortunate with a graceful mien, he continued to use diligence and perseverance.

'All this lighted a spark in his heart that changed his whole character, and, like the unyielding Deity that follows the storm to check its rage in the forest, he resolves for the first time to shake off

his embarrassment, and return where he had before
only worshipped.'

At last we begin to get the Major's measure. We
are able to put this and that casual fact together,
and build the man up before our eyes, and look at
him. And after we have got him built, we find him
worth the trouble. By the above comparison
between his age and Ambulinia's, we guess the
war-worn veteran to be twenty-two; and the other
facts stand thus : he had grown up in the Cherokee
country with the same equal proportions as one of
the natives—how flowing and graceful the language,
and yet how tantalising as to meaning!—he had
been turned adrift by his father, to whom he had
been ' somewhat of a dutiful son ' ; he wandered in
distant lands ; came back frequently ' to the scenes
of his boyhood, almost destitute of many of the
comforts of life,' in order to get into the presence of
his father's winter-worn locks, and spread a humid
veil of darkness around his expectations ; but he was
always promptly sent back to the cold charity of the
combat again ; he learned to play the fiddle, and
made a name for himself in that line ; he had
dwelt among the wild tribes ; he had philosophised
about the despoilers of the kingdoms of the earth,
and found out—the cunning creature—that they

refer their differences to the learned for settlement;
he had achieved a vast fame as a military chieftain,
the Achilles of the Florida campaigns, and then had
got him a spelling-book and started to school; he
had fallen in love with Ambulinia Valeer while she
was teething, but had kept it to himself awhile, out
of the reverential awe which he felt for the child;
but now at last, like the unyielding deity who
follows the storm to check its rage in the forest, he
resolves to shake off his embarrassment, and to
return where before he had only worshipped. The
Major, indeed, has made up his mind to rise up
and shake his faculties together, and to see if *he*
can't do that thing himself. This is not clear.
But no matter about that: there stands the hero,
compact and visible; and he is no mean structure,
considering that his creator had never created
anything before, and hadn't anything but rags and
wind to build with this time. It seems to me that
no one can contemplate this odd creature, this
quaint and curious blatherskite, without admiring
McClintock, or, at any rate, loving him and feeling
grateful to him; for McClintock made him;
he gave him to us; without McClintock we
could not have had him, and would now be
poor.

But we must come to the feast again. Here is a courtship scene, down there in the romantic glades among the raccoons, alligators, and things, that has merit, peculiar literary merit. See how Achilles wooes. Dwell upon the second sentence (particularly the close of it), and the beginning of the third. Never mind the new personage, Leos, who is intruded upon us unheralded and unexplained. That is McClintock's way; it is his habit; it is a part of his genius; he cannot help it; he never interrupts the rush of his narrative to make introductions:

'It could not escape Ambulinia's penetrating eye that he sought an interview with her, which she as anxiously avoided, and assumed a more distant calmness than before, seemingly to destroy all hope. After many efforts and struggles with his own person, with timid steps the Major approached the damsel, with the same caution as he would have done in a field of battle. "Lady Ambulinia," said he, trembling, "I have long desired a moment like this. I dare not let it escape. I fear the consequences; yet I hope your indulgence will at least hear my petition. Can you not anticipate what I would say, and what I am about to express? Will you not, like Minerva, who sprung from the brain

of Jupiter, release me from thy winding chains or
cure me——" " Say no more, Elfonzo," answered
Ambulinia, with a serious look, raising her hand as
if she intended to swear eternal hatred against the
whole world; "another lady in my place would
have perhaps answered your question in bitter coldness. I know not the little arts of my sex. I care
but little for the vanity of those who would chide
me, and am unwilling as well as ashamed to be
guilty of anything that would lead you to think 'all
is not gold that glitters'; so be not rash in your
resolution. It is better to repent now, than to do
it in a more solemn hour. Yes, I know what you
would say. I know you have a costly gift for me—
the noblest that man can make—your heart! You
should not offer it to one so unworthy. Heaven,
you know, has allowed my father's house to be made
a house of solitude, a home of silent obedience,
which my parents say is more to be admired than
big names and high-sounding titles. Notwithstanding all this, let me speak the emotions of an honest
heart—allow me to say in the fulness of my hopes
that I anticipate better days. The bird may stretch
its wings towards the sun which it can never reach;
and flowers of the field appear to ascend in the same
direction, because they cannot do otherwise: but

man confides his complaints to the saints in whom he believes; for in their abodes of light they know no more sorrow. From your confession and indicative looks, I must be that person: if so, deceive not yourself."

'Elfonzo replied, "Pardon me, my dear madam, for my frankness. I have loved you from my earliest days—everything grand and beautiful hath borne the image of Ambulinia: while precipices on every hand surrounded me, your guardian angel stood and beckoned me away from the deep abyss. In every trial—in every misfortune, I have met with your helping hand; yet I never dreamed or dared to cherish thy love, till a voice impaired with age encouraged the cause, and declared they who acquired thy favour should win a victory. I saw how Leos worshipped thee. I felt my own unworthiness. I began to know jealousy, a strong guest indeed, in my bosom, yet I could see if I gained your admiration, Leos was to be my rival. I was aware that he had the influence of your parents, and the wealth of a deceased relative, which is too often mistaken for permanent and regular tranquillity; yet I have determined by your permission to beg an interest in your prayers—to ask you to animate my drooping spirits by your smiles and

your winning looks; for, if you but speak, I shall
be conqueror, my enemies shall stagger like Olympus
shakes. And though earth and sea may tremble,
and the charioteer of the sun may forget his dashing steed; yet I am assured that it is only to arm
me with divine weapons, which will enable me to
complete my long-tried intention." "Return to
yourself, Elfonzo," said Ambulinia, pleasantly, "a
dream of vision has disturbed your intellect—you
are above the atmosphere, dwelling in the celestial
regions, nothing is there that urges or hinders,
nothing that brings discord into our present litigation. I entreat you to condescend a little, and be a
man, and forget it all. When Homer describes the
battle of the gods and noble men, fighting with
giants and dragons, they represent under this image
our struggles with the delusions of our passions.
You have exalted me, an unhappy girl, to the
skies; you have called me a saint, and portrayed
in your imagination an angel in human form.
Let her remain such to you—let her continue to
be as you have supposed, and be assured that she
will consider a share in your esteem as her highest
treasure. Think not that I would allure you from
the path in which your conscience leads you; for
you know I respect the conscience of others, as I

would die for my own. Elfonzo, if I am worthy of thy love, let such conversation never again pass between us. Go, seek a nobler theme! we will seek it in the stream of time as the sunset in the Tigris." As she spake these words she grasped the hand of Elfonzo, saying at the same time— "Peace and prosperity attend you, my hero: be up and doing." Closing her remarks with this expression, she walked slowly away, leaving Elfonzo astonished and amazed. He ventured not to follow, or detain her. Here he stood alone, gazing at the stars—confounded as he was, here he stood.'

Yes; there he stood. There seems to be no doubt about that. Nearly half of this delirious story has now been delivered to the reader. It seems a pity to reduce the other half to a cold synopsis. Pity! it is more than a pity, it is a crime; for, to synopsise McClintock is to reduce a sky-flushing conflagration to dull embers, it is to reduce barbaric splendour to ragged poverty. McClintock never wrote a line that was not precious; he never wrote one that could be spared; he never framed one from which a word could be removed without damage. Every sentence that this master has produced may be likened to a perfect set of teeth—white, uniform, beautiful. If you pull one, the charm is gone. Still, it is now necessary to begin to pull, and to keep it up; for lack of space requires us to synopsise.

We left Elfonzo standing there, amazed. At what, we do not know. Not at the girl's speech. No; we ourselves should have been amazed at it, of course, for none of us has ever heard anything resembling it: but Elfonzo was used to speeches made up of noise and vacancy, and could listen to them with undaunted mind like the 'topmost topaz of an ancient tower'; he was used to making them himself; he—but let it go, it cannot be guessed out; we shall never know what it was that astonished him. He stood there awhile; then he said, 'Alas! am I now Grief's disappointed son at last.' He did not stop to examine his mind, and to try to find out what he probably meant by that, because, for one reason, 'a mixture of ambition and greatness of soul moved upon his young heart,' and started him for the village. He resumed his bench in school, 'and reasonably progressed in his education.' His heart was heavy, but he went into society, and sought surcease of sorrow in its light distractions. He made himself popular with his violin, 'which seemed to have a thousand chords—

more symphonious than the Muses of Apollo, and more enchanting than the ghost of the Hills.' This is obscure, but let it go.

During this interval Leos did some unencouraged courting, but at last, 'choked by his undertaking,' he desisted.

Presently 'Elfonzo again wends his way to the stately walls and new-built village.' He goes to the house of his beloved; she opens the door herself. To my surprise—for Ambulinia's heart had still seemed free at the time of their last interview—love beamed from the girl's eyes. One sees that Elfonzo was surprised, too; for when he caught that light 'a halloo of smothered shouts ran through every vein.' A neat figure—a very neat figure, indeed! Then he kissed her. 'The scene was overwhelming.' They went into the parlour. The girl said it was safe, for her parents were abed and would never know. Then we have this fine picture—flung upon the canvas with hardly an effort, as you will notice.

'Advancing towards him she gave a bright display of her rosy neck, and from her head the ambrosial locks breathed divine fragrance; her robe hung waving to his view, while she stood like a goddess confessed before him.'

There is nothing of interest in the couple's interview. Now, at this point the girl invites Elfonzo to a village show, where jealousy is the motive of the play, for she wants to teach him a wholesome lesson if he is a jealous person. But this is a sham, and pretty shallow. McClintock merely wants a pretext to drag in a plagiarism of his upon a scene or two in ' Othello.'

The lovers went to the play. Elfonzo was one of the fiddlers. He and Ambulinia must not be seen together, lest trouble follow with the girl's malignant father; we are made to understand that clearly. So the two sit together in the orchestra, in the midst of the musicians. This does not seem to be good art. In the first place, the girl would be in the way, for orchestras are always packed closely together, and there is no room to spare for people's girls; in the next place, one cannot conceal a girl in an orchestra without everybody taking notice of it. There can be no doubt, it seems to me, that this is bad art.

Leos is present. Of course one of the first things that catches his eye is the maddening spectacle of Ambulinia ' leaning upon Elfonzo's chair.' This poor girl does not seem to understand even the rudiments of concealment. But she is ' in her seventeenth,' as the author phrases it, and that is her justification.

Leos meditates, constructs a plan—with personal violence as a basis, of course. It was their way, down there. It is a good plain plan, without any imagination in it. He will go out and stand at the front door, and when these two come out he will 'arrest Ambulinia from the hands of the insolent Elfonzo,' and thus make for himself a 'more prosperous field of immortality than ever was decreed by Omnipotence, or ever pencil drew, or artist imagined.' But, dear me, while he is waiting there the couple climb out at the back window and scurry home! This is romantic enough, but there is a lack of dignity in the situation.

At this point McClintock puts in the whole of his curious play—which we skip.

Some correspondence follows now. The bitter father and the distressed lovers write the letters. Elopements are attempted. They are idiotically planned, and they fail. Then we have several pages of romantic powwow and confusion signifying nothing. Another elopement is planned; it is to take place on Sunday, when everybody is at church. But the 'hero' cannot keep the secret;

he tells everybody. Another author would have found another instrument when he decided to defeat this elopement; but that is not McClintock's way. He uses the person that is nearest at hand.

The evasion failed, of course. Ambulinia, in her flight, takes refuge in a neighbour's house. Her father drags her home. The villagers gather, attracted by the racket.

'Elfonzo was moved at this sight. The people followed on to see what was going to become of Ambulinia, while he, with downcast looks, kept at a distance, until he saw them enter the abode of the father, thrusting her, that was the sigh of his soul, out of his presence into a solitary apartment, when she exclaimed, "Elfonzo! Elfonzo! oh! Elfonzo! where art thou, with all thy heroes? haste, oh! haste, come thou to my relief. Ride on the wings of the wind! Turn thy force loose like a tempest, and roll on thy army like a whirlwind, over this mountain of trouble and confusion. Oh, friends! if any pity me, let your last efforts throng upon the green hills, and come to the relief of Ambulinia, who is guilty of nothing but innocent love." Elfonzo called out with a loud voice, "My God, can I stand this! arouse up, I beseech you, and put an end to this tyranny.  Come, my brave boys," said he, " are you ready to go forth to your duty ?"  They stood around him.  " Who," said he, " will call us to arms ?  Where are my thunderbolts of war ?  Speak ye, the first who will meet the foe ! Who will go forth with me in this ocean of grievous temptation ?  If there is one who desires to go, let him come and shake hands upon the altar of devotion, and swear that he will be a hero; yes, a Hector in a cause like this, which calls aloud for a speedy remedy."  " Mine be the deed," said a young lawyer, " and mine alone; Venus alone shall quit her station before I will forsake one jot or tittle of my promise to you; what is death to me? what is all this warlike army, if it is not to win a victory ? I love the sleep of the lover and the mighty; nor would I give it over till the blood of my enemies should wreak with that of my own.  But God forbid that our fame should soar on the blood of the slumberer."  Mr. Valeer stands at his door with the frown of a demon upon his brow, with his dangerous weapon[1] ready to strike the first man who should enter his door.  " Who will arise and go forward through blood and carnage to the rescue of my Ambulinia ?" said Elfonzo.  " All," exclaimed

[1] It is a crowbar.

the multitude; and onward they went, with their implements of battle. Others, of a more timid nature, stood among the distant hills to see the result of the contest.'

It will hardly be believed that after all this thunder and lightning not a drop of rain fell; but such is the fact. Elfonzo and his gang stood up and blackguarded Mr. Valeer with vigour all night, getting their outlay back with interest; then in the early morning the army and its general retired from the field, leaving the victory with their solitary adversary and his crowbar. This is the first time this has happened in romantic literature. The invention is original. Everything in this book is original; there is nothing hackneyed about it anywhere. Always, in other romances, when you find the author leading up to a climax, you know what is going to happen. But in this book it is different; the thing which seems inevitable and unavoidable never happens; it is circumvented by the art of the author every time.

Another elopement was attempted. It failed.

We have now arrived at the end. But it is not exciting. McClintock thinks it is; but it isn't. One day Elfonzo sends Ambulinia another note—a note proposing elopement No. 16. This time the plan is admirable; admirable, sagacious, ingenious, imaginative, deep—oh, everything, and perfectly easy. One wonders why it was never thought of before. This is the scheme. Ambulinia is to leave the breakfast table, ostensibly to 'attend to the placing of those flowers, which ought to have been done a week ago '—artificial ones, of course; the others wouldn't keep so long—and then, instead of fixing the flowers, she is to walk out to the grove, and go off with Elfonzo. The invention of this plan overstrained the author, that is plain, for he straightway shows failing powers. The details of the plan are not many or elaborate. The author shall state them himself—this good soul, whose intentions are always better than his English :

' " You walk carelessly towards the academy grove, where you will find me with a lightning steed, elegantly equipped to bear you off where we shall be joined in wedlock with the first connubial rights." '

Last scene of all, which the author, now much enfeebled, tries to smarten up and make acceptable to his spectacular heart by introducing some new properties—silver bow, golden harp, olive branch, —things that can all come good in an elopement, no doubt, yet are not to be compared to an umbrella for real handiness and reliability in an excursion of that kind.

'And away she ran to the sacred grove, surrounded with glittering pearls, that indicated her coming. Elfonzo hails her with his silver bow and his golden harp. They meet—Ambulinia's countenance brightens—Elfonzo leads up his winged steed. "Mount," said he, "ye true-hearted, ye fearless soul—the day is ours." She sprang upon the back of the young thunderbolt; a brilliant star sparkles upon her head, with one hand she grasps the reins, and with the other she holds an olive branch. "Lend thy aid, ye strong winds," they exclaimed, "ye moon, ye sun, and all ye fair host of heaven, witness the enemy conquered." "Hold," said Elfonzo, "thy dashing steed." "Ride on," said Ambulinia, "the voice of thunder is behind us." And onward they went with such rapidity that they very soon arrived at Rural Retreat, where they dismounted, and were united with all the solemnities that usually attend such divine operations.'

There is but one Homer, there was but one Shakspeare, there is but one McClintock—and his immortal book is before you. Homer could not have written this book, Shakspeare could not have written it, I could not have done it myself. There is nothing just like it in the literature of any country or of any epoch. It stands alone, it is monumental. It adds G. Ragsdale McClintock's to the sum of the republic's imperishable names.

# THE
# CURIOUS BOOK

## COMPLETE

.

[The foregoing review of the great work of G. Ragsdale McClintock is liberally illuminated with sample extracts, but these cannot appease the appetite. Only the complete book, unabridged, can do that. Therefore it is here printed.—M. T.]

## THE ENEMY CONQUERED; OR, LOVE TRIUMPHANT

> Sweet girl, thy smiles are full of charms,
> Thy voice is sweeter still,
> It fills the breast with fond alarms,
> Echoed by every rill.

I BEGIN this little work with an eulogy upon woman, who has ever been distinguished for her perseverance, her constancy, and her devoted attention to those upon whom she has been pleased to place her *affections*. Many have been the themes upon which writers and public speakers have dwelt with intense and increasing interest. Among these delightful themes stands that of woman, the balm to all our sighs and disappointments, and the most pre-eminent of all other topics. Here the poet and orator have stood and gazed with wonder and with admiration; they have dwelt upon her innocence, the ornament of all her virtues. First viewing her external charms, such as are set forth in her form and her benevolent countenance, and then passing to the deep hidden springs of loveliness and disinterested devotion. In every clime, and in every age, she has been the pride of her *nation.* Her watchfulness is untiring; she who guarded the sepulchre was the first to approach it, and the last to depart from its awful yet sublime scene. Even here, in this highly-favoured land, we look to her for the security of our institutions, and for our future greatness as a nation. But, strange as it may appear, woman's charms and virtues are but slightly appreciated by thousands. Those who should raise the standard of female worth, and paint her value with her virtues, in living colours, upon the banners that are fanned by the zephyrs of heaven, and hand them down to posterity as emblematical of a rich inheritance, do not properly estimate them.

Man is not sensible, at all times, of the nature and the emotions which bear that name; he does not understand, he will not comprehend; his intelligence has not expanded to that degree of glory which drinks in the vast revolution of humanity, its end, its mighty destination, and the causes which operated, and are still operating, to produce a more elevated station, and the objects which energise and enliven its consummation.

This he is a stranger to; he is not aware that woman is the recipient of celestial love, and that man is dependent upon her to perfect his character; that without her, philosophically and truly speaking, the brightest of his intelligence is but the coldness of a winter moon, whose beams can produce no fruit, whose solar light is not its own, but borrowed from the great dispenser of effulgent beauty. We have no disposition in the world to flatter the fair sex; we would raise them above those dastardly principles which only exist in little souls, contracted hearts, and a distracted brain. Often does she unfold herself in all her fascinating loveliness, presenting the most captivating charms; yet we find man frequently treats such purity of purpose with indifference. Why does he do it? Why does he baffle that which is inevitably the source of his better days? Is he so much of a stranger to those excellent qualities, as not to appreciate woman, as not to have respect to her dignity? Since her art and beauty first captivated man, she has been his delight and his comfort; she has shared alike in his misfortunes and in his prosperity.

Whenever the billows of adversity and the tumultuous waves of trouble beat high, her smiles subdue their fury. Should the tear of sorrow and the mournful sigh of grief interrupt the peace of his mind, her voice removes them all, and she bends from her circle to encourage him onward. When darkness would obscure his mind, and a thick cloud of gloom would bewilder its operations, her intelligent eye darts a ray of streaming light into his heart. Mighty and charming is that disinterested devotion which she is ever ready to exercise towards man, not waiting till the last moment of his danger, but seeks to relieve him in his early afflictions. It gushes forth from the expansive fulness of a tender and devoted heart, where the noblest, the purest, and the most elevated and refined feelings are matured, and developed in those many kind offices which invariably make her character.

In the room of sorrow and sickness, this unequalled characteristic may always be seen, in the performance of the most charitable acts; nothing that she can do to promote the happiness of him who she claims to be her protector will be omitted; all is invigorated by the animating sunbeams which awaken the heart to songs of gaiety. Leaving this point, to notice another prominent consideration, which is generally one of great moment and of vital importance. Invariably she is firm and steady in all her pursuits and aims. There is required a combination of forces and extreme opposition to drive her from her position; she takes her stand, not to be moved by the sound of Apollo's lyre, or the curved bow of pleasure.

Firm and true to what she undertakes, and that which she requires by her own aggrandisement, and regards as being within the strict rules of propriety, she will remain stable and unflinching to the last. A more genuine principle is not to be found in the most determined, resolute heart of man. For this she deserves to be held in the highest commendation, for this she deserves the purest of all other blessings, and for this she deserves the most laudable reward of all others. It is a noble characteristic, and is worthy the imitation of any age. And when we look at it in one particular aspect, it is still magnified, and grows brighter and brighter the more we reflect upon its eternal duration. What will she not do, when her word as well as her affections and *love* are pledged to her lover? Everything that is dear to her on earth, all the hospitalities of kind and loving parents, all the sincerity and loveliness of sisters, and the benevolent devotion of brothers, who have surrounded her with every comfort; she will forsake them all, quit the harmony and sweet sound of the lute and the harp, and throw herself upon the affections of some devoted admirer, in whom she fondly hopes to find more than she has left behind, which is not often realised by many. Truth and virtue all combined! How deserving our admiration and love! Ah! cruel would it be in man, after she has thus manifested such an unshaken confidence in him, and said by her determination to abandon all the endearments and blandishments of home, to act a villainous part, and prove a traitor in the revolution of his mission, and then turn Hector over the innocent victim whom he swore to protect, in the presence of Heaven, recorded by the pen of an angel.

Striking as this trait may unfold itself in her character, and as pre-eminent as it may stand among the fair display of her other qualities, yet there is another, which struggles into existence, and adds an additional lustre to what she already possesses. I mean that disposition in woman which enables her, in sorrow, in grief, and in distress, to bear all with enduring patience. This she has done, and can and will do, amid the din of war and clash of arms. Scenes and occurrences which, to every appearance, are calculated to rend the heart with the profoundest emotions of trouble, do not fetter that exalted principle imbued in her very nature.   It is true, her tender and feeling heart may often be moved (as she is thus constituted), but still she is not conquered, she has not given up to the harlequin of disappointments, her energies have not become clouded in the last moment of misfortune, but she is continually invigorated by the archetype of her affections.   She may bury her face in her hands, and let the tear of anguish roll, she may promenade the delightful walks of some garden, decorated with all the flowers of nature, or she may steal out along some gently rippling stream, and there, as the silver waters uninterruptedly move forward, sheds her silent tears, they mingle with the waves, and take a last farewell of their agitated home, to seek a peaceful dwelling among the rolling floods;  yet there is a voice rushing from her breast, that proclaims *victory* along the whole line and battlement of her affections.   That voice is the voice of patience and resignation; that voice is one that bears everything calmly and dispassionately; amid the most distressing scenes, when the fates are arrayed against her peace, and apparently plotting for her destruction, still she is resigned. Woman's affections are deep, consequently her troubles may be made to sink deep. Although you may not be able to mark the traces of her grief and the furrowings of her anguish upon her winning countenance, yet be assured they are nevertheless preying upon her inward person, sapping the very foundation of that heart which alone was made for the weal and not the woe of man. The deep recesses of the soul are fields for their operation. But they are not destined simply to take the regions of the heart for their dominion, they are not satisfied merely with interrupting her better feelings ; but after a while you may see the blooming cheek beginning to droop and fade, her intelligent eye no longer sparkles with the starry light of heaven, her vibrating pulse long since changed its regular motion, and her palpitating bosom beats once more for the mid-day of her glory. Anxiety and care ultimately throw her into the arms of the haggard and grim monster, Death. But, oh, how patient, under every pining influence! Let us view the matter in bolder colours ; see her when the dearest object of her affections recklessly seeks every bacchanalian pleasure, contents himself with the last rubbish of creation. With what solicitude she awaits his return! Sleep fails to perform its office—she weeps while the nocturnal shades of the night triumph in the stillness. Bending over some favourite book, whilst the author throws before her mind the most beautiful imagery, she startles at every sound. The midnight silence is broken by the solemn announcement of the return of another morning. He is still absent: she listens for that voice which has so often been greeted by the melodies of her own; but, alas! stern silence is all that she receives for her vigilance.

Mark her unwearied watchfulness, as the night passes away. At last, brutalised by the accursed thing, he staggers along with rage, and, shivering with cold, he makes his appearance. Not a murmur is heard from her lips. On the contrary, she meets him with a smile—she caresses him with her tender arms, with all the gentleness and softness of her sex. Here, then, is seen her disposition, beautifully arrayed. Woman, thou art more to be admired than the spicy gales of Arabia, and more sought for than the gold of Golconda. We believe that woman should associate freely with man, and we believe that it is for the preservation of her rights. She should become acquainted with the metaphysical designs of those who condescend to sing the siren song of flattery. This, we think, should be according to the unwritten law of decorum, which is stamped upon every innocent heart. The precepts of prudery are often steeped in the guilt of contamination, which blasts the expectations of better moments. Truth, and beautiful dreams—loveliness, and delicacy of character, with cherished affections of the ideal woman—gentle hopes and aspirations, are enough to uphold her in the storms of darkness, without the transferred colourings of a stained sufferer. How often have we seen it in our public prints, that woman occupies a false station in the world! and some have gone so far as to say it was an unnatural one. So long has she been regarded a weak creature, by the rabble and illiterate—they have looked upon her as an insufficient actress on the great stage of human life—a mere puppet, to fill up the drama of human existence—a thoughtless inactive being,—that she has too often come to the same conclusion herself, and has sometimes forgotten her high destination, in the meridian of her glory. We have but little sympathy or patience for those who treat her as a mere Rosy Melinda—who are always fishing for pretty compliments—who are satisfied by the gossamer of romance, and who can be allured by the verbosity of high-flown words, rich in language, but poor and barren in sentiment. Beset, as she has been, by the intellectual vulgar, the selfish, the designing, the cunning, the hidden, and the artful—no wonder she has sometimes folded her wings in despair, and forgotten her *heavenly* mission in the delirium of imagination ; no wonder she searches out some wild desert, to find a peaceful home.  But this cannot always continue.  A new era is moving gently onward, old things are rapidly passing away; old superstitions, old prejudices, and old notions are now bidding farewell to their old associates and companions, and giving way to one whose wings are plumed with the light of heaven, and tinged by the dews of the morning.  There is a remnant of blessedness that clings to her in spite of all evil influence—there is enough of the Divine Master left, to accomplish the noblest work ever achieved under the canopy of the vaulted skies ; and that time is fast approaching, when the picture of the true woman will shine from its frame of glory, to captivate, to win back, to restore, and to call into being once more, *the object of her mission.*

> Star of the brave !  thy glory shed,
> O'er all the earth, thy army led—
> Bold meteor of immortal birth !
> Why come from Heaven to dwell on earth ?

Mighty and glorious are the days of youth; happy the moments of the *lover*, mingled with smiles and tears of his devoted, and long to be remembered are the achievements which he gains with a palpitating heart and a trembling hand. A bright and lovely dawn, the harbinger of a fair and prosperous day, had arisen over the beautiful little village of Cumming, which is surrounded by the most romantic scenery in the Cherokee country. Brightening clouds seemed to rise from the mist of the fair Chattahoochee, to spread their beauty over the thick forest, to guide the hero whose bosom beats with aspirations to conquer the enemy that would tarnish his name, and to win back the admiration of his long-tried friend. He endeavoured to make his way through Sawney's Mountain, where many meet to catch the gales that are continually blowing for the refreshment of the stranger and the traveller. Surrounded as he was, by hills on every side, naked rocks dared the efforts of his energies. Soon the sky became overcast, the sun buried itself in the clouds, and the fair day gave place to gloomy twilight, which lay heavily on the Indian Plains. He remembered an old Indian Castle, that once stood at the foot of the mountain. He thought if he could make his way to this, he would rest contented for a short time.   The mountain air breathed fragrance—a rosy tinge rested on the glassy waters that murmured at its base.   His resolution soon brought him to the remains of the red man's hut : he surveyed with wonder and astonishment the decayed building, which time had buried in the dust, and thought to himself, his happiness was not yet complete.   Beside the shore of the brook sat a young man, about eighteen or twenty, who seemed to be reading some favourite book, and who had a remarkably noble countenance—eyes which betrayed more than a common mind.   This of course made the youth a welcome guest, and gained him friends in whatever condition of life he might be placed. The traveller observed that he was a well-built figure which showed strength and grace in every movement.   He accordingly addressed him in quite a gentlemanly manner, and inquired of him the way to the village. After he had received the desired information, and was about taking his leave, the youth said, ' Are you not Major Elfonzo, the great musician—the champion of a noble cause —the modern Achilles, who gained so many victories in the Florida War ? '  ' I bear that name,' said the Major, 'and those titles, trusting at the same time, that the ministers of grace will carry

me triumphantly through all my laudable undertakings, and if,' continued the Major, ' you, sir, are
the patroniser of noble deeds, I should like to make
you my confidant, and learn your address.' The
youth looked somewhat amazed, bowed low, mused
for a moment, and began : ' My name is Roswell.
I have been recently admitted to the bar, and can
only give a faint outline of my future success in
that honourable profession ; but I trust, sir, like
the Eagle, I shall look down from lofty rocks upon
the dwellings of man, and shall ever be ready to
give you any assistance in my official capacity, and
whatever this muscular arm of mine can do, whenever it shall be called from its buried *greatness.*'
The Major grasped him by the hand, and exclaimed:
' O ! thou exalted spirit of inspiration—thou flame
of burning prosperity, may the Heaven-directed
blaze be the glare of thy soul, and battle down
every rampart that seems to impede your progress ! '

The road which led to the town presented many
attractions. Elfonzo had bid farewell to the youth
of deep feeling, and was now wending his way to
the dreaming spot of his fondness. The south
winds whistled through the woods, as the waters
dashed against the banks, as rapid fire in the pent

furnace roars. This brought him to remember while alone, that he quietly left behind the hospitality of a father's house, and gladly entered the world, with higher hopes than are often realised. But as he journeyed onward, he was mindful of the advice of his father, who had often looked sadly on the ground, when tears of cruelly deceived hope moistened his eye. Elfonzo had been somewhat of a dutiful son ; yet fond of the amusements of life —had been in distant lands—had enjoyed the pleasure of the world, and had frequently returned to the scenes of his boyhood, almost destitute of many of the comforts of life. In this condition he would frequently say to his father, ' Have I offended you, that you look upon me as a stranger, and frown upon me with stinging looks ?  Will you not favour me with the sound of your voice ?  If I have trampled upon your veneration, or have spread a humid veil of darkness around your expectations, send me back into the world where no heart beats for me—where the foot of man has never yet trod; but give me at least one kind word—allow me to come into the presence sometimes of thy winter-worn locks.'  ' Forbid it, Heaven, that I should be angry with thee,' answered the father, ' my son, and yet I send thee back to the children of the

world—to the cold charity of the combat, and to a
land of victory. I read another destiny in thy
countenance—-I learn thy inclinations from the
flame that has already kindled in my soul a strange
sensation. It will seek thee, my dear Elfonzo, it
will find thee—thou canst not escape that lighted
torch which shall blot out from the remembrance
of men a long train of prophecies which they have
foretold against thee. I once thought not so.
Once I was blind; but now the path of life is plain
before me, and my sight is clear; yet, Elfonzo,
return to thy worldly occupation—take again in
thy hand that chord of sweet sounds—struggle
with the civilised world, and with your own heart;
fly swiftly to the enchanted ground—let the night-
owl send forth its screams from the stubborn oak
—let the sea sport upon the beach, and the stars
sing together; but learn of these, Elfonzo, thy
doom, and thy hiding-place. Our most innocent
as well as our most lawful desires must often be
denied us, that we may learn to sacrifice them to a
Higher will.'

Remembering such admonitions with gratitude,
Elfonzo was immediately urged by the recollection
of his father's family to keep moving. His steps
became quicker and quicker—he hastened through

the piny woods, dark as the forest was, and with joy he very soon reached the little village of repose, in whose bosom rested the boldest chivalry. His close attention to every important object—his modest questions about whatever was new to him—his reverence for wise old age, and his ardent desire to learn many of the fine arts, soon brought him into respectable notice.

One mild winter day, as he walked along the streets towards the Academy, which stood upon a small eminence, surrounded by native growth—some venerable in its appearance, others young and prosperous—all seemed inviting, and seemed to be the very place for learning as well as for genius to spend its research beneath its spreading shades. He entered its classic walls in the usual mode of Southern manners. The principal of the Institution begged him to be seated, and listen to the recitations that were going on. He accordingly obeyed the request, and seemed to be much pleased. After the school was dismissed, and the young hearts regained their freedom, with the songs of the evening, laughing at the anticipated pleasures of a happy home, while others tittered at the actions of the past day, he addressed the teacher in a tone that indicated a resolution—with an undaunted mind. He said he had determined to become a student, if he could meet with his approbation. 'Sir,' said he, 'I have spent much time in the world. I have travelled among the uncivilised inhabitants of America. I have met with friends, and combated with foes; but none of these gratify my ambition, or decide what is to be my destiny. I see the learned world have an influence with the voice of the people themselves. The despoilers of the remotest kingdoms of the earth refer their differences to this class of persons. This the illiterate and inexperienced little dream of; and now if you will receive me as I am, with these deficiencies—with all my misguided opinions, I will give you my honour, sir, that I will never disgrace the Institution, or those who have placed you in this honourable station.' The instructor, who had met with many disappointments, knew how to feel for a stranger who had been thus turned upon the charities of an unfeeling community. He looked at him earnestly, and said: 'Be of good cheer—look forward, sir, to the high destination you may attain. Remember, the more elevated the mark at which you aim, the more sure, the more glorious, the more magnificent the prize.' From wonder to wonder, his encouragement led the impatient lis-

tener. A strange nature bloomed before him—
giant streams promised him success—gardens of
hidden treasures opened to his view. All this, so
vividly described, seemed to gain a new witchery
from his glowing fancy.

In 1842 he entered the class, and made rapid
progress in the English and Latin departments.
Indeed, he continued advancing with such rapidity,
that he was like to become the first in his class,
and made such unexpected progress, and was so
studious, that he had almost forgotten the pictured
saint of his affections. The fresh wreaths of the
pine and cypress had waited anxiously to drop once
more the dews of Heaven upon the heads of those
who had so often poured forth the tender emotions
of their souls under its boughs. He was aware of
the pleasure that he had seen there. So one evening, as he was returning from his reading, he concluded he would pay a visit to this enchanting
spot. Little did he think of witnessing a shadow
of his former happiness, though no doubt he wished
it might be so. He continued sauntering by the
road-side, meditating on the past. The nearer he
approached the spot, the more anxious he became.
At that moment, a tall female figure flitted across
his path, with a bunch of roses in her hand; her

countenance showed uncommon vivacity, with a resolute spirit; her ivory teeth already appeared as she smiled beautifully promenading, while her ringlets of hair dangled unconsciously around her snowy neck. Nothing was wanting to complete her beauty. The tinge of the rose was in full bloom upon her cheek; the charms of sensibility and tenderness were always her associates. In Ambulinia's bosom dwelt a noble soul—one that never faded—one that never was conquered. Her heart yielded to no feeling but the love of Elfonzo, on whom she gazed with intense delight, and to whom she felt herself more closely bound because he sought the hand of no other. Elfonzo was roused from his apparent reverie. His books no longer were his inseparable companions — his thoughts arrayed themselves to encourage him to the field of victory. He endeavoured to speak to his supposed Ambulinia, but his speech appeared not in words. No, his effort was a stream of fire, that kindled his soul into a flame of admiration, and carried his senses away captive. Ambulinia had disappeared, to make him more mindful of his duty. As she walked speedily away through the piny woods, she calmly echoed: 'O! Elfonzo, thou wilt now look from thy sunbeams. Thou shalt now walk in a new path—perhaps thy way leads through darkness; but fear not, the stars foretell happiness.'

Not many days afterwards, as surrounded by fragrant flowers, she sat one evening at twilight, to enjoy the cool breeze that whispered notes of melody along the distant groves, the little birds perched on every side, as if to watch the movements of their new visitor. The bells were tolling, when Elfonzo silently stole along by the wild wood flowers, holding in his hand his favourite instrument of music—his eye continually searching for Ambulinia, who hardly seemed to perceive him, as she played carelessly with the songsters that hopped from branch to branch. Nothing could be more striking than the difference between the two. Nature seemed to have given the more tender soul to Elfonzo, and the stronger and more courageous to Ambulinia. A deep feeling spoke from the eyes of Elfonzo—such a feeling as can only be expressed by those who are blessed as admirers, and by those who are able to return the same with sincerity of heart. He was a few years older than Ambulinia, she had turned a little into her seventeenth. He had almost grown up in the Cherokee country, with the same equal proportions as one of the natives. But little intimacy had existed between them until the year forty-one—because the youth felt that the character of such a lovely girl was too exalted to inspire any other feeling than that of quiet reverence. But as lovers will not always be insulted, at all times and under all circumstances, by the frowns and cold looks of crabbed old age, which should continually reflect dignity upon those around, and treat the unfortunate as well as the fortunate with a graceful mien, he continued to use diligence and perseverance. All this lighted a spark in his heart that changed his whole character, and like the unyielding Deity that follows the storm to check its rage in the forest, he resolves for the first time to shake off his embarrassment, and return where he had before only worshipped.

It could not escape Ambulinia's penetrating eye, that he sought an interview with her, which she as anxiously avoided, and assumed a more distant calmness than before, seemingly to destroy all hope. After many efforts and struggles with his own person, with timid steps the Major approached the damsel, with the same caution as he would have done in a field of battle. 'Lady Ambulinia,' said he, trembling, 'I have long desired a moment like this. I dare not let it escape. I fear the consequences; yet I hope your indulgence will at least hear my petition. Can you not anticipate what I would say, and what I am about to express? Will you not, like Minerva, who sprung from the brain of Jupiter, release me from thy winding chains, or cure me——' 'Say no more, Elfonzo,' answered Ambulinia, with a serious look, raising her hand as if she intended to swear eternal hatred against the whole world, 'another lady in my place would have perhaps answered your question in bitter coldness. I know not the little arts of my sex. I care but little for the vanity of those who would chide me, and am unwilling, as well as ashamed to be guilty of anything that would lead you to think "all is not gold that glitters:" so be not rash in your resolution. It is better to repent now, than to do it in a more solemn hour. Yes, I know what you would say. I know you have a costly gift for me— the noblest that man can make—*your heart!* you should not offer it to one so unworthy. Heaven, you know, has allowed my father's house to be made a house of solitude, a home of silent obedi- ence, which, my parents say, is more to be admired than big names and high-sounding titles. Not- withstanding all this, let me speak the emotions of an honest heart—allow me to say in the fulness of my hopes that I anticipate better days. The bird may stretch its wings towards the sun, which it can never reach ; and flowers of the field appear to ascend in the same ·direction, because they cannot do otherwise : but man confides his complaints to the saints in whom he believes : for in their abodes of light they know no more sorrow. From your confession and indicative looks, I must be that person : if so, deceive not yourself.'

Elfonzo replied, ' Pardon me, my dear madam, for my frankness. I have loved you from my earliest days—everything grand and beautiful hath borne the image of Ambulinia : while precipices on every hand surrounded me, your *guardian angel* stood and beckoned me away from the deep abyss. In every trial—in every misfortune, I have met with your helping hand ; yet I never dreamed or dared to cherish thy love, till a voice impaired with age encouraged the cause, and declared they who acquired thy favour should win a victory. I saw how Leos worshipped thee. I felt my own unworthiness. I began to *know jealousy*, a strong guest indeed, in my bosom ; yet I could see, if I gained your admiration, Leos was to be my rival. I was aware that he had the influence of your parents, and the wealth of a deceased relative, which is too often mistaken for permanent and regular tranquillity; yet I have determined by your permission to beg an interest in your prayers—to ask you to animate my drooping spirits by your smiles and your winning looks; for, if you but speak, I shall be conqueror, my enemies shall stagger like Olympus shakes. And though earth and sea may tremble, and the charioteer of the sun may forget his dashing steed; yet I am assured that it is only to arm me with divine weapons, which will enable me to complete my long-tried intention.' 'Return to yourself, Elfonzo,' said Ambulinia, pleasantly, 'a dream of vision has disturbed your intellect—you are above the atmosphere, dwelling in the celestial regions; nothing is there that urges or hinders, nothing that brings discord into our present litigation. I entreat you to condescend a little, and be a man and forget it all. When Homer describes the battle of the gods and noble men, fighting with giants and dragons, they represent under this image our struggles with the delusions of our passions. You have exalted me, an unhappy girl, to the skies— you have called me a saint, and portrayed in your imagination an angel in human form. Let her remain such to you—let her continue to be as you have supposed, and be assured that she will consider a share in your esteem as her highest treasure. Think not that I would allure you from the path in which your conscience leads you; for you know I respect the conscience of others, as I would die for my own. Elfonzo, if I am worthy of thy love, let such conversation never again pass between us. Go, seek a nobler theme; we will seek it in the stream of time, as the sun set in the Tigris.' As she spake these words, she grasped the hand of Elfonzo, saying at the same time, 'Peace and prosperity attend you, my hero; be up and doing.' Closing her remarks with this expression, she walked slowly away, leaving Elfonzo astonished and amazed. He ventured not to follow or detain her. Here he stood alone, gazing at the stars;—confounded as he was, here he stood. The rippling stream rolled on at his feet. Twilight had already begun to draw her sable mantle over the earth, and now and then the fiery smoke would ascend from the little town which lay spread out before him. The citizens seemed to be full of life and good humour; but poor Elfonzo saw not a brilliant scene. No, his future life stood before him, stripped of the hopes that once adorned all his sanguine desires. 'Alas!' said he, 'am I now

Grief's disappointed son at last!' Ambulinia's image rose before his fancy. A mixture of ambition and greatness of soul moved upon his young heart, and encouraged him to bear all his crosses with the patience of a Job, notwithstanding he had to encounter with so many obstacles. He still endeavoured to prosecute his studies, and reasonably progressed in his education. Still he was not content; there was something yet to be done before his happiness was complete. He would visit his friends and acquaintances. They would invite him to social parties, insisting that he should partake of the amusements that were going on. This he enjoyed tolerably well. The ladies and gentlemen were generally well pleased with the Major, as he delighted all with his violin, which seemed to have a thousand chords—more symphonious than the Muses of Apollo, and more enchanting than the ghost of the Hills. He passed some days in the country. During that time Leos had made many calls upon Ambulinia, who was generally received with a great deal of courtesy by the family. They thought him to be a young man worthy of attention, though he had but little in his soul to attract the attention, or even win the affections of her whose graceful manners had almost made him a slave to every bewitching look that fell from her eyes. Leos made several attempts to tell her of his fair prospects—how much he loved her, and how much it would add to his bliss if he could but think she would be willing to share these blessings with him; but, choked by his undertaking, he made himself more like an inactive drone than he did like one who bowed at beauty's shrine.

Elfonzo again wends his way to the stately walls and new-built village. He now determines to see the end of the prophecy which had been foretold to him. The clouds burst from his sight; he believes if he can but see his Ambulinia, he can open to her view the bloody altars that have been misrepresented to stigmatise his name. He knows that her breast is transfixed with the sword of reason, and ready at all times to detect the hidden villainy of her enemies. He resolves to see her in her own home, with the consoling theme: 'I can but perish if I go. Let the consequences be what they may,' said he, 'if I die, it shall be contending and struggling for my own rights.'

Night had almost overtaken him when he arrived in town. Colonel Elder, a noble-hearted, high-minded, and independent man, met him at

his door as usual, and seized him by the hand.
'Well, Elfonzo,' said the Colonel, 'how does the
world use you in your efforts?'   'I have no objection to the world,' said Elfonzo, 'but the people
are rather singular in some of their opinions.'
'Aye, well,' said the Colonel, 'you must remember
that creation is made up of many mysteries: just
take things by the right handle—be always sure you
know which is the smooth side before you attempt
your polish—be reconciled to your fate, be it what
it may, and never find fault with your condition,
unless your complaining will benefit it.   Perseverance is a principle that should be commendable in
those who have judgment to govern it.   I should
never have been so successful in my hunting ex-
cursions, had I waited till the deer by some magic
dream had been drawn to the muzzle of the gun,
before I made an attempt to fire at the game that
dared my boldness in the wild forest.   The great
mystery in hunting seems to be—a good marks-
man, a resolute mind, a fixed determination, and
my word for it, you will never return home without sounding your horn with the breath of a new
victory.   And so with every other undertaking.
Be confident that your ammunition is of the right
kind—always pull your trigger with a steady hand,

and so soon as you perceive a calm, touch her off, and the spoils are yours.'

This filled him with redoubled vigour, and he set out with a stronger anxiety than ever to the home of Ambulinia. A few short steps soon brought him to the door, half out of breath. He rapped gently. Ambulinia, who sat in the parlour alone, suspecting Elfonzo was near, ventured to the door, opened it, and beheld the hero, who stood in an humble attitude, bowed gracefully, and as they caught each other's looks, the light of peace beamed from the eyes of Ambulinia. Elfonzo caught the expression; a halloo of smothered shouts ran through every vein, and for the first time he dared to impress a kiss upon her cheek. The scene was overwhelming; had the temptation been less animating, he would not have ventured to have acted so contrary to the desired wish of his Ambulinia; but who could have withstood the irresistible temptation? What society condemns the practice, but a cold, heartless, uncivilised people, that know nothing of the warm attachments of refined society? Here the dead was raised to his long-cherished hopes, and the lost was found. Here all doubt and danger were buried in the vortex of oblivion; sectional differences no

longer disunited their opinions'; like the freed bird
from the cage, sportive claps its rustling wings,
wheels about to Heaven in a joyful strain, and
raises its notes to the upper sky. Ambulinia in-
sisted upon Elfonzo to be seated, and give her a
history of his unnecessary absence; assuring him
the family had retired, consequently they would
ever remain ignorant of his visit. Advancing
towards him, she gave a bright display of her rosy
neck, and from her head the ambrosial locks
breathed divine fragrance; her robe hung waving
to his view, while she stood like a goddess confessed
before him.

'It does seem to me, my dear sir,' said Ambulinia, 'that you have been gone an age. Oh, the
restless hours I have spent since I last saw you, in
yon beautiful grove! There is where I trifled with
your feelings for the express purpose of trying your
attachment for me. I now find you are devoted;
but ah! I trust you live not unguarded by the
powers of Heaven. Though oft did I refuse to join
my hand with thine, and as oft did I cruelly mock
thy entreaties with borrowed shapes: yes, I feared
to answer thee by terms, in words sincere and
undissembled. O! could I pursue, and you had
leisure to hear the annals of my woes, the evening

star would shut Heaven's gates upon the impending day, before my tale would be finished, and this night would find me soliciting your forgiveness. 'Dismiss thy fears and thy doubts,' replied Elfonzo. 'Look O! look: that angelic look of thine—bathe not thy visage in tears; banish those floods that are gathering; let my confession and my presence bring thee some relief.' 'Then, indeed, I will be cheerful,' said Ambulinia; 'and I think, if we will go to the exhibition this evening, we certainly will see something worthy of our attention. One of the most tragical scenes is to be acted that has ever been witnessed, and one that every jealous-hearted person should learn a lesson from. It cannot fail to have a good effect, as it will be performed by those who are young and vigorous, and learned as well as enticing. You are aware, Major Elfonzo, who are to appear on the stage, and what the characters are to represent.' 'I am acquainted with the circumstances,' replied Elfonzo, 'and as I am to be one of the musicians upon that interesting occasion, I should be much gratified if you would favour me with your company during the hours of the exercises.'

'What strange notions are in your mind?' inquired Ambulinia. 'Now I know you have something in view, and I desire you to tell me why it is that you are so anxious that I should continue with you while the exercises are going on ; though, if you think I can add to your happiness and predilections, I have no particular objection to acquiesce in your request.   Oh, I think I foresee, now, what you anticipate.'   'And will you have the goodness to tell me what you think it to be?' inquired Elfonzo.  'By all means,' answered Ambulinia ; 'a rival, sir, you would fancy in your own mind; but let me say to you, fear not! fear not!   I will be one of the last persons to disgrace my sex, by thus encouraging every one who may feel disposed to visit me, who may honour me with their graceful bows and their choicest compliments.   It is true that young men too often mistake civil politeness for the finer emotions of the heart, which is tantamount to courtship ; but, ah ! how often are they deceived when they come to test the weight of sunbeams, with those on whose strength hangs the future happiness of an untried life.'

The people were now rushing to the Academy with impatient anxiety; the band of music was closely followed by the students ; then the parents and guardians ; nothing interrupted the glow of spirits which ran through every bosom, tinged with the songs of a Virgil and the tide of a Homer. Elfonzo and Ambulinia soon repaired to the scene, and, fortunately for them both, the house was so crowded that they took their seats together in the music department, which was not in view of the auditory. This fortuitous circumstance added more to the bliss of the Major than a thousand such exhibitions would have done. He forgot that he was man; music had lost its charms for him; whenever he attempted to carry his part, the string of the instrument would break, the bow became stubborn, and refused to obey the loud calls of the audience. Here, he said, was the paradise of his home, the long-sought-for opportunity; he felt as though he could send a million supplications to the throne of heaven for such an exalted privilege. Poor Leos, who was somewhere in the crowd, looking as attentively as if he was searching for a needle in a haystack; here he stood, wondering to himself why Ambulinia was not there. 'Where can she be? Oh! if she was only here, how I could relish the scene! Elfonzo is certainly not in town; but what if he is? I have got the wealth, if I have not the dignity, and I am sure that the squire and his lady have always been particular friends of mine, and I think with this assurance I shall be able to get upon the blind side of the rest of the family, and make the heaven-born Ambulinia the mistress of all I possess.' Then, again, he would drop his head, as if attempting to solve the most difficult problem in Euclid. While he was thus conjecturing in his own mind, a very interesting part of the exhibition was going on, which called the attention of all present. The curtains of the stage waved continually by the repelled forces that were given to them, which caused Leos to behold Ambulinia leaning upon the chair of Elfonzo. Her lofty beauty, seen by the glimmering of the chandelier, filled his heart with rapture, he knew not how to contain himself; to go where they were would expose him to ridicule; to continue where he was, with such an object before him, without being allowed an explanation in that trying hour, would be to the great injury of his mental as well as of his physical powers; and, in the náme of high heaven, what must he do? Finally, he resolved to contain himself as well as he conveniently could, until the scene was over, and then he would plant himself at the door, to arrest Ambulinia from the hands of the insolent Elfonzo, and thus make for himself a more prosperous field of immortality than ever was decreed by Omnipotence, or ever pencil drew or artist imagined. Accordingly he made himself sentinel, immediately after the performance of the evening—retained his position apparently in defiance of all the world, he waited, he gazed at every lady, his whole frame trembled; here he stood until everything like human shape had disappeared from the Institution, and he had done nothing; he had failed to accomplish that which he so eagerly sought for. Poor, unfortunate creature! he had not the eyes of an Argus, or he might have seen his Juno and Elfonzo, assisted by his friend Sigma, make their escape from the window, and, with the rapidity of a race-horse, hurry through the blast of the storm, to the residence of her father, without being recognised. He did not tarry long, but assured Ambulinia the endless chain of their existence was more closely connected than ever, since he had seen the virtuous, innocent, imploring, and the constant Amelia murdered by the jealous-hearted Farcillo, the accursed of the land.

The following is the tragical scene, which is only introduced to show the subject matter that enabled Elfonzo to come to such a determinate resolution, that nothing of the kind should ever dispossess him of his true character, should he be so fortunate as to succeed in his present undertaking.

Amelia was the wife of Farcillo, and a virtuous woman; Gracia, a young lady, was her particular friend and confidant. Farcillo grew jealous of Amelia, murders her, finds out that he was deceived, *and stabs himself.* Amelia appears alone, talking to herself.

*A.* Hail, ye solitary ruins of antiquity, ye sacred tombs and silent walks! it is your aid I invoke; it is to you, my soul, wrapt in deep meditation, pours forth its prayer. Here I wander upon the stage of mortality, since the world hath turned against me. Those whom I believed to be my friends, alas! are now my enemies, planting thorns in all my paths, poisoning all my pleasures, and turning the past to pain. What a lingering catalogue of sighs and tears lies just before me, crowding my aching bosom with the fleeting dream of humanity, which must shortly terminate! And to what purpose will all this bustle of life, these agitations and emotions of the heart, have conduced, if it leave behind it nothing of utility, if it leave no traces of improvement? Can it be that I am deceived in my conclusion? No, I see that I have nothing to hope for, but everything to fear, which tends to drive me from the walks of time.

> Oh! in this dead night, if loud winds arise,
> To lash the surge and bluster in the skies,
> May the west its furious rage display,
> Toss me with storms in the watery way.

*(Enter Gracia.)*

*G.* Oh, Amelia, is it you, the object of grief, the daughter of opulence, of wisdom and philosophy, that thus complaineth? It cannot be you are the child of misfortune, speaking of the monuments of former ages, which were allotted not for the reflection of the distressed, but for the fearless and bold.

*A.* Not the child of poverty, Gracia, or the heir of glory and peace, but of fate. Remember, I have wealth more than wit can number; I have had power more than kings could encompass; yet the world seems a desert; all nature appears an afflictive spectacle of warring passions. This blind fatality, that capriciously sports with the rules and lives of mortals, tells me that the mountains will never again send forth the water of their springs to my thirst. Oh, that I might be freed and set at liberty from wretchedness! But I fear, I fear this will never be.

*G.* Why, Amelia, this untimely grief? What

has caused the sorrows that bespeak better and happier days, to thus lavish out such heaps of misery? You are aware that your instructive lessons embellish the mind with holy truths, by wedding its attention to none but great and noble affections.

*A.* This, of course, is some consolation. I will ever love my own species with feelings of a fond recollection, and while I am studying to advance the universal philanthropy, and the spotless name of my own sex, I will try to build my own upon the pleasing belief that I have accelerated the advancement of one who whispers of departed confidence.

> And I, like some poor peasant fated to reside
> Remote from friends, in a forest wide.
> Oh, see what woman's woes and human wants require,
> Since that great day hath spread the seed of sinful fire.

*G.* Look up, thou poor disconsolate; you speak of quitting earthly enjoyments. Unfold thy bosom to a friend, who would be willing to sacrifice every enjoyment for the restoration of that dignity and gentleness of mind which used to grace your walks, and which is so natural to yourself; not only that, but your paths were strewed with flowers of every hue and of every order.

> With verdant green the mountains glow,
> For thee, for thee, the lilies grow;
> Far stretched beneath the tented hills,
> A fairer flower the valley fills.

*A.* Oh, would to heaven I could give you a short narrative of my former prospects for happiness, since you have acknowledged to be an unchangeable confidant — the richest of all other blessings! Oh, ye names for ever glorious, ye celebrated scenes, ye renowned spot of my hymeneal moments; how replete is your chart with sublime reflections! How many profound vows, decorated with immaculate deeds, are written upon the surface of that precious spot of earth, where I yielded up my life of celibacy, bade youth with all its beauties a final adieu, took a last farewell of the laurels that had accompanied me up the hill of my juvenile career! It was then I began to descend towards the valley of disappointment and sorrow; it was then I cast my little bark upon a mysterious ocean of wedlock, with him who then smiled and caressed me, but, alas! now frowns with bitterness, and has grown jealous and cold towards me, because the ring he gave me is misplaced or lost. Oh, bear me, ye flowers of memory, softly through the eventful history of past times; and ye places that have witnessed the progression of man in the

circle of so many societies, aid, oh aid my recollection, while I endeavour to trace the vicissitudes of
a life devoted in endeavouring to comfort him that
I claim as the object of my wishes !

> Ah ! ye mysterious men, of all the world, how few
> Act just to Heaven and to your promise true !
> But He who guides the stars with a watchful eye,
> The deeds of men lay open without disguise ;
> Oh, this alone will avenge the wrongs I bear,
> For all the oppressed are his peculiar care.

*(F. makes a slight noise.)*

*A.* Who is there—Farcillo ?

*G.* Then I must be gone.   Heaven protect you.
Oh, Amelia, farewell, be of good cheer.

> May you stand, like Olympus' towers,
> Against earth and all jealous powers !
> May you, with loud shouts ascend on high,
> Swift as an eagle in the upper sky.

*A.* Why so cold and distant to-night, Farcillo ?
Come, let us each other greet, and forget all the
past, and give security for the future.

*F.* Security ! talk to me about giving security
for the future—what an insulting requisition !
Have you said your prayers to-night, Madam
Amelia ?

*A.* Farcillo, we sometimes forget our duty,
particularly when we expect to be caressed by others.

*F.* If you bethink yourself of any crime, or of any fault, that is yet concealed from the courts of Heaven and the thrones of grace, I bid you ask and solicit forgiveness for it now.

*A.* Oh, be kind, Farcillo, don't treat me so! What do you mean by all this?

*F.* Be kind, you say; you, madam, have forgot that kindness you owe to me, and bestowed it upon another; you shall suffer for your conduct when you make your peace with your God. I would not slay thy unprotected spirit. I call to Heaven to be my guard and my watch—I would not kill thy soul, in which all once seemed just, right, and perfect; but I must be brief, woman.

*A.* What, talk you of killing? Oh, Farcillo, Farcillo, what is the matter?

*F.* Aye, I do, without doubt; mark what I say, Amelia.

*A.* Then, O God, O Heaven, and Angels, be propitious, and have mercy upon me!

*F.* Amen to that, madam, with all my heart and with all my soul.

*A.* Farcillo, listen to me one moment; I hope you will not kill me.

*F.* Kill you, aye, that I will; attest it, ye fair host of light; record it, ye dark imps of hell!

*A.* Oh, I fear you—you are fatal when darkness covers your brow; yet I know not why I should fear, since I never wronged you in all my life. I stand, sir, guiltless before you.

*F.* You pretend to say you are guiltless! Think of thy sins, Amelia ; think, oh think, hidden woman !

*A.* Wherein have I not been true to you? That death is unkind, cruel, and unnatural, that kills for loving.

*F.* Peace, and be still while I unfold to thee.

*A.* I will, Farcillo, and while I am thus silent, tell me the cause of such cruel coldness in an hour like this.

*F.* That *ring*, oh that ring I so loved, and gave thee as the ring of my heart; the allegiance you took to be faithful, when it was presented; the kisses and smiles with which you honoured it. You became tired of the donor, despised it as a plague, and finally gave it to Malos, the hidden, the vile traitor !

*A.* No, upon my word and honour, I never did; I appeal to the Most High to bear me out in this matter. Send for Malos, and ask him.

*F.* Send for Malos, aye ! Malos you wish to see ; I thought so. I knew you could not keep his name concealed. Amelia, sweet Amelia, take heed, take heed of perjury; you are on the stage of death, to suffer for *your sins.*

*A.* What, not to die I hope, my Farcillo, my ever beloved?

*F.* Yes, madam, to die a traitor's death. Shortly your spirit shall take its exit; therefore confess freely thy sins, for to deny tends only to make me groan under the bitter cup thou hast made for me. Thou art to die with the name of traitor on thy brow!

*A.* Then, O Lord, have mercy upon me; give me courage, give me grace and fortitude to stand this hour of trial!

*F.* Amen, I say, with all my heart.

*A.* And, oh, Farcillo, will you have mercy, too? I never intentionally offended you in all my life; never *loved* Malos, never gave him cause to think so, as the high court of Justice will acquit me before its tribunal.

*F.* Oh, false, perjured woman, thou dost chill my blood, and makest me a demon like thyself. I saw the ring.

*A.* He found it, then, or got it clandestinely; send for him, and let him confess the truth; let his confession be sifted.

*F.* And you still wish to see him ! I tell you, madam, he hath already confessed, and thou knowest the darkness of thy heart.

*A.* What, my deceived Farcillo, that I gave him the ring, in which all my affections were concentrated ? Oh, surely not.

*F.* Aye, he did. Ask thy conscience, and it will speak with a voice of thunder to thy soul.

*A.* He will not say so, he dare not, he cannot.

*F.* No, he will not say so now, because his mouth, I trust, is hushed in death, and his body stretched to the four winds of heaven, to be torn to pieces by carnivorous birds.

*A.* What, is he dead, and gone to the world of spirits with that declaration in his mouth ? Oh, unhapy man ! Oh, insupportable hour !

*F.* Yes, and had all his sighs and looks and tears been lives, my great revenge could have slain them all, without the least condemnation.

*A.* Alas ! he is ushered into eternity without testing the matter for which I am abused and sentenced and condemned to die.

*F.* Cursed, infernal woman ! Weepest thou for him to my face ? He that hath robbed me of my peace, my energy, the whole love of my life ? Could I call the fabled Hydra, I would have him live and perish, survive and die, until the sun itself would grow dim with age. I would make him have the thirst of a Tantalus, and roll the wheel of an Ixion, until the stars of heaven should quit their brilliant stations.

*A.* Oh, invincible God, save me! Oh, unsupportable moment! Oh, heavy hour! Banish me, Farcillo—send me where no eye can ever see me, where no sound shall ever greet my ear; but, oh, slay me not, Farcillo; vent thy rage and thy spite upon this emaciated frame of mine, only spare my life!

*F.* Your petitions avail nothing, cruel Amelia.

*A.* Oh, Farcillo, perpetrate the dark deed to-morrow; let me live till then, for my past kindness to you, and it may be some kind angel will show to you that I am not only the object of innocence, but one who never loved another but your noble self.

*F.* Amelia, the decree has gone forth, it is to be done, and that quickly; thou art to die, madam.

*A.* But half an hour allow me, to see my father and my only child, to tell her the treachery and vanity of this world.

*F.* There is no alternative, there is no pause; my daughter shall not see its deceptive mother die; your father shall not know that his daughter fell disgraced, despised by all but her enchanting Malos.

*A.* Oh, Farcillo, put up thy threatening dagger into its scabbard ; let it rest and be still, just while I say one prayer for thee and for my child.

*F.* It is too late, thy doom is fixed, thou hast not confessed to Heaven or to me, my child's protector—thou art to die. Ye powers of earth and heaven, protect and defend me in this alone. (*Stabs her, while imploring for mercy.*)

*A.* Oh, Farcillo, Farcillo, a guiltless death I die.

*F.* Die ! die ! die !

(*Gracia enters running, falls to her knees weeping, and kisses Amelia.*)

*G.* Oh, Farcillo, Farcillo ! oh, Farcillo !

*F.* I am here, the genius of the age, and the avenger of my wrongs.

*G.* Oh, lady, speak once more ; sweet Amelia, oh, speak again ! Gone, gone—yes, for ever gone ! Farcillo, oh, cold-hearted Farcillo, some evil fiend hath urged you to do this, Farcillo.

*F.* Say you not so again, or you shall receive the same fate. I did the glorious deed, madam— beware, then, how you talk.

*G.* I fear not your implements of war ; I will

let you know you have not the power to do me harm. If you have a heart of triple brass, it shall be reached and melted, and thy blood shall chill thy veins and grow stiff in thy arteries. Here is the ring of the virtuous and innocent murdered Amelia; I obtained it from Malos, who yet lives, in hopes that he will survive the wound given him, and says he got it clandestinely—declares Amelia to be the princess of truth and virtue, invulnerable to anything like forgetting her first devotion to thee. The world has heard of your conduct and your jealousy, and with one universal voice declares her to be the best of all in piety; that she is the star of this great universe, and a more virtuous woman never lived since the wheels of time began. Oh, had you waited till to-morrow, or until I had returned, some kind window would have been opened to her relief. But, alas! she is gone—yes, for ever gone, to try the realities of an unknown world!

(*Farcillo leaning over the body of Amelia.*)

*F.* Malos not dead, and here is my ring! Oh, Amelia! falsely, falsely murdered! Oh, bloody deed! Oh, wretch that I am! Oh, angels, forgive me! Oh, God, withhold Thy vengeance! Oh,

Amelia, if Heaven would make a thousand worlds like this, set with diamonds, and all of one perfect chrysolite, I would not have done this for them all, I would not have frowned and cursed as I did. Oh, she was heavenly true, nursed in the very lap of bright angels! Cursed slave that I am! Jealousy, oh! thou infernal demon! Lost, lost to every sense of honour! Oh! Amelia—heaven-born Amelia—dead, dead! Oh! oh! oh!—then let me die with thee. Farewell! farewell! ye world that deceived me! (*Stabs himself.*)

Soon after the excitement of this tragical scene was over, and the enlisted feeling for Amelia had grown more buoyant with Elfonzo and Ambulinia, he determined to visit his retired home, and make the necessary improvements to enjoy a better day; consequently he conveyed the following lines to Ambulinia:

> Go tell the world that hope is glowing,
>   Go bid the rocks their silence break,
> Go tell the stars that love is glowing,
>   Then bid the hero his lover take.

In the region where scarcely the foot of man hath ever trod, where the woodman hath not found his way, lies a blooming grove, seen only by the sun when he mounts his lofty throne, visited only by the light of the stars, to whom are entrusted the guardianship of earth, before the sun sinks to rest in his rosy bed. High cliffs of rock surround the romantic place, and in the small cavity of the rocky wall grows the daffodil clear and pure; and as the wind blows along the enchanting little mountain which surrounds the lonely spot, it nourishes the flowers with the dew-drops of heaven. Here is the seat of Elfonzo; Darkness claims but little victory over this dominion, and in vain does she spread out her gloomy wings. Here the waters flow perpetually, and the trees lash their tops together to bid the welcome visitor a happy muse. Elfonzo, during his short stay in the country, had fully persuaded himself that it was his duty to bring this solemn matter to an issue. A duty that he individually owed, as a gentleman, to the parents of Ambulinia, a duty in itself involving not only his own happiness and his own standing in society, but one that called aloud the act of the parties to make it perfect and complete. How he should communicate his intentions to get a favourable reply, he was at a loss to know; he knew not whether to address Squire Valeer in prose or in poetry, in a jocular or an argumentative manner, or

whether he should use moral suasion, legal injunction, or seize and take by reprisal; if it was to do
the latter, he would have no difficulty in deciding
in his own mind, but his gentlemanly honour was
at stake; so he concluded to address the following
letter to the father and mother of Ambulinia,
as his address in person he knew would only
aggravate the old gentleman, and perhaps his lady.

'Cumming, Ga., January 22, 1844.

'Mr. and Mrs. Valeer,—

' Again I resume the pleasing task of addressing
you, and once more beg an immediate answer to
my many salutations. From every circumstance
that has taken place, I feel in duty bound to
comply with my obligations; to forfeit my word
would be more than I dare do: to break my pledge,
and my vows that have been witnessed, sealed, and
delivered in the presence of an unseen Deity,
would be disgraceful on my part, as well as ruinous
to Ambulinia. I wish no longer to be kept in
suspense about this matter. I wish to act gentlemanly in every particular. It is true the promises
I have made are unknown to any but Ambulinia,
and I think it unnecessary to here enumerate
them, as they who promise the most generally

perform the least. Can you for a moment doubt my sincerity or my character? My only wish is, sir, that you may calmly and dispassionately look at the situation of the case, and if your better judgment should dictate otherwise, my obligations may induce me to pluck the flower that you so diametrically opposed. We have sworn by the saints—by the gods of battle, and by that faith whereby just men are made perfect, to be united. I hope, my dear sir, you will find it convenient as well as agreeable to give me a favourable answer, with the signature of Mrs. Valeer as well as yourself.

'With very great esteem,

'Your humble servant,

'J. I. ELFONZO.'

The moon and stars had grown pale when Ambulinia had retired to rest. A crowd of unpleasant thoughts passed through her bosom. Solitude dwelt in her chamber—no sound from the neighbouring world penetrated its stillness; it appeared a temple of silence, of repose, and of mystery. At that moment she heard a still voice calling her father. In an instant, like a flash of lightning, a thought ran through her mind, that it must be the bearer of Elfonzo's communication.

'It is not a dream!' she said, 'no, I cannot read
dreams.  Oh! I would to Heaven I was near that
glowing eloquence—that poetical language,—it
charms the mind in an inexpressible manner, and
warms the coldest heart.'  While consoling herself
with this strain, her father rushed into her room
almost frantic with rage, exclaiming: 'O, Ambulinia! Ambulinia!! undutiful, ungrateful daughter!
What does this mean?  Why does this letter bear
such heartrending intelligence?  Will you quit a
father's house with this debased wretch, without a
place to lay his distracted head; going up and
down the country, with every novel · object that
may chance to wander through this region?  He is
a pretty man to make love known to his superiors,
and you, Ambulinia, have done but little credit to
·yourself by honouring his visits.  O wretchedness!
can it be that my hopes of happiness are for ever
blasted?  Will you not listen to a father's entreaties, and pay some regard to a mother's tears?
I know, and I do pray that God will give me
fortitude to bear with this sea of troubles, and
rescue my daughter, my Ambulinia, as a brand
from the eternal burning.'  'Forgive me, father.
Oh! forgive thy child,' replied Ambulinia.  'My
heart is ready to break, when I see you in this

grieved state of agitation. Oh! think not so meanly of me, as that I mourn for my own danger. Father, I am only woman. Mother, I am only the templement of thy youthful years; but will suffer courageously whatever punishment you think proper to inflict upon me, if you will but allow me to comply with my most sacred promises—if you will but give me my personal right, and my personal liberty. Oh, father! if your generosity will but give me these, I ask nothing more. When Elfonzo offered me his heart, I gave him my hand, never to forsake him; and now may the mighty God banish me before I leave him in adversity! What a heart must I have to rejoice in prosperity with him whose offers I have accepted, and then, when poverty comes, haggard as it may be,—for me to trifle with the oracles of Heaven, and change with every fluctuation that may interrupt our happiness,—like the politician who runs the political gauntlet for office one day, and the next day, because the horizon is darkened a little, he is seen running for his life, for fear he might perish in its ruins. Where is the philosophy; where is the consistency; where is the charity; in conduct like this? Be happy, then, my beloved father, and forget me; let the sorrow of parting break down the wall of separation and make us equal in our feeling; let me now say how ardently I love you; let me kiss that age-worn cheek, and should my tears bedew thy face, I will wipe them away. Oh, I never can forget you; no, never, never!'

'Weep not,' said the father, 'Ambulinia. I will forbid Elfonzo my house, and desire that you may keep retired a few days. I will let him know that my friendship for my family is not linked together by cankered chains; and if he ever enters upon my premises again, I will send him to his long home.' 'Oh, father! let me entreat you to be calm upon this occasion; and though Elfonzo may be the sport of the clouds and winds, yet I feel assured that no fate will send him to the silent tomb until the God of the Universe calls him hence with a triumphant voice.'

Here the father turned away, exclaiming: 'I will answer his letter in a very few words, and you, madam, will have the goodness to stay at home with your mother: and remember, I am determined to protect you from the consuming fire that looks so fair to your view.'

'Cumming : January 22, 1844.

'Sir,—In regard to your request, I am as I ever have been, utterly opposed to your marrying into

my family; and if you have any regard for yourself, or any gentlemanly feeling, I hope you will
mention it to me no more; but seek some other
one who is not so far superior to you in standing.

' W. W. VALEER.'

When Elfonzo read the above letter, he became
so much depressed in spirits, that many of his
friends thought it advisable to use other means to
bring about the happy union. 'Strange,' said he,
'that the contents of this diminutive letter should
cause me to have such depressed feelings; but
there is a nobler theme than this. I know not why
my *military title* is not as great as that of *Squire
Valeer*. For my life I cannot see that my ancestors
are inferior to those who are so bitterly opposed to
my marriage with Ambulinia. I know I have seen
huge mountains before me; yet, when I think that
I know gentlemen will insult me upon this delicate
matter, should I become angry at fools and babblers
who pride themselves in their impudence and
ignorance? No. My equals! I know not where to
find them. My inferiors! I think it beneath me:
and my superiors! I think it presumption: therefore, if this youthful heart is protected by any of
the divine rights, I never will betray my trust.'

He was aware that Ambulinia had a confidence that was, indeed, as firm and as resolute as she was beautiful and interesting. He hastened to the cottage of Louisa, who received him in her usual mode of pleasantness, and informed him that Ambulinia had just that moment left. 'Is it possible?' said Elfonzo. 'Oh, murdered hour! Why did she not remain and be the guardian of my secrets? But hasten and tell me how she has stood this trying scene, and what are her future determinations.' 'You know,' said Louisa, 'Major Elfonzo, that you have Ambulinia's first love, which is of no small consequence. She came here about twilight, and shed many precious tears in consequence of her own fate with yours. We walked silently in yon little valley, you see, where we spent a momentary repose. She seemed to be quite as determined as ever, and before we left that beautiful spot she offered up a prayer to Heaven for thee.' 'I will see her, then,' replied Elfonzo, 'though legions of enemies may oppose. She is mine by foreordination—she is mine by prophecy—she is mine by her own free will, and I will rescue her from the hands of her oppressors. Will you not, Miss Louisa, assist me in my capture?' 'I will certainly, by the aid of Divine Providence,' answered Louisa, ' endeavour to break those slavish chains that bind the richest of prizes ; though allow me, Major, to entreat you to use no harsh means on this important occasion ; take a decided stand, and write freely to Ambulinia upon this subject, and I will see that no intervening cause hinders its passage to her. God alone will save a mourning people. Now is the day, and now is the hour to obey a command of such valuable worth.' The Major felt himself grow stronger after this short interview with Louisa. He felt as if he could whip his weight in wild-cats—he knew he was master of his own feelings, and could now write a letter that would bring this litigation to *an issue.*

' Cumming, January 24, 1844.

' DEAR AMBULINIA,—

' We have now reached the most trying moment of our lives ; we are pledged not to forsake our trust ; we have waited for a favourable hour to come, thinking your friends would settle the matter agreeably among themselves, and finally be reconciled to our marriage ; but as I have waited in vain, and looked in vain, I have determined in my own mind to make a proposition to you, though you may think it not in accordance with your station, or compatible with your rank ; yet, " sub hoc signo vinces." You know I cannot resume my visits, in consequence of the utter hostility that your father has to me ; therefore the consummation of our union will have to be sought for in a more sublime sphere, at the residence of a respectable friend of this village. You cannot have any scruples upon this mode of proceeding, if you will but remember it emanates from one who loves you better than his own life—who is more than anxious to bid you welcome to a new and a happy home. Your warmest associates say, come ; the talented, the learned, the wise and the experienced say, come ;— all these with their friends say, come. Viewing these, with many other inducements, I flatter myself that you will come to the embraces of your Elfonzo ; for now is the time of your acceptance and the day of your liberation. You cannot be ignorant, Ambulinia, that thou art the desire of my heart; its thoughts are too noble, and too pure, to conceal themselves from you. I shall wait for your answer to this impatiently, expecting that you will set the time to make your departure, and to be in readiness at a moment's warning to share the joys of a more preferable life. This will be handed you by Louisa, who will take a pleasure in communicating anything to you that may relieve your dejected spirits, and will assure you that I now stand ready, willing and waiting to make good my vows.

'I am, dear Ambulina,

'Yours truly and for ever,

'J. I. Elfonzo.'

Louisa made it convenient to visit Mr. Valeer's, though they did not suspect her in the least the bearer of love epistles: consequently, she was invited in the room to console Ambulinia, where they were left alone. Ambulinia was seated by a small table—her head resting on her hand—her brilliant eyes were bathed in tears. Louisa handed her the letter of Elfonzo, when another spirit animated her features—the spirit of renewed confidence that never fails to strengthen the female character in an hour of grief and sorrow like this; and as she pronounced the last accent of his name, she exclaimed, 'And does he love me yet? I never will forget your generosity, Louisa. Oh, unhappy and yet blessed Louisa! may you never feel what I have felt—may you never know the pangs of love! Had I never loved, I never would have been unhappy; but I turn to Him who can save, and if His wisdom does not will my expected union, I know He will give me strength to bear my lot. Amuse yourself with this little book, and take it as an apology for my silence,' said Ambulinia, 'while I attempt to answer this volume of consolation.' 'Thank you,' said Louisa, 'you are excusable upon this occasion; but I pray you, Ambulinia, to be expert upon this momentous subject, that there may be nothing mistrustful upon my part.' 'I will,' said Ambulinia, and immediately resumed her seat and addressed the following to Elfonzo:—

'Cumming, Ga., January 28, 1844.

' DEVOTED ELFONZO,—

'I hail your letter as a welcome messenger of faith, and can now say truly and firmly, that my feelings correspond with yours.   Nothing shall be wanting on my part to make my obedience your fidelity.   Courage and perseverance will accomplish success.   Receive this as my oath, that while I grasp your hand in my own imagination, we stand united before a higher tribunal than any on earth. All the powers of my life, soul, and body, I devote to thee.   Whatever dangers may threaten me, I fear not to encounter them.   Perhaps I have determined upon my own destruction, by leaving the house of the best of parents; be it so, I flee to you, I share your destiny, faithful to the end. The day that I have concluded upon for this task is *Sabbath* next, when the family with the citizens are generally at church. For Heaven's sake let not that day pass unimproved: trust not till to-morrow, it is the cheat of life—the future that never comes—the grave of many noble births—the cavern of ruined enterprise: which like the lightning's flash is born, and dies, and perishes, ere the voice of him who sees can cry, *Behold! behold!!* You may trust to what I say; no power shall tempt me to betray confidence. Suffer me to add one word more.

> I will soothe thee, in all thy grief,
>    Beside the gloomy river:
> And though thy love may yet be brief,
>    Mine is fixed for ever.

' Receive the deepest emotions of my heart for thy constant love, and may the power of inspiration be thy guide, thy portion, and thy all. In great haste,        ' Yours faithfully,

' AMBULINIA.'

' I now take my leave of you, sweet girl,' said Louisa, ' sincerely wishing you success on Sabbath next.' When Ambulinia's letter was handed to Elfonzo, he perused it without doubting its contents. Louisa charged him to make but few confidants; but, like most young men who happened to win the heart of a beautiful girl, he was so elated with the idea, that he felt as a commanding general on parade, who had confidence in all, consequently gave orders to all. The appointed Sabbath, with a delicious breeze and cloudless sky, made its appearance. The people gathered in crowds to the church—the streets were filled with the neighbouring citizens, all marching to the house of worship. It is entirely useless for me to attempt to describe the feelings of Elfonzo and Ambulinia, who were silently watching the movements of the multitude, apparently counting them as they entered the house of God, looking for the last one to darken the door. The impatience and anxiety with which they waited, and the bliss they anticipated on the eventful day, is altogether indescribable. Those that have been so fortunate as to embark in such a noble enterprise, know all its realities; and those who have not had this inestimable privilege, will have to taste its sweets, before they can tell to others its joys, its comforts, and its Heaven-born worth. Immediately after Ambulinia had assisted the family off to church, she took the advantage of that oppor--

tunity to make good her promises. She left a
home of enjoyment to be wedded to one whose
love had been justifiable. A few short steps brought
her to the presence of Louisa, who urged her to
make good use of her time, and not to delay a
moment, but to go with her to her brother's house,
where Elfonzo would for ever make her happy.
With lively speed, and yet a graceful air, she
entered the door and found herself protected by
the champion of her confidence. The necessary
arrangements were fast making to have the two
lovers united—everything was in readiness except
the Parson ; and as they are generally very sancti-
monious on such occasions, the news got to the
parents of Ambulinia before the everlasting knot
was tied, and they both came running, with uplifted hands and injured feelings, to arrest their
daughter from an unguarded and hasty resolution.
Elfonzo desired to maintain his ground, but
Ambulinia thought it best for him to leave, to
prepare for a greater contest. He accordingly
obeyed, as it would have been a vain endeavour
for him to have battled against a man who was
armed with deadly weapons ; and, besides, he could
not resist the request of such a pure heart.
Ambulinia concealed herself in the upper story of

the house, fearing the rebuke of her father; the door was locked, and no chastisement was now expected.  Squire Valeer, whose pride was already touched, resolved to preserve the dignity of his family.  He entered the house almost exhausted, looking wildly for Ambulinia.  'Amazed and astonished indeed I am,' said he, 'at a people who call themselves civilised, to allow such behaviour as this.  Ambulinia, Ambulinia!' he cried, 'come to the calls of your first, your best, and your only friend.  I appeal to you, sir,' turning to the gentleman of the house, 'to know where Ambulinia has gone, or where is she?'  'Do you mean to insult me, sir, in my own house?' inquired the confounded gentleman.  'I will burst,' said Mr. V., 'asunder every door in your dwelling, in search of my daughter, if you do not speak quickly, and tell me where she is.  I care nothing about that outcast rubbish of creation, that mean, low-lived Elfonzo, if I can but obtain Ambulinia!  Are you not going to open this door?' said he.  'By the Eternal that made heaven and earth! I will go about the work instantly, if it is not done.'  The confused citizens gathered from all parts of the village to know the cause of this commotion.  Some rushed into the house; the door that was locked flew open, and there stood Ambulinia, weeping. 'Father, be still,' said she, 'and I will follow thee home.' But the agitated man seized her, and bore her off through the gazing multitude. 'Father,' she exclaimed, 'I humbly beg your pardon—I will be dutiful—I will obey thy commands. Let the sixteen years I have lived in obedience to thee be my future security.' 'I don't like to be always giving credit, when the old score is not paid up, madam,' said the father. The mother followed almost in a state of derangement, crying and imploring her to think beforehand, and ask advice from experienced persons, and they would tell her it was a rash undertaking. 'Oh!' said she, 'Ambulinia, my daughter, did you know what I have suffered—did you know how many nights I have whiled away in agony, in pain, and in fear, you would pity the sorrows of a heartbroken mother.'

'Well, mother,' replied Ambulinia, 'I know I have been disobedient; I am aware that what I have done might have been done much better; but oh! what shall I do with my honour? it is so dear to me; I am pledged to Elfonzo. His high moral worth is certainly worth some attention; moreover, my vows, I have no doubt, are recorded in the book of life, and must I give these all up?

must my fair hopes be for ever blasted?   Forbid it,
father; oh! forbid it, mother; forbid it, heaven.'
'I have seen so many beautiful skies overclouded,'
replied the mother, 'so many blossoms nipped by
the frost, that I am afraid to trust you to the care
of those fair days, which may be interrupted by
thundering and tempestuous nights.   You no doubt
think as I did—life's devious ways were strewed
with sweet-scented flowers; but ah! how long they
have lingered around me and took their flight in
the vivid hope that laughs at the drooping victims
it has murdered.'   Elfonzo was moved at this sight.
The people followed on to see what was going to
become of Ambulinia, while he, with downcast
looks, kept at a distance, until he saw them enter
the abode of the father, thrusting her, that was the
sigh of his soul, out of his presence into a solitary
apartment, when she exclaimed, 'Elfonzo! Elfonzo! oh, Elfonzo! where art thou, with all thy
heroes? haste, oh! haste, come thou to my relief.
Ride on the wings of the wind! Turn thy force
loose like a tempest, and roll on thy army like a
whirlwind over this mountain of trouble and confusion.   Oh, friends! if any pity me, let your last
efforts throng upon the green hills, and come to the
relief of Ambulinia, who is guilty of nothing but

innocent love.' Elfonzo called out with a loud voice, 'My God, can I stand this? Arouse up, I beseech you, and put an end to this tyranny. Come, my brave boys,' said he, 'are you ready to go forth to your duty?' They stood around him. 'Who,' said he, 'will call us to arms? Where are my thunderbolts of war? Speak ye, the first who will meet the foe! Who will go forward with me in this ocean of grievous temptation? If there is one who desires to go, let him come and shake hands upon the altar of devotion, and swear that he will be a hero; yes, a Hector in a cause like this, which calls aloud for a speedy remedy.' 'Mine be the deed,' said a young lawyer, 'and mine alone; Venus alone shall quit her station before I will forsake one jot or tittle of my promise to you; what is death to me? what is all this warlike army, if it is not to win a victory? I love the sleep of the lover and the mighty; nor would I give it over till the blood of my enemies should wreak with that of my own. But God forbid that our fame should soar on the blood of the slumberer.' Mr. Valeer stands at his door with the frown of a demon upon his brow, with his dangerous weapon ready to strike the first man who should enter his door. 'Who will arise and go forward through blood and carnage to the rescue of my Ambulinia?' said Elfonzo. 'All,' exclaimed the multitude; and onward they went, with their implements of battle. Others, of a more timid nature, stood among the distant hills to see the result of the contest.

Elfonzo took the lead of his band. Night arose in clouds; darkness concealed the heavens; but the blazing hopes that stimulated them gleamed in every bosom. All approached the anxious spot; they rushed to the front of the house, and with one exclamation demanded Ambulinia. 'Away, begone, and disturb my peace no more,' said Mr. Valeer. 'You are a set of base, insolent, and infernal rascals. Go, the northern star points your path through the dim twilight of the night; go, and vent your spite upon the lonely hills; pour forth your love, you poor, weak-minded wretch, upon your idleness and upon your guitar, and your fiddle; they are fit subjects for your admiration, for, let me assure you, though this sword and iron lever are cankered, yet they frown in sleep, and let one of you dare to enter my house this night and you shall have the contents and the weight of these instruments.' 'Never yet did base dishonour blur my name,' said Elfonzo; 'mine is a cause of renown; here are my warriors, fear and tremble, for this night, though hell itself should oppose, I will endeavour to avenge her whom thou hast banished in solitude. The voice of Ambulinia shall be heard from that dark dungeon.' At that moment Ambulinia appeared at the window above, and with a tremulous voice said, 'Live, Elfonzo! oh! live to raise my stone of moss! why should such language enter your heart? why should thy voice rend the air with such agitation? I bid thee live, once more remembering these tears of mine are shed alone for thee, in this dark and gloomy vault, and should I perish under this load of trouble, join the song of thrilling accents with the raven above my grave, and lay this tattered frame beside the banks of the Chattahoochee, or the stream of Sawney's brook; sweet will be the song of death to your Ambulinia. My ghost shall visit you in the smiles of Paradise, and tell your high fame to the minds of that region, which is far more preferable than this lonely cell. My heart shall speak for thee till the latest hour; I know faint and broken are the sounds of sorrow, yet our souls, Elfonzo, shall hear the peaceful songs together. One bright name shall be ours on high, if we are not permitted to be united here; bear in mind that I still cherish my old sentiments, and the poet will mingle the names of Elfonzo and Ambulinia in the tide of other days.' 'Fly, Elfonzo,' said the voices of his united band, 'to the wounded heart of your beloved. All enemies shall fall beneath thy sword. Fly through the clefts, and the dim spark shall sleep in death.' Elfonzo rushes forward and strikes his shield against the door, which was barricaded, to prevent any intercourse. His brave sons throng round him. The people pour along the streets, both male and female, to prevent or witness the melancholy scene.

'To arms, to arms!' cried Elfonzo, 'here is a victory to be won, a prize to be gained, that is more to me than the whole world beside.' 'It cannot be done to-night,' said Mr. Valeer. 'I bear the clang of death; my strength and armour shall prevail. My Ambulinia shall rest in this hall until the break of another day, and if we fall, we fall together. If we die, we die clinging to our tattered rights, and our blood alone shall tell the mournful tale of a murdered daughter and a ruined father.' Sure enough, he kept watch all night, and was successful in defending his house and family. The bright morning gleamed upon the hills, night vanished away, the Major and his associates felt somewhat ashamed that they had not been as fortunate as they expected to have been; however, they still leaned upon their arms in dispersed groups; some were walking the streets, others were talking in the Major's behalf. Many of the citizens suspended business, as the town presented nothing but consternation. A novelty that might end in the destruction of some worthy and respectable citizens. Mr. Valeer ventured in the streets, though not without being well armed. Some of his friends congratulated him on the decided stand he had taken, and hoped he would settle the matter amicably with Elfonzo, without any serious injury. 'Me,' he replied, ' what, me, condescend to fellowship with a coward, and a low-lived, lazy, undermining villain? No, gentlemen, this cannot be; I had rather be borne off, like the bubble upon the dark blue ocean, with Ambulinia by my side, than to have him in the ascending or descending line of relationship. Gentlemen,' continued he, 'if Elfonzo is so much of a distinguished character, and is so learned in the fine arts, why do you not patronise such men? why not introduce him into your families as a gentleman of taste and of unequalled magnanimity? why are you so very anxious that he should become a relative of mine? Oh, gentlemen, I fear you yet are tainted with the curiosity of our first parents, who were beguiled by the poisonous kiss of an old ugly serpent, and who, for one *apple, damned* all mankind. I wish to divest myself, as far as possible, of that untutored custom. I have long since learned that the perfection of wisdom and the end of true philosophy is to proportion our wants to our possessions, our ambition to our capacities; we will then be a happy and a virtuous people.' Ambulinia was sent off to prepare for a long and tedious journey. Her new acquaintances had been instructed by her father how to treat her, and in what manner, and to keep the anticipated visit entirely secret. Elfonzo was watching the movements of everybody; some friends had told him of the plot that was laid to carry off Ambulinia. At night, he rallied some two or three of his forces, and went silently along to the stately mansion; a faint and glimmering light showed through the windows; lightly he steps to the door, there were many voices rallying fresh in fancy's eye; he tapped the shutter, it was opened instantly, and he beheld once more, seated beside several ladies, the hope of all his toils; he rushed towards her, she rose from her seat, rejoicing: he made one mighty grasp, when Ambulinia exclaimed, ' Huzza for Major Elfonzo!  I will defend myself and you, too, with this conquering instrument I hold in my hand; huzza, I say, I now invoke time's broad wing to shed around us some dewdrops of verdant spring.'

But the hour had not come for this joyous re-union; her friends struggled with Elfonzo for some time, and finally succeeded in arresting her from his hands. He dared not injure them, because they were matrons whose courage needed no spur; she was snatched from the arms of Elfonzo, with so much eagerness and yet with such expressive signification, that he calmly withdrew from this lovely enterprise, with an ardent hope that he should be lulled to repose by the zephyrs which whispered peace to his soul. Several long days and nights passed unmolested, all seemed to have grounded their arms of rebellion, and no callidity appeared to be going on with any of the parties. Other arrangements were made by Ambulinia; she feigned herself to be entirely the votary of a mother's care, and said, by her graceful smiles, that manhood might claim his stern dominion in some other region, where such boisterous love was not so prevalent. This gave the parents a confidence that yielded some hours of sober joy; they believed that Ambulinia would now cease to love Elfonzo, and that her stolen affections would now expire with her misguided opinions. They therefore declined the idea of sending her to a distant land. But oh! they dreamed not of the rapture that dazzled the fancy of Ambulinia, who would say, when alone, youth should not fly away on his rosy pinions, and leave her to grapple in the conflict with unknown admirers.

> No frowning age shall control
> The constant current of my soul,
> Nor a tear from pity's eye
> Shall check my sympathetic sigh.

With this resolution fixed in her mind, one dark and dreary night, when the winds whistled and the tempest roared, she received intelligence that Elfonzo was then waiting, and every preparation was then ready, at the residence of Dr. Tully, and for her to make a quick escape while the family were reposing. Accordingly she gathered her books, went to the wardrobe supplied with a variety of ornamental dressing, and ventured alone in the streets to make her way to Elfonzo, who was near at hand, impatiently looking and watching her arrival. 'What forms,' said she, 'are those rising before me ? What is that dark spot on the clouds? I do wonder what frightful ghost that is, gleaming

on the red tempest?  Oh, be merciful and tell me
what region you are from.  Oh tell me, ye strong
spirits, or ye dark and fleeting clouds, that I yet
have a friend.'  'A friend,' said a low, whispering
voice.  'I am thy unchanging, thy aged, and thy
disappointed mother.  Oh, Ambulinia, why hast
thou deceived me?  Why brandish in that hand
of thine a javelin of pointed steel?  Why
suffer that lip I have kissed a thousand times, to
equivocate?  My daughter, let these tears sink
deep into thy soul, and no longer persist in that
which may be your destruction and ruin.  Come,
my dear child, retrace your steps, and bear me
company to your welcome home.'  Without one
retorting word, or frown from her brow, she yielded
to the entreaties of her mother, and with all the
mildness of her former character she went along
with the silver lamp of age, to the home of candour
and benevolence.  Her father received her with cold
and formal politeness—'Where has Ambulinia been,
this blustering evening, Mrs. Valeer?' inquired he.
'Oh, she and I have been taking a solitary walk,'
said the mother; 'all things, I presume, are now
working for the best.'

Elfonzo heard this news shortly after it happened.  'What,' said he, 'has heaven and earth

turned against me ?  I have been disappointed
times without number.  Shall I despair ?  Must I
give it over ?  Heaven's decrees will not fade ; I
will write again—I will try again ; and if it traverses
a gory field, I pray forgiveness at the altar of
justice.'

'Desolate Hill, Cumming, Geo., 1844.

'UNCONQUERED AND BELOVED AMBULINIA,—

'I have only time to say to you, not to despair;
thy fame shall not perish ; my visions are brightening before me.  The whirlwind's rage is past, and
we now shall subdue our enemies without doubt.
On Monday morning, when your friends are at
breakfast, they will not suspect your departure, or
even mistrust me being in town, as it has been
reported advantageously that I have left for the
west.  You walk carelessly towards the academy
grove, where you will find me with a lightning steed,
elegantly equipped to bear you off where we shall be
joined in wedlock with the first connubial rights.
Fail not to do this—think not of the tedious relations
of our wrongs—be invincible.  You alone occupy
all my ambition, and I alone will make you my
happy spouse, with the same unimpeached veracity.
I remain, for ever, your devoted friend and
admirer,                                  'J. I. ELFONZO.'

The appointed day ushered in undisturbed by any clouds; nothing disturbed Ambulinia's soft beauty. With serenity and loveliness she obeys the request of Elfonzo. The moment the family seated themselves at the table—'Excuse my absence for a short time,' said she, 'while I attend to the placing of those flowers which should have been done a week ago.' And away she ran to the sacred grove, surrounded with glittering pearls that indicated her coming. Elfonzo hails her with his silver bow and his golden harp. They meet—Ambulinia's countenance brightens—Elfonzo leads up his winged steed. 'Mount,' said he, 'ye true-hearted, ye fearless soul—the day is ours.' She sprang upon the back of the young thunderbolt, a brilliant star sparkles upon her head, with one hand she grasps the reins, and with the other she holds an olive branch. 'Lend thy aid, ye strong winds,' they exclaimed; 'ye moon, ye sun, and all ye fair host of heaven, witness the enemy conquered.' 'Hold,' said Elfonzo, 'thy dashing steed.' 'Ride on,' said Ambulinia, 'the voice of thunder is behind us.' And onward they went, with such rapidity that they very soon arrived at Rural Retreat, where they dismounted, and were united with all the solemnities that usually attend such divine operations. They passed the day in thanksgiving and great rejoicing, and on that evening they visited their uncle, where many of their friends and acquaintances had gathered to congratulate them in the field of untainted bliss. The kind old gentleman met them in the yard: ' Well,' said he, ' I wish I may die, Elfonzo, if you and Ambulinia haven't tied a knot with your tongue that you can't untie with your teeth. But come in, come in; never mind, all is right—the world still moves on, and no one has fallen in this great battle.'

Happy now is their lot! Unmoved by misfortune, they live among the fair beauties of the South. Heaven spreads their peace and fame upon the arch of the rainbow, and smiles propitiously at their triumph, *through the tears of the storm.*

THE MODERN STEAMER AND THE OBSOLETE STEAMER

WE are victims of one common superstition—the superstition that we realise the changes that are daily taking place in the world because we read about them and know what they are.  I should not have supposed that the modern ship could be a surprise to me, but it is.  It seems to be as much of a surprise to me as it could have been if I had never read anything about it.  I walk about this great vessel, the ' Havel,' as she ploughs her way through the Atlantic, and every detail that comes under my eye brings up the miniature counterpart of it as it existed in the little ships I crossed the ocean in, fourteen, seventeen, eighteen, and twenty years ago.

In the ' Havel ' one can be in several respects more comfortable than he can be in the best hotels on the Continent of Europe.  For instance, she has several bath-rooms, and they are as convenient and as nicely equipped as the bath-rooms in a fine private house in America; whereas in the hotels of the Continent one bath-room is considered sufficient, and it is generally shabby and located in some out-of-the-way corner of the house; moreover, you need to give notice so long beforehand that you get over wanting a bath by the time you get it. In the hotels there are a good many different kinds of noises, and they spoil sleep; in my room in the ship I hear no sounds. In the hotels they usually shut off the electric light at midnight; in the ship one may burn it in one's room all night.

In the steamer 'Batavia,' twenty years ago, one candle set in the bulkhead between two state-rooms was there to light both rooms, but did not light either of them. It was extinguished at eleven at night, and so were all the saloon lamps, except one or two, which were left burning to help the passenger see how to break his neck trying to get around in the dark. The passengers sat at table on long benches made of the hardest kind of wood; in the 'Havel' one sits on a swivel chair with a cushioned back to it. In those old times the dinner bill of fare was always the same: a pint of some simple, homely soup or other, boiled codfish and

potatoes, slab of boiled beef; stewed prunes for des-
sert—on Sundays 'dog in a blanket,' on Thursdays
'plum duff.' In the modern ship the *menu* is
choice and elaborate, and is changed daily. In the
old times dinner was a sad occasion; in our day a
concealed orchestra enlivens it with charming music.
In the old days the decks were always wet; in our
day they are usually dry, for the promenade-deck is
roofed over, and a sea seldom comes aboard. In a
moderately disturbed sea, in the old days, a lands-
man could hardly keep his legs, but in such a sea
in our day, the decks are as level as a table. In
the old days the inside of a ship was the plainest
and barrenest thing, and the most dismal and uncomfortable, that ingenuity could devise; the modern
ship is a marvel of rich and costly decoration and
sumptuous appointment, and is equipped with every
comfort and convenience that money can buy. The
old ships had no place of assembly but the dining-
room; the new ones have several spacious and
beautiful drawing-rooms. The old ships offered
the passenger no chance to smoke except in the
place that was called the ' fiddle.' It was a repul-
sive den made of rough boards (full of cracks), and
its office was to protect the main hatch. It was
grimy and dirty; there were no seats; the only

light was a lamp of the rancid-oil-and-rag kind ;
the place was very cold, and never dry, for the seas
broke in through the  cracks every little while and
drenched the cavern  thoroughly.   In the modern
ship there are three or four large smoking-rooms,
and they have card tables and cushioned sofas, and
are  heated  by  steam  and  lighted  by  electricity.
There are few European hotels with such smoking-
rooms.

The former ships were built of wood, and had
two or three water-tight compartments in the  hold
with doors in them, which were often left open, particularly when the  ship was  going  to  hit  a  rock.
The modern leviathan is built of steel, and the water-
tight bulkheads have no doors in them ; they divide
the ship into nine or ten water-tight compartments
and endow her with as many lives as a cat.   Their
complete efficiency was established by the happy
results  following  the  memorable  accident  to  the
' City of Paris ' a year or two ago.

One curious thing which is at once noticeable in
the great  modern ship  is  the  absence  of  hubbub,
clatter, rush of feet, roaring of orders.   That is all
gone by.   The elaborate manœuvres necessary in
working  the  vessel  into  her  dock  are  conducted
without sound : one sees nothing of the processes,

hears no commands. A Sabbath stillness and solemnity reign in place of the turmoil and racket of the earlier days. The modern ship has a spacious bridge, fenced chin-high with sail-cloth, and floored with wooden gratings; and this bridge, with its fenced fore-and-aft annexes, could accommodate a seated audience of a hundred and fifty men. There are three steering equipments, each competent if the others should break. From the bridge the ship is steered, and also handled. The handling is not done by shout or whistle, but by signalling with patent automatic gongs. There are three tell-tales with plainly lettered dials—for steering, handling the engines, and for communicating orders to the invisible mates who are conducting the landing of the ship or casting off. The officer who is astern is out of sight, and too far away to hear trumpet calls; but the gongs near him tell him to haul in, pay out, make fast, let go, and so on; he hears, but the passengers do not, and so the ship seems to land herself without human help.

This great bridge is thirty or forty feet above the water, but the sea climbs up there sometimes; so there is another bridge twelve or fifteen feet higher still, for use in these emergencies. The force of water is a strange thing. It slips between one's fingers like air, but upon occasion it acts like a solid body, and will bend a thin iron rod. In the 'Havel' it has splintered a heavy oaken rail into broom-straws, instead of merely breaking it in two as would have been the seemingly natural thing for it to do. At the time of the awful Johnstown disaster, according to the testimony of several witnesses, rocks were carried some distance on the surface of the stupendous torrent; and at St. Helena, many years ago, a vast sea-wave carried a battery of cannon forty feet up a steep slope, and deposited the guns there in a row. But the water has done a still stranger thing, and it is one which is credibly vouched for. A marlinspike is an implement about a foot long which tapers from its butt to the other extremity, and ends in a sharp point. It is made of iron, and is heavy. A wave came aboard a ship in a storm and raged aft, breast high, carrying a marlinspike point-first with it, and with such lightning-like swiftness and force as to drive it three or four inches into a sailor's body and kill him.

In all ways the ocean greyhound of to-day is imposing and impressive to one who carries in his head no ship-pictures of a recent date. In bulk she comes near to rivalling the Ark; yet this monstrous mass of steel is driven five hundred miles through the waves in twenty-four hours. I remember the brag run of a steamer which I travelled in once on the Pacific—it was two hundred and nine miles in twenty-four hours; a year or so later I was a passenger in the excursion-tub 'Quaker City,' and on one occasion, in a level and glassy sea, it was claimed that she reeled off two hundred and eleven miles between noon and noon, but it was probably a campaign lie. That little steamer had seventy passengers and a crew of forty men, and seemed a good deal of a bee-hive; but in this present ship we are living in a sort of solitude, these soft summer days, with sometimes a hundred passengers scattered about the spacious distances, and sometimes nobody in sight at all; yet, hidden somewhere in the vessel's bulk, there are (including crew) near eleven hundred people.

The stateliest lines in the literature of the sea are these:

> Britannia needs no bulwark, no towers along the steep—
> Her march is o'er the mountain wave, her home is on the
> deep !

There it is. In those old times the little ships climbed over the waves and wallowed down into the trough on the other side; the giant ship of our day does not climb over the waves, but crushes her way through them. Her formidable weight and mass and impetus give her mastery over any but extraordinary storm-waves.

The ingenuity of man! I mean in this passing generation. To-day I found in the chart-room a frame of removable wooden slats on the wall, and on the slats was painted uninforming information like this:

| | | | | |
|---|---|---|---|---|
| Trim-Tank | . | . | . | Empty |
| Double-Bottom No. 1 | | . | . | Full |
| Double-Bottom No. 2 | | . | . | Full |
| Double-Bottom No. 3 | | . | . | Full |
| Double-Bottom No. 4 | | . | . | Full |

While I was trying to think out what kind of a game this might be, and how a stranger might best go to work to beat it, a sailor came in and pulled out the 'Empty' end of the first slat and put it back with its reverse side to the front, marked 'Full.' He made some other change, I did not notice what. The slat-frame was soon explained. Its function was to indicate how the ballast in the ship was distributed. The striking thing was, that that ballast was water. I did not know that a ship had ever been ballasted with water. I had merely read, some time or other, that such an experiment was to be tried. But that is the modern way; between the experimental trial of a new thing and its adoption there is no wasted time, if the trial proves its value.

On the wall, near the slat-frame, there was an outline drawing of the ship, and this betrayed the fact that this vessel has twenty-two considerable lakes of water in her. These lakes are in her bottom; they are imprisoned between her real bottom and a false bottom. They are separated from each other, thwartships, by water-tight bulkheads, and separated down the middle by a bulkhead running from the bow four-fifths of the way to the stern. It is a chain of lakes four hundred feet long and from five to seven feet deep. Fourteen of the lakes contain fresh water brought from shore, and the aggregate weight of it is four hundred tons. The rest of the lakes contain salt water—six hundred and eighteen tons. Upwards of a thousand tons of water altogether.

Think how handy this ballast is. The ship leaves port with the lakes all full. As she lightens forward, through consumption of coal, she loses trim—her head rises, her stern sinks down. Then they spill one of the sternward lakes into the sea, and the trim is restored. This can be repeated right along as occasion may require. Also, a lake at one end of the ship can be moved to the other end by pipes and steam pumps. When the sailor changed the slat-frame to-day, he was posting a transference of that kind. The seas had been increasing, and the vessel's head needed more weighting, to keep it from rising on the waves instead of ploughing through them ; therefore, twenty-five tons of water had been transferred to the bow from a lake situated well towards the stern.

A water compartment is kept either full or empty. The body of water must be compact, so that it cannot slosh around. A shifting ballast would not do, of course.

The modern ship is full of beautiful ingenuities, but it seems to me that this one is the king. I would rather be the originator of that idea than of any of the others. Perhaps the trim of a ship was never perfectly ordered and preserved until now. A vessel out of trim will not steer, her speed is maimed, she strains and labours in the seas. Poor creature! for six thousand years she has had no comfort until these latest days. For six thousand years she swam through the best and cheapest ballast in the world, the only perfect ballast, but she couldn't tell her master, and he had not the wit to find it out for himself. It is odd to reflect that there is nearly as much water inside of this ship as there is outside, and yet there is no danger.

## NOAH'S ARK

The progress made in the great art of ship-building since Noah's time is quite noticeable. Also, the looseness of the navigation laws in the time of Noah is in quite striking contrast with the strictness of the navigation laws of our time. It would not be possible for Noah to do in our day what he was permitted to do in his own. Experience has taught us the necessity of being more particular, more conservative, more careful of human life. Noah would not be allowed to sail from Bremen in our day. The inspectors would come and examine the Ark, and make all sorts of objections. A person who knows Germany can imagine the scene and the conversation without difficulty and without missing a detail. The inspector would be in a beautiful military uniform; he would be respectful, dignified, kindly, the perfect gentleman, but steady as the north star to the last requirement of his duty. He would make Noah tell him where he was born, and how old he was, and what religious sect he belonged to, and the amount of his income, and the grade and position he claimed socially, and the name and style of his occupation, and how many wives and children he had, and how many servants, and the name, sex, and age of the whole of them ; and if he hadn't a passport he would be courteously required to get one right away.   Then he would take up the matter of the Ark :

'What is her length ?'

'Six hundred feet.'

'Depth ?'

'Sixty-five.'

'Beam ?'

'Fifty or sixty.'

'Built of——'

'Wood.'

'What kind ?'

'Shittim and gopher.'

'Interior and exterior decorations ?'

'Pitched within and without.

'Passengers ?'

'Eight.'

'Sex ?'

'Half male, the others female.'

'Ages ?'

'From a hundred years up.'

'Up to where ?'

'Six hundred.'

'Ah! going to Chicago; good idea, too.  Surgeon's name?'

'We have no surgeon.'

'Must provide a surgeon.   Also an undertaker
—particularly the undertaker.   These people must
not be left without the necessities of life at their age.
Crew?'

'The same eight.'

'The same eight?'

'The same eight.'

'And half of them women?'

'Yes, sir.'

'Have they ever served as seamen?'

'No, sir.'

'Have the men?'

'No, sir.'

'Have any of you ever been to sea?'

'No, sir.'

'Where were you reared?'

'On a farm—all of us.'

'This vessel requires a crew of eight hundred
men, she not being a steamer.   You must provide
them.   She must have four mates and nine cooks.
Who is captain?'

'I am, sir.'

'You must get a captain.   Also a chambermaid.
Also sick nurses for the old people.   Who designed
this vessel ? '

'I did, sir.'

'Is it your first attempt ? '

'Yes, sir.'

'I partly suspected it.   Cargo ? '

'Animals.'

'Kind ? '

'All kinds.'

'Wild or tame ? '

'Mainly wild.'

'Foreign or domestic ? '

'Mainly foreign.'

'Principal wild ones ? '

'Megatherium, elephant, rhinoceros, lion, tiger,
wolf, snakes—all the wild things of all climes—two
of each.'

'Securely caged ? '

'No, not caged.'

'They must have iron cages.   Who feeds and
waters the menagerie ? '

'We do.'

'The old people ? '

'Yes, sir.'

'It is dangerous—for both.   The animals must

be cared for by a competent force.   How many animals are there ? '

'Big ones, seven thousand ;  big and little together, ninety-eight thousand.'

'You must provide twelve hundred keepers.   How is the vessel lighted ? '

' By two windows.'

' Where are they ? '

' Up under the eaves.'

' Two windows for a tunnel six hundred feet long and sixty-five feet deep ? You must put in the electric light—a few arc lights and fifteen hundred incandescents.   What do you do in case of leaks ? How many pumps have you ? '

' None, sir.'

'You must provide pumps.   How do you get water for the passengers and the animals ? '

' We let down the buckets from the windows.'

' It is inadequate.   What is your motive power ? '

' What is my which ? '

'Motive power.   What power do you use in driving the ship ? '

' None.'

' You must provide sails or steam.   What is the nature of your steering apparatus ? '

' We haven't any.'

'Haven't you a rudder?'

'No, sir.'

'How do you steer the vessel?'

'We don't.'

'You must provide a rudder, and properly equip it.   How many anchors have you?'

'None.'

'You must provide six.   One is not permitted to sail a vessel like this without that protection.   How many life-boats have you?'

'None, sir.'

'Provide   twenty-five.   How   many   life-preservers?'

'None.'

'You will provide two thousand.   How long are you expecting your voyage to last?'

'Eleven or twelve months.'

'Eleven or twelve months.   Pretty slow—but you will be in time for the Exposition.   What is your ship sheathed with—copper?'

'Her hull is bare—not sheathed at all.'

'Dear man, the wood-boring creatures of tho sea would riddle her like a sieve and send her to the bottom in three months.   She *cannot* be allowed to go away in this condition; she must be sheathed. Just a word more: Have you reflected that Chicago is an inland city, and not reachable with a vessel like this?'

'Shecargo? What is Shecargo? I am not going to Shecargo.'

'Indeed? Then may I ask what the animals are for?'

'Just to breed others from.'

'Others? Is it possible that you haven't enough?'

'For the present needs of civilisation, yes; but the rest are going to be drowned in a flood, and these are to renew the supply.'

'A flood?'

'Yes, sir.'

'Are you sure of that?'

'Perfectly sure. It is going to rain forty days and forty nights.'

'Give yourself no concern about that, dear sir, it often does that here.'

'Not this kind of rain. This is going to cover the mountain-tops, and the earth will pass from sight.'

'Privately—but of course not officially—I am sorry you revealed this, for it compels me to withdraw the option I gave you as to sails or steam. I must require you to use steam. Your ship cannot carry the hundredth part of an eleven-months' water-supply for the animals. You will have to have condensed water.'

'But I tell you I am going to dip water from outside with buckets.'

'It will not answer. Before the flood reaches the mountain-tops the fresh waters will have joined the salt seas, and it will all be salt. You must put in steam and condense your water. I will now bid you good-day, sir. Did I understand you to say that this was your very first attempt at ship-building?'

'My very first, sir, I give you the honest truth. I built this Ark without having ever had the slightest training or experience or instruction in marine architecture.'

' It is a remarkable work, sir, a most remarkable work. I consider that it contains more features that are new—absolutely new and unhackneyed—than are to be found in any other vessel that swims the seas.'

'This compliment does me infinite honour, dear sir, infinite; and I shall cherish the memory of it while life shall last. Sir, I offer my duty, and most grateful thanks. Adieu.'

No, the German inspector would be limitlessly courteous to Noah, and would make him feel that he was among friends, but he wouldn't let him go to sea with that Ark.

### COLUMBUS'S CRAFT

Between Noah's time and the time of Columbus naval architecture underwent some changes, and from being unspeakably bad was improved to a point which may be described as less unspeakably bad. I have read somewhere, some time or other, that one of Columbus's ships was a ninety-ton vessel. By comparing that ship with the ocean greyhounds of our time one is able to get down to a comprehension of how small that Spanish bark was, and how little fitted she would be to run opposition in the Atlantic passenger trade to-day. It would take seventy-four of her to match the tonnage of the 'Havel' and carry the 'Havel's' trip. If I remember rightly, it took her ten weeks to make the passage. With our ideas this would now be considered an objectionable gait. She probably had a captain, a mate, and a crew consisting of four seamen and a boy. The crew of a modern greyhound numbers two hundred and fifty persons.

Columbus's ship being small and very old, we know that we may draw from these two facts several absolute certainties in the way of minor details which history has left unrecorded. For instance, being small, we know that she rolled and pitched and tumbled in any ordinary sea, and stood on her head or her tail, or lay down with her ear in the water, when storm-seas ran high; also, that she was used to having billows plunge aboard and wash her decks from stem to stern; also, that the storm-racks were on the table all the way over, and that, nevertheless, a man's soup was oftener landed in his lap than in his stomach; also, that the dining-saloon was about ten feet by seven, dark, airless, and suffocating with oil-stench; also, that there was only about one state-room—the size of a grave—with a tier of two or three berths in it, of the dimensions and comfortableness of coffins, and that when the light was out, the darkness in there was so thick and real that you could bite into it and chew it like gum; also, that the only promenade was on the lofty poop-deck astern (for the ship was shaped like a high-quarter shoe)—a streak sixteen feet long by three feet wide, all the rest of the vessel being littered with ropes and flooded by the seas.

We know all these things to be true, from the mere fact that we know the vessel was small. As the vessel was old, certain other truths follow as matters of course.  For instance, she was full of rats, she was full of cockroaches, the heavy seas made her seams open and shut like your fingers, and she leaked like a basket; where leakage is, there also, of necessity, is bilgewater; and where bilgewater is, only the dead can enjoy life.  This is on account of the smell.  In the presence of bilgewater, Limburger cheese becomes odourless and ashamed.

From these absolutely sure data we can competently picture the daily life of the great discoverer.  In the early morning he paid his devotions at the shrine of the Virgin.  At eight bells he appeared on the poop-deck promenade.  If the weather was chilly, he came up clad from plumed helmet to spurred heel in magnificent plate armour inlaid with arabesques of gold, having previously warmed it at the galley fire.  If the weather was warm, he came up in the ordinary sailor toggery of the time: great slouch hat of blue velvet, with a flowing brush of snowy ostrich plumes, fastened on with a flashing cluster of diamonds and emeralds; gold-embroidered doublet of green velvet, with slashed sleeves exposing under-sleeves of crimson satin; deep collar and cuff-ruffles of rich limp lace; trunk hose of pink velvet, with big knee knots of brocaded yellow ribbon; pearl-tinted silk stockings, clocked and daintily embroidered; lemon-coloured buskins of unborn kid, funnel-topped, and drooping low to expose the pretty stockings; deep gauntlets of finest white heretic skin, from the factory of the Holy Inquisition, formerly part of the person of a lady of rank; rapier with sheath crusted with jewels, and hanging from a broad baldric upholstered with rubies and sapphires.

He walked the promenade thoughtfully; he noted the aspects of the sky and the course of the wind; he kept an eye out for drifting vegetation and other signs of land; he jawed the man at the wheel for pastime; he got out an imitation egg and kept himself in practice on his old trick of making it stand on its end; now and then he hove a life-line below and fished up a sailor who was drowning on the quarter-deck; the rest of his watch he gaped and yawned and stretched and said he wouldn't make the trip again to discover six Americas. For that was the kind of natural human person Columbus was when not posing for posterity.

At noon he took the sun and ascertained that the good ship had made three hundred yards in twenty-four hours, and this enabled him to win the pool. Anybody can win the pool when nobody but himself has the privilege of straightening out the ship's run and getting it right.

The Admiral has breakfasted alone, in state: bacon, beans, and gin; at noon he dines alone in state: bacon, beans, and gin; at six he sups alone in state: bacon, beans, and gin; at 11 P.M. he takes a night relish, alone, in state: bacon, beans, and gin. At none of these orgies is there any music; the ship-orchestra is modern. After his final meal he returned thanks for his many blessings, a little over-rating their value, perhaps, and then he laid off his silken splendours or his gilded hardware, and turned in, in his little coffin-bunk, and blew out his flickering stencher, and began to refresh his lungs with inverted sighs freighted with the rich odours of rancid oil and bilgewater. The sighs returned as snores, and then the rats and the cockroaches swarmed out in brigades and divisions and army corps and had a circus all over him. Such was the daily life of the great discoverer in his marine basket during several historic weeks; and the difference between his ship and his comforts and ours is visible almost at a glance.

When he returned, the King of Spain, marvelling, said—as history records:

'This ship seems to be leaky.  Did she leak badly?'

'You shall judge for yourself, sire.  I pumped the Atlantic Ocean through her sixteen times on the passage.'

This is General Horace Porter's account.  Other authorities say fifteen.

It can be shown that the differences between that ship and the one I am writing these historical contributions in, are in several respects remarkable. Take the matter of decoration, for instance.  I have been looking around again, yesterday and to-day, and have noted several details which I conceive to have been absent from Columbus's ship, or at least slurred over and not elaborated and perfected.  I observe state-room doors three inches thick, of solid oak, and polished.  I note companionway vestibules with walls, doors, and ceilings panelled in polished hard-woods, some light, some dark, all dainty and delicate joiner-work, and yet every joint compact and tight; with beautiful pictures inserted, composed of blue tiles—some of the pictures containing as many as sixty tiles— and the joinings of those tiles perfect.  These are daring experiments.  One would have said that the first time the ship went straining and labouring through a storm-tumbled sea those tiles would gape apart and drop out. That they have not done so is evidence that the joiner's art has advanced a good deal since the days when ships were so shackly that when a giant sea gave them a wrench the doors came unbolted. I find the walls of the dining-saloon upholstered with mellow pictures wrought in tapestry, and the ceiling aglow with pictures done in oil. In other places of assembly I find great panels filled with embossed Spanish leather, the figures rich with gilding and bronze. Everywhere I find sumptuous masses of colour—colour, colour, colour—colour all about, colour of every shade and tint and variety; and as a result, the ship is bright and cheery to the eye, and this cheeriness invades one's spirit and contents it. To fully appreciate the force and spiritual value of this radiant and opulent dream of colour, one must stand outside at night in the pitch dark and the rain, and look in through a port, and observe it in the lavish splendour of the electric lights. The old-time ships were dull, plain, graceless, gloomy, and horribly depressing. They compelled the blues; one could not escape the blues in them. The modern idea is right: to surround the passenger with conveniences, luxuries, and abundance of inspiriting colour.  As a result, the ship is the pleasantest place one can be in, except, perhaps, one's home.

## A VANISHED SENTIMENT

One thing is gone, to return no more for ever— the romance of the sea.  Soft sentimentality about the sea has retired from the activities of this life, and is but a memory of the past, already remote and much faded.  But within the recollection of men still living, it was in the breast of every individual; and the further any individual lived from salt water the more of it he kept in stock.  It was as pervasive, as universal, as the atmosphere itself.  The mere mention of the sea, the romantic sea, would make any company of people sentimental and mawkish at once.  The great majority of the songs that were sung by the young people of the back settlements had the melancholy wanderer for subject, and his mouthings about the sea for refrain.  Picnic parties, paddling down a creek in a canoe when the twilight shadows were gathering, always sang

> Homeward bound, homeward bound
> From a foreign shore;

and this was also a favourite in the West with the

passengers on sternwheel steamboats. There was another—

> My boat is by the shore,
>     And my bark is on the sea,
> But before I go, Tom Moore,
>     Here's a double health to thee.

And this one, also—

> Oh, pilot, 'tis a fearful night,
> There's danger on the deep.

And this—

> A life on the ocean wave,
>     And a home on the rolling deep,
> Where the scattered waters rave,
>     And the winds their revels keep !

And this—

> A wet sheet and a flowing sea,
> And a wind that follows fair.

And this—

> My foot is on my gallant deck,
> Once more the rover is free !

And the ' Larboard Watch '—the person referred to below is at the masthead, or somewhere up there—

> Oh, who can tell what joy he feels,
> As o'er the foam his vessel reels,
> And his tired eyelids slumb'ring fall,
> He rouses at the welcome call
>         Of ' Larboard watch—ahoy ! '

Yes, and there was for ever and always some jackass-voiced person braying out—

> Rocked in the cradle of the deep,
> I lay me down in peace to sleep!

Other favourites had these suggestive titles: 'The Storm at Sea;' 'The Bird at Sea;' 'The Sailor Boy's Dream;' 'The Captive Pirate's Lament;' 'We are far from Home on the Stormy Main'—and so on, and so on, the list is endless. Everybody on a farm lived chiefly amid the dangers of the deep on those days, in fancy.

But all that is gone now. Not a vestige of it is left. The iron-clad, with her unsentimental aspect and frigid attention to business, banished romance from the war-marine, and the unsentimental steamer has banished it from the commercial marine. The dangers and uncertainties which made sea life romantic have disappeared and carried the poetic element along with them. In our day the passengers never sing sea-songs on board a ship, and the band never plays them. Pathetic songs about the wanderer in strange lands far from home, once so popular and contributing such fire and colour to the imagination by reason of the rarity of that kind of wanderer, have lost their charm and fallen silent, because everybody is a wanderer in the far lands now, and the interest in that detail is dead. Nobody is worried about the wanderer; there are no perils of the sea for him, there are no uncertainties. He is safer in the ship than he would probably be at home, for there he is always liable to have to attend some friend's funeral, and stand over the grave in the sleet, bareheaded—and that means pneumonia for him, if he gets his deserts; and the uncertainties of his voyage are reduced to whether he will arrive on the other side in the appointed afternoon, or have to wait till morning.

The first ship I was ever in was a sailing vessel. She was twenty-eight days going from San Francisco to the Sandwich Islands. But the main reason for this particularly slow passage was, that she got becalmed, and lay in one spot fourteen days in the centre of the Pacific, two thousand miles from land. I hear no sea-songs in this present vessel, but I heard the entire layout in that one. There were a dozen young people—they are pretty old now I reckon—and they used to group themselves on the stern, in the starlight or the moonlight, every evening, and sing sea-songs till after midnight, in that hot, silent, motionless calm. They had no sense of humour, and they always sang 'Homeward Bound,' without reflecting that that was practically ridiculous, since they were standing still and not proceeding in any direction at all; and they often followed that song with 'Are we almost there, are we almost there, said the dying girl as she drew near home?'

It was a very pleasant company of young people, and I wonder where they are now. Gone, oh, none knows whither; and the bloom and grace and beauty of their youth, where is that? Among them was a liar; all tried to reform him, but none could do it. And so, gradually, he was left to himself, none of us would associate with him. Many a time since I have seen in fancy that forsaken figure, leaning forlorn against the taffrail, and have reflected that perhaps if we had tried harder, and been more patient, we might have won him from his fault and persuaded him to relinquish it. But it is hard to tell; with him the vice was extreme, and was probably incurable. I like to think—and, indeed, I do think—that I did the best that in me lay to lead him to higher and better ways.

There was a singular circumstance. The ship lay becalmed that entire fortnight in exactly the same spot. Then a handsome breeze came fanning over the sea, and we spread our white wings for flight.

But the vessel did not budge. The sails bellied out, the gale strained at the ropes, but the vessel moved not a hair's breadth from her place. The captain was surprised. It was some hours before we found out what the cause of the detention was. It was barnacles. They collect very fast in that part of the Pacific. They had fastened themselves to the ship's bottom; then others had fastened themselves to the first bunch, others to these, and so on, down and down and down, and the last bunch had glued the column hard and fast to the bottom of the sea, which is five miles deep at that point. So the ship was simply become the handle of a walking-cane five miles long—yes, and no more movable by wind and sail than a continent is. It was regarded by every one as remarkable.

Well, the next week—however, Sandy Hook is in sight.

## *PLAYING COURIER*

A TIME would come when we must go from Aix-les-Bains to Geneva, and from thence, by a series of day-long and tangled journeys, to Bayreuth in Bavaria. I should have to have a courier, of course, to take care of so considerable a party as mine.

But I procrastinated. The time slipped along, and at last I woke up one day to the fact that we were ready to move and had no courier. I then resolved upon what I felt was a foolhardy thing, but I was in the humour of it. I said I would make the first stage without help—I did it.

I brought the party from Aix to Geneva by myself—four people. The distance was two hours and more, and there was one change of cars. There was not an accident of any kind, except leaving a valise and some other matters on the platform—a thing which can hardly be called an accident, it is so common.  So I offered to conduct the party all the way to Bayreuth.

This was a blunder, though it did not seem so at the time.  There was more detail than I thought there would be : 1. Two persons whom we had left in a Genevan pension some weeks before must be collected and brought to the hotel.  2. I must notify the people on the Grand Quay who store trunks to bring seven of our stored trunks to the hotel and carry back seven which they would find piled in the lobby.  3. I must find out what part of Europe Bayreuth was in and buy seven railway tickets for that point.  4. I must send a telegram to a friend in the Netherlands.  5. It was now two in the afternoon, and we must look sharp and be ready for the first night train, and make sure of sleeping-car tickets.  6. I must draw money at the bank.

It seemed to me that the sleeping-car tickets must be the most important thing, so I went to the station myself to make sure ; hotel messengers are not always brisk people.  It was a hot day and I ought to have driven, but it seemed better economy to walk.  It did not turn out so, because I lost my way and trebled the distance.  I applied for the tickets, and they asked me which route I wanted to go by, and that embarrassed me and made me lose my head, there were so many people standing around, and I not knowing anything about the routes, and not supposing there were going to be two; so I judged it best to go back and map out the road and come again.

I took a cab this time, but on my way upstairs at the hotel I remembered that I was out of cigars, so I thought it would be well to get some while the matter was in my mind. It was only round the corner and I didn't need the cab. I asked the cabman to wait where he was. Thinking of the telegram and trying to word it in my head, I forgot the cigars and the cab, and walked on indefinitely. I was going to have the hotel people send the telegram, but as I could not be far from the Post Office by this time, I thought I would do it myself. But it was further than I had supposed. I found the place at last, and wrote the telegram and handed it in. The clerk was a severe-looking, fidgety man, and he began to fire French questions at me in such a liquid form that I could not detect the joints between his words, and this made me lose my head again. But an Englishman stepped up and said the clerk wanted to know where he was to send the telegram. I could not tell him, because it was not my telegram, and I explained that I was merely sending it for a member of my party. But nothing would pacify the clerk but the address ; so I said that if he was so particular I would go back and get it.

However, I thought I would go and collect those lacking two persons first, for it would be best.to do everything systematically and in order, and one detail at a time. Then I remembered the cab was eating up my substance down at the hotel yonder ; so I called another cab, and told the man to go down and fetch it to the Post Office and wait till I came.

I had a long hot walk to collect those people, and when I got there they couldn't come with me because they had heavy satchels, and must have a cab. I went away to find one, but before I ran across any I noticed that I had reached the neighbourhood of the Grand Quay—at least, I thought I had—so I judged I could save time by stepping around and arranging about the trunks. I stepped around about a mile, and although I did not find the Grand Quay, I found a cigar shop, and remembered about the cigars. I said I was going to Bayreuth, and wanted enough for the journey. The man asked me which route I was going to take.

I said I did not know.  He said he would recommend me to go by Zurich and various other places
which he named, and offered to sell me seven
second-class through tickets for *$22* apiece, which
would be throwing off the discount which the
railroads allowed him.  I was already tired of
riding second class on first-class tickets, so I took
him up.

By-and-by I found Natural & Co.'s storage
office, and told them to send seven of our trunks
to the hotel and pile them up in the lobby.  It
seemed to me that I was not delivering the whole
of the message; still, it was all I could find in my
head.

Next I found the bank, and asked for some
money, but I had left my letter of credit somewhere
and was not able to draw.  I remembered now that
I must have left it lying on the table where I wrote
my telegram; so I got a cab and drove to the Post
Office and went upstairs, and they said that a letter
of credit had indeed been left on the table, but that
it was now in the hands of the police authorities,
and it would be necessary for me to go there and
prove property.  They sent a boy with me, and we
went out the back way and walked a couple of miles
and found the place; and then I remembered about

my cabs, and asked the boy to send them to me when he got back to the Post Office. It was night-fall now, and the Mayor had gone to dinner. I thought I would go to dinner myself, but the officer on duty thought differently, and I stayed. The Mayor dropped in at half past ten, but said it was too late to do anything to-night—come at 9.30 in the morning. The officer wanted to keep me all night, and said I was a suspicious-looking person, and probably did not own the letter of credit, and didn't know what a letter of credit was, but merely saw the real owner leave it lying on the table, and wanted to get it because I was probably a person that would want anything he could get, whether it was valuable or not. But the Mayor said he saw nothing suspicious about me, and that I seemed a harmless person, and nothing the matter with me but a wandering mind, and not much of that. So I thanked him and he set me free, and I went home in my three cabs.

As I was dog-tired, and in no condition to answer questions with discretion, I thought I would not disturb the Expedition at that time of night, as there was a vacant room I knew of at the other end of the hall; but I did not quite arrive there, as a watch had been set, the Expedition being anxious about me.   I was placed in a galling situation. The Expedition sat stiff and forbidding, on four chairs in a row, with shawls and things all on, satchels and guide-books in lap.   They had been sitting like that for four hours, and the glass going down all the time.   Yes, and they were waiting— waiting for me.   It seemed to me that nothing but a sudden, happily contrived, and brilliant *tour de force* could break this iron front and make a diversion in my favour; so I shied my hat into the arena, and followed it with a skip and a jump, shouting blithely:

'Ha, ha, here we all are, Mr. Merryman!'

Nothing could be deeper or stiller than the absence of applause which followed.   But I kept on; there seemed no other way, though my confidence, poor enough before, had got a deadly check, and was in effect gone.

I tried to be jocund out of a heavy heart; I tried to touch the other hearts there and soften the bitter resentment in those faces by throwing off bright and airy fun, and making of the whole ghastly thing a joyously humorous incident; but this idea was not well conceived.   It was not the right atmosphere for it.   I got not one smile; not one line in those offended faces relaxed; I thawed nothing of the winter that looked out of those frosty eyes.  I started one more breezy, poor effort, but the head of the Expedition cut into the centre of it, and said :

'Where have you been ?'

I saw by the manner of this that the idea was to get down to cold business now.  So I began my travels, but was cut short again.

'Where are the two others?  We have been in frightful anxiety about them.'

'Oh, they're all right.  I was to fetch a cab.  I will go straight off, and——'

'Sit down!  Don't you know it is 11 o'clock?  Where did you leave them ?'

'At the pension.'

'Why didn't you bring them ?'

'Because we couldn't carry the satchels.  And so I thought——'

'Thought!  You should not try to think.  One cannot think without the proper machinery.  It is two miles to that pension.  Did you go there without a cab ?'

'I—well, I didn't intend to; it only happened so.'

'How did it happen so ?'

'Because I was at the Post Office, and I re-

membered that I had left a cab waiting here,
and so, to stop the expense, I sent another cab to—
to—— '

'To what?'

'Well, I don't remember now, but I think the
new cab was to have the hotel pay the old cab, and
send it away.'

'What good would that do?'

'What good would it do? It would stop the
expense, wouldn't it?'

'By putting the new cab in its place to ccn-
tinue the expense?'

'I didn't say anything.

'Why didn't you have the new cab come back
for you?'

'Oh, that is what I did! I remember now.
Yes, that is what I did. Because I recollect that
when I—— '

'Well, then, why didn't it come back for you?'

'To the Post Office? Why, it did.'

'Very well, then, how did you come to walk to
the pension?'

'I—I don't quite remember how that happened.
Oh, yes, I do remember now. I wrote the despatch
to send to the Netherlands, and—— '

'Oh, thank goodness, you did accomplish something! I wouldn't have had you fail to send—— What makes you look like that? You are trying to avoid my eye. That despatch is the most important thing that—— You haven't sent that despatch!'

'I haven't said I didn't send it.'

'You don't need to. Oh, dear, I wouldn't have had that telegram fail for anything. Why didn't you send it?'

'Well, you see, with so many things to do and think of, I—they're very particular there, and after I had written the telegram——'

'Oh, never mind, let it go, explanations can't help the matter now—what will he think of us?'

'Oh, that's all right, that's all right! He'll think we gave the telegram to the hotel people, and that they——'

'Why, certainly! Why didn't you do that? There was no other rational way.'

'Yes, I know, but then I had it on my mind that I must be sure and get to the bank and draw some money——'

'Well, you are entitled to some credit, after all, for thinking of that, and I don't wish to be too hard on you, though you must acknowledge yourself that you have cost us all a good deal of trouble, and some of it not necessary.  How much did you draw ?'

'Well, I—I had an idea that—that——'

'That what ?'

'That—well, it seems to me that in the circumstances—so many of us, you know, and—and——'

'What are you mooning about ?  Do turn your face this way and let me—— Why, you haven't drawn any money ! '

'Well, the banker said——'

'Never mind what the banker said.  You must have had a reason of your own.  Not a reason, exactly, but something which——'

'Well, then, the simple fact was that I hadn't my letter of credit.'

'Hadn't your letter of credit ? '

'Hadn't my letter of credit.'

'Don't repeat me like that.  Where was it ? '

'At the Post Office.'

'What was it doing there ? '

'Well, I forgot it, and left it there.'

'Upon my word, I've seen a good many couriers, but of all the couriers that ever I——'

'I've done the best I could.'

'Well, so you have, poor thing, and I'm wrong to abuse you so when you've been working yourself

to death while we've been sitting here, only thinking of our vexations instead of feeling grateful for
what you were trying to do for us.   It will all come
out right.   We can take the 7.30 train in the
morning just as well.   You've bought the tickets?'

'I have—and it's a bargain, too.   Second class.'

'I'm glad of it.   Everybody else travels second
class, and we might just as well save that ruinous
extra charge.   What did you pay?'

'Twenty-two dollars apiece—through to Bayreuth.'

'Why, I didn't know you could buy through
tickets anywhere but in London and Paris.'

'Some people can't, maybe; but some people
can—of whom I am one of which, it appears.'

'It seems a rather high price.'

'On the contrary, the dealer knocked off his
commission.'

'Dealer?'

'Yes—I bought them at a cigar shop.'

'That reminds me.   We shall have to get up
pretty early, and so there should be no packing to
do.   Your umbrella, your rubbers, your cigars——
What is the matter?'

'Hang it! I've left the cigars at the bank.'

'Just think of it!   Well, your umbrella?'

' I'll have that all right.   There's no hurry.'

' What do you mean by that ? '

' Oh, that's all right; I'll take care of——'

' Where is that umbrella ? '

' It's just the merest step—it won't take me——'

' Where is it ? '

' Well, I think I left it at the cigar shop; but any way——'

' Take your feet out from under that thing.   It's just as I expected !   Where are your rubbers ? '

' They—well——'

' Where are your rubbers ? '

' It's got so dry now—well, everybody says there's not going to be another drop of——'

' Where—are —your—rubbers ? '

' Well, you see—well, it was this way.  First, the officer said——'

' What officer ? '

' Police officer ; but the Mayor, he——'

' What Mayor ? '

' Mayor of Geneva ; but I said——'

' Wait.   What is the matter with you ? '

' Who, me ?   Nothing.   They both tried to persuade me to stay, and——'

' Stay where ? '

'Well—the fact is——

'Where have you been?  What's kept you out till half past ten at night?'

'Oh, you see, after I lost my letter of credit, I——'

'You are beating around the bush a good deal. Now, answer the question in just one straightforward word.   Where are those rubbers?'

'They—well, they're in the county jail.'

I started a placating smile, but it petrified. The climate was unsuitable.   Spending three or four hours in jail did not seem to the Expedition humorous.   Neither did it to me, at bot·tom.

I had to explain the whole thing, and of course it came out then that we couldn't take the early train, because that would leave my letter of credit in hock still.   It did look as if we had all got to go to bed estranged and unhappy, but by good luck that was prevented.   There happened to be mention of the trunks, and I was able to say I had attended to that feature.

'There, you are just as good and thoughtful and painstaking and intelligent as you can be, and it's a shame to find so much fault with you, and there shan't be another word of it!   You've done beauti·

fully, admirably, and I'm sorry I ever said one un-grateful word to you.'

This hit deeper than some of the other things, and made me uncomfortable, because I wasn't feeling as solid about that trunk errand as I wanted to. There seemed, somehow, to be a defect about it somewhere, though I couldn't put my finger on it, and didn't like to stir the matter just now, it being late and maybe well enough to let well enough alone.

Of course there was music in the morning, when it was found that we couldn't leave by the early train. But I had no time to wait; I got only the opening bars of the overture, and then started out to get my letter of credit.

It seemed a good time to look into the trunk business and rectify it if it needed it, and I had a suspicion that it did. I was too late. The con-cierge said he had shipped the trunks to Zurich the evening before. I asked him how he could do that without exhibiting passage tickets.

'Not necessary in Switzerland. You pay for your trunks and send them where you please. Nothing goes free but your hand baggage.'

'How much did you pay on them?'

'A hundred and forty francs.'

'Twenty-eight dollars. There's something wrong about that trunk business, sure.'

Next I met the porter. He said:

'You have not slept well, is it not? You have the worn look. If you would like a courier, a good one has arrived last night, and is not engaged for five days already, by the name of Ludi. We recommend him; "das heisst," the Grande Hotel Beau Rivage recommends him.'

I declined with coldness. My spirit was not broken yet. And I did not like having my condition taken notice of in this way. I was at the county jail by nine o'clock, hoping that the Mayor might chance to come before his regular hour; but he didn't. It was dull there. Every time I offered to touch anything, or look at anything, or do anything, or refrain from doing anything, the policeman said it was 'defendu.' I thought I would practise my French on him, but he wouldn't have that either. It seemed to make him particularly bitter to hear his own tongue.

The Mayor came at last, and then there was no trouble; for the minute he had convened the Supreme Court—which they always do whenever there is valuable property in dispute—and got everything shipshape, and sentries posted, and had prayer, by the chaplain, my unsealed letter was brought and opened, and there wasn't anything in it but some photographs : because, as I remembered now, I had taken out the letter of credit so as to make room for the photographs, and had put the letter in my other pocket, which I proved to everybody's satisfaction by fetching it out and showing it with a good deal of exultation. So then the court looked at each other in a vacant kind of way, and then at me, and then at each other again, and finally let me go, but said it was imprudent for me to be at large, and asked me what my profession was. I said I was a courier. They lifted up their eyes in a kind of reverent way and said, ' Du lieber Gott ! ' and I said a word of courteous thanks for their apparent admiration and hurried off to the bank.

However, being a courier was already making me a great stickler for order and system and one thing at a time and each thing in its own proper turn ; so I passed by the bank and branched off and started for the two lacking members of the Expedition. A cab lazied by and I took it upon persuasion. I gained no speed by this, but it was a reposeful turn out and I liked reposefulness. The week-long jubilations over the six-hundredth anniversary of the birth of Swiss liberty and the Signing of the

Compact was at flood tide, and all the streets were clothed in fluttering flags.

The horse and the driver had been drunk three days and nights, and had known no stall nor bed meantime.  They looked as I felt—dreamy and seedy.  But we arrived in course of time.  I went in and rang, and asked a housemaid to rush out the lacking members.  She said something which I did not understand, and I returned to the chariot.  The girl had probably told me that those people did not belong on her floor, and that it would be judicious for me to go higher, and ring from floor to floor till I found them; for in those Swiss flats there does not seem to be any way to find the right family but to be patient and guess your way along up.  I calculated that I must wait fifteen minutes, there being three details inseparable from an occasion of this sort: 1, put on hats and come down and climb in; 2, return of one to get 'my other glove'; 3, presently, return of the other one to fetch 'my French Verbs at a Glance.'  I would muse during the fifteen minutes and take it easy.

A very still and blank interval ensued, and then I felt a hand on my shoulder and started.  The intruder was a policeman.  I glanced up and perceived that there was new scenery.  There was a good deal of a crowd, and they had that pleased and interested look which such a crowd wears when they see that somebody is out of luck. The horse was asleep, and so was the driver, and some boys had hung them and me full of gaudy decorations stolen from the innumerable banner poles. It was a scandalous spectacle. The officer said:

'I'm sorry, but we can't have you sleeping here all day.'

I was wounded, and said with dignity:

'I beg your pardon, I was not sleeping; I was thinking.'

'Well, you can think, if you want to, but you've got to think to yourself; you disturb the whole neighbourhood.'

It was a poor joke, and it made the crowd laugh. I snore at night sometimes, but it is not likely that I would do such a thing in the daytime and in such a place. The officer undecorated us, and seemed sorry for our friendlessness, and really tried to be humane, but he said we mustn't stop there any longer or he would have to charge us rent—it was the law, he said, and he went on to say in a sociable way that I was looking pretty mouldy, and he wished he knew——

I shut him off pretty austerely, and said I hoped

one might celebrate a little, these days, especially when one was personally concerned.

' Personally ? ' he asked.　' How ? '

' Because six hundred years ago an ancestor of mine signed the Compact.'

He reflected a moment, then looked me over and said :

' Ancestor ! It's my opinion you signed it yourself.　For of all the old ancient relics that ever I— but never mind about that.　What is it you are waiting here for so long ? '

I said :

' I'm not waiting here so long at all.　I'm waiting fifteen minutes till they forget a glove and a book and go back and get them.'　Then I told him who they were that I had come for.

He was very obliging, and began to shout inquiries to the tiers of heads and shoulders projecting from the windows above us.　Then a woman away up there sang out :

' Oh, they ?　Why, I got them a cab and they left here long ago—half-past eight, I should say.'

It was annoying.　I glanced at my watch, but didn't say anything.　The officer said :

' It is a quarter of twelve, you see.　You should have inquired better.　You have been asleep three-quarters of an hour, and in such a sun as this! You are baked—baked black. It is wonderful. And you will miss your train, perhaps. You interest me greatly. What is your occupation ? '

I said I was a courier. It seemed to stun him, and before he could come to we were gone.

When I arrived in the third story of the hotel I found our quarters vacant. I was not surprised. The moment a courier takes his eye off his tribe they go shopping. The nearer it is to train time the surer they are to go. I sat down to try and think out what I had best do next, but presently the hall boy found me there, and said the Expedition had gone to the station half an hour before. It was the first time I had known them to do a rational thing, and it was very confusing. This is one of the things that make a courier's life so difficult and un-certain. Just as matters are going the smoothest, his people will strike a lucid interval, and down go all his arrangements to wreck and ruin.

The train was to leave at twelve noon sharp. It was now ten minutes after twelve. I could be at the station in ten minutes. I saw I had no great amount of leeway, for this was the lightning express, and on the Continent the lightning expresses are pretty fastidious about getting away some time during the advertised day. My people were the only ones remaining in the waiting room; everybody else had passed through and 'mounted the train,' as they say in those regions. They were exhausted with nervousness and fret, but I comforted them and heartened them up, and we made our rush.

But no; we were out of luck again. The door-keeper was not satisfied with the tickets. He examined them cautiously, deliberately, suspiciously: then glared at me awhile, and after that he called another official. The two examined the tickets and called another official. These called others, and the convention discussed and discussed, and gesticulated and carried on until I begged that they would consider how time was flying, and just pass a few resolutions and let us go. Then they said very courteously that there was a defect in the tickets, and asked me where I got them.

I judged I saw what the trouble was, now. You see, I had bought the tickets in a cigar shop, and of course the tobacco smell was on them: without doubt the thing they were up to was to work the tickets through the Custom House and to collect duty on that smell. So I resolved to be perfectly frank: itis sometimes the best way. I said:

'Gentlemen, I will not deceive you. These railway tickets——'

'Ah! **pardon,** monsieur! These are not railway tickets.'

'Oh,' I said, 'is that the defect?'

'Ah, truly yes, monsieur. These are lottery tickets, yes; and it is a lottery which has been drawn two years ago.'

I affected to be greatly amused; it is all one can do in such circumstances; it is all one can do, and yet there is no value in it; it deceives nobody, and you can see that everybody around pities you and is ashamed of you. One of the hardest situations in life, I think, is to be full of grief and a sense of defeat and shabbiness that way, and yet have to put on an outside of archness and gaiety, while all the time you know that your own expedition, the treasures of your heart, and whose love and reverence you are by the custom of our civilisation entitled to, are being consumed with humiliation before strangers to see you earning and getting a compassion, which is a stigma, a brand—a brand which certifies you to be—oh, anything and everything which is fatal to human respect.

I said, cheerily, it was all right, just one of those little accidents that was likely to happen to anybody—I would have the right tickets in two minutes, and we would catch the train yet, and, moreover, have something to laugh about all through the journey. I did get the tickets in time, all stamped and complete; but then it turned out that I couldn't take them, because, in taking so much pains about the two missing members, I had skipped the bank and hadn't the money. So then the train left, and there didn't seem to be anything to do but go back to the hotel, which we did; but it was kind of melancholy and not much said. I tried to start a few subjects, like scenery and transubstantiation, and those sorts of things, but they didn't seem to hit the weather right.

We had lost our good rooms, but we got some others which were pretty scattering, but would answer. I judged things would brighten now, but the Head of the Expedition said, ' Send up the trunks.' It made me feel pretty cold. There was a doubtful something about that trunk business. I was almost sure of it. I was going to suggest——

But a wave of the hand sufficiently restrained me, and I was informed that we would now camp for three days and see if we could rest up.

I said all right, never mind ringing; I would go

down and attend to the trunks myself. I got a cab and went straight to Mr. Charles Natural's place, and asked what order it was I had left there.

'To send seven trunks to the hotel.'

'And were you to bring any back?'

'No.'

'You are sure I didn't tell you to bring back seven that would be found piled in the lobby?'

'Absolutely sure you didn't.'

'Then the whole fourteen are gone to Zurich or Jericho or somewhere, and there is going to be more débris around that hotel when the Expedition——'

I didn't finish, because my mind was getting to be in a good deal of a whirl, and when you are that way you think you have finished a sentence when you haven't, and you go mooning and dreaming away, and the first thing you know you get run over by a dray or a cow or something.

I left the cab there—I forgot it—and on my way back I thought it all out and concluded to resign, because otherwise I should be nearly sure to be discharged. But I didn't believe it would be a good idea to resign in person; I could do it by message. So I sent for Mr. Ludi and explained that there was a courier going to resign on account of incompatibility or fatigue or something, and as he had four or five vacant days, I would like to insert him into that vacancy if he thought he could fill it. When everything was arranged I got him to go up and say to the Expedition that, owing to an error made by Mr. Natural's people, we were out of trunks here, but would have plenty in Zurich, and we'd better take the first train, freight, gravel, or construction, and move right along.

He attended to that and came down with an invitation for me to go up—yes, certainly; and, while we walked along over to the bank to get money, and collect my cigars and tobacco, and to the cigar shop to trade back the lottery tickets and get my umbrella, and to Mr. Natural's to pay that cab and send it away, and to the county jail to get my rubbers and leave p. p. c. cards for the Mayor and Supreme Court, he described the weather to me that was prevailing on the upper levels there with the Expedition, and I saw that I was doing very well where I was.

I stayed out in the woods till 4 P.M., to let the weather moderate, and then turned up at the station just in time to take the three o'clock express for Zurich along with the Expedition, now in the hands of Ludi, who conducted its complex affairs with little apparent effort or inconvenience.

Well, I had worked like a slave while I was in office, and done the very best I knew how; yet all that these people dwelt upon or seemed to care to remember was the defects of my administration, not its creditable features. They would skip over a thousand creditable features to remark upon and reiterate and fuss about just one fact, till it seemed to me they would wear it out; and not much of a fact, either, taken by itself—the fact that I elected myself courier in Geneva, and put in work enough to carry a circus to Jerusalem, and yet never even got my gang out of the town. I finally said I didn't wish to hear any more about the subject, it made me tired. And I told them to their faces that I would never be a courier again to save anybody's life. And if I live long enough I'll prove it. I think it's a difficult, brain-racking, overworked, and thoroughly ungrateful office, and the main bulk of its wages is a sore heart and a bruised spirit.

# THE GERMAN CHICAGO

I FEEL lost, in Berlin. It has no resemblance to
the city I had supposed it was. There was once a
Berlin, which I would have known, from descriptions
in books—the Berlin of the last century and the
beginning of the present one: a dingy city in a
marsh, with rough streets, muddy and lantern-
lighted, dividing straight rows of ugly houses all
alike, compacted into blocks as square and plain
and uniform and monotonous and serious as so
many dry-goods boxes. But that Berlin has disappeared. It seems to have disappeared totally,
and left no sign. The bulk of the Berlin of to-day
has about it no suggestion of a former period. The
site it stands on has traditions and a history, but
the city itself has no traditions and no history. It
is a new city, the newest I have ever seen. Chicago
would seem venerable beside it; for there are
many old-looking districts in Chicago, but not

many in Berlin.  The main mass of the city looks
as if it had been built last week; the rest of it has
a just perceptibly graver tone, and looks as if it
might be six or even eight months old.

The next feature that strikes one is the spaciousness, the roominess of the city.  There is no other
city, in any country, whose streets are so generally
wide.  Berlin is not merely *a* city of wide streets,
it is *the* city of wide streets.  As a wide-street city
it has never had its equal, in any age of the world.
' Unter den Linden ' is three streets in one; the
Potsdamerstrasse is bordered on both sides by
sidewalks which are themselves wider than some
of the historic thoroughfares of the old European
capitals; there seem to be no lanes or alleys;
there are no short-cuts; here and there, where
several important streets empty into a common
centre, that centre's circumference is of a magni-
tude calculated to bring that word spaciousness
into your mind again.  The park in the middle of
the city is so huge that it calls up that expression
once more.

The next feature that strikes one is the straight-
ness of the streets.  The short ones haven't so
much as a waver in them; the long ones stretch
out to prodigious distances and then tilt a little to

the right or left, then stretch out on another immense reach as straight as a ray of light. A result of this arrangement is, that at night Berlin is an inspiring sight to see. Gas and the electric light are employed with a wasteful liberality, and so, wherever one goes, he has always double ranks of brilliant lights stretching far down into the night on every hand, with here and there a wide and splendid constellation of them spread out over an intervening 'Platz'; and between the interminable double procession of street lamps one has the swarming and darting cab lamps, a lively and pretty addition to the fine spectacle, for they counterfeit the rush and confusion and sparkle of an invasion of fire-flies.

There is one other noticeable feature—the absolutely level surface of the site of Berlin. Berlin —to capitulate—is newer to the eye than is any other city, and also blonder of complexion and tidier; no other city has such an air of roominess, freedom from crowding; no other city has so many straight streets; and with Chicago it contests the chromo for flatness of surface and for phenomenal swiftness of growth. Berlin is the European Chicago. The two cities have about the same population—say a million and a half. I cannot speak in exact terms, because I only know what Chicago's population was week before last; but at that time it was about a million and a half. Fifteen years ago Berlin and Chicago were large cities, of course, but neither of them was the giant it now is.

But now the parallels fail. Only parts of Chicago are stately and beautiful, whereas all of Berlin is stately and substantial, and it is not merely in parts but uniformly beautiful. There are buildings in Chicago that are architecturally finer than any in Berlin, I think, but what I have just said above is still true. These two flat cities would lead the world for phenomenal good health if London were out of the way. As it is, London leads, by a point or two. Berlin's death rate is only nineteen in the thousand. Fourteen years ago the rate was a third higher.

Berlin is a surprise in a great many ways—in a multitude of ways, to speak strongly and be exact. It seems to be the most governed city in the world, but one must admit that it also seems to be the best governed. Method and system are observable on every hand—in great things, in little things, in all details, of whatsoever size. And it is not method and system on paper, and there an end—

it is method and system in practice. It has a rule for everything, and puts the rule in force; puts it in force against the poor and powerful alike, without favour or prejudice. It deals with great matters and minute particulars with equal faithfulness, and with a plodding and painstaking diligence and persistency which compel admiration—and sometimes regret. There are several taxes, and they are collected quarterly. Collected is the word; they are not merely levied, they are collected— every time. This makes light taxes. It is in cities and countries where a considerable part of the community shirk payment that taxes have to be lifted to a burdensome rate. Here the police keep coming, calmly and patiently, until you pay your tax. They charge you five or ten cents per visit after the first call. By experiment you will find that they will presently collect that money.

In one respect the million and a half of Berlin's population are like a family; the head of this large family knows the names of its several members, and where the said members are located, and when and where they were born, and what they do for a living, and what their religious brand is. Whoever comes to Berlin must furnish these particulars to the police immediately; moreover, if he knows how long he is going to stay, he must say so. If he take a house he will be taxed on the rent and taxed also on his income. He will not be asked what his income is, and so he may save some lies for home consumption. The police will estimate his income from the house-rent he pays, and tax him on that basis.

Duties on imported articles are collected with inflexible fidelity, be the sum large or little; but the methods are gentle, prompt, and full of the spirit of accommodation. The postman attends to the whole matter for you, in cases where the article comes by mail, and you have no trouble, and suffer no inconvenience. The other day a friend of mine was informed that there was a package in the post-office for him, containing a lady's silk belt with gold clasp, and a gold chain to hang a bunch of keys on. In his first agitation he was going to try to bribe the postman to chalk it through, but acted upon his sober second thought and allowed the matter to take its proper and regular course. In a little while the postman brought the package and made these several collections: duty on the silk belt, 7½ cents; duty on the gold chain, 10 cents; charge for fetching the package, 5 cents. These devastating imposts are exacted for the protection of German home industries.

The calm, quiet, courteous, cussed persistence of the police is the most admirable thing I have encountered on this side. They undertook to persuade me to send and get a passport for a Swiss maid whom we had brought with us, and at the end of six weeks of patient, tranquil, angelic daily effort they succeeded. I was not intending to give them trouble, but I was lazy, and I thought they would get tired. Meanwhile they probably thought I would be the one. It turned out just so.

One is not allowed to build unstable, unsafe, or unsightly houses in Berlin ; the result is this comely and conspicuously stately city, with its security from conflagrations and break-downs. It is built of architectural Gibraltars. The Building Commissioners inspect while the building is going up. It has been found that this is better than to wait till it falls down. These people are full of whims.

One is not allowed to cram poor folk into cramped and dirty tenement houses. Each individual must have just so many cubic feet of room-space, and sanitary inspections are systematic and frequent.

Everything is orderly. The fire brigade march

in rank, curiously uniformed, and so grave is their demeanour that they look like a Salvation Army under conviction of sin.  People tell me that when a fire alarm is sounded, the firemen assemble calmly, answer to their names when the roll is called, then proceed to the fire.  There they are ranked up, military fashion, and told off in detachments by the chief, who parcels out to the detachments the several parts of the work which they are to undertake in putting out that fire.  This is all done with low-voiced propriety, and strangers think these people are working a funeral.  As a rule the fire is confined to a single floor in these great masses of bricks and masonry, and consequently there is little or no interest attaching to a fire here for the rest of the occupants of the house.

There are abundance of newspapers in Berlin, and there was also a newsboy, but he died.  At intervals of half a mile on the thoroughfares there are booths, and it is at these that you buy your papers.  There are plenty of theatres, but they do not advertise in a loud way.  There are no big posters of any kind, and the display of vast type and of pictures of actors and performance, framed on a big scale and done in rainbow colours, is a thing unknown.  If the big show-bills existed there would be no place to exhibit them; for there are no poster-fences, and one would not be allowed to disfigure dead walls with them. Unsightly things are forbidden here; Berlin is a rest to the eye.

And yet the saunterer can easily find out what is going on at the theatres. All over the city, at short distances apart, there are neat round pillars eighteen feet high and about as thick as a hogshead, and on these the little black-and-white theatre bills and other notices are posted. One generally finds a group around each pillar reading these things. There are plenty of things in Berlin worth importing to America. It is these that I have particularly wished to make a note of. When Buffalo Bill was here his biggest poster was probably not larger than the top of an ordinary trunk.

There is a multiplicity of clean and comfortable horse-cars, but whenever you think you know where a car is going to, you would better stop ashore, because that car is not going to that place at all. The car-routes are marvellously intricate, and often the drivers get lost and are not heard of for years. The signs on the cars furnish no details as to the course of the journey; they name the end of it, and then experiment around to see how much territory

they can cover before they get there. The con-
ductor will collect your fare over again, every few
miles, and give you a ticket which he hasn't
apparently kept any record of, and you keep it till
an inspector comes aboard by-and-by and tears a
corner off it (which he does not keep), then you
throw the ticket away and get ready to buy another.
Brains are of no value when you are trying to
navigate Berlin in a horse-car. When the ablest of
Brooklyn's editors was here on a visit he took a
horse-car in the early morning and wore it out trying to go to a point in the centre of the city. He
was on board all day and spent many dollars in
fares, and then did not arrive at the place which
he had started to go to. This is the most thorough
way to see Berlin, but it is also the most expensive.

But there are excellent features about the car
system, nevertheless. The car will not stop for you
to get on or off, except at certain places a block or
two apart, where there is a sign to indicate that
that is a halting station. This system saves many
bones. There are twenty places inside the car;
when these seats are filled, no more can enter.
Four or five persons may stand on each platform—
the law decrees the number—and when these
standing places are all occupied the next applicant

is refused. As there is no crowding, and as no rowdyism is allowed, women stand on the platforms as well as men ; they often stand there when there are vacant seats inside, for these places are comfortable, there being little or no jolting. A native tells me that when the first car was put on, thirty or forty years ago, the public had such a terror of it that they didn't feel safe inside of it, or outside either. They made the company keep a man at every crossing with a red flag in his hand. Nobody would travel in the car except convicts on the way to the gallows. This made business in only one direction, and the car had to go back light. To save the company, the city government transferred the convict cemetery to the other end of the line. This made traffic in both directions, and kept the company from going under. This sounds like some of the information which travelling foreigners are furnished with in America. To my mind it has a doubtful ring about it.

The first-class cab is neat and trim, and has leather-cushion seats and a swift horse. The second-class cab is an ugly and lubberly vehicle, and is always old. It seems a strange thing that they have never built any new ones. Still, if such a thing were done everybody that had time to flock would flock to see it, and that would make a crowd, and the police do not like crowds and disorder here. If there were an earthquake in Berlin the police would take charge of it, and conduct it in that sort of orderly way that would make you think it was a prayer meeting. That is what an earthquake generally ends in, but this one would be different from those others; it would be kind of soft and self-contained, like a republican praying for a mugwump.

For a course (a quarter of an hour or less), one pays twenty-five cents in a first-class cab, and fifteen cents in a second-class. The first-class will take you along faster, for the second-class horse is old—always old—as old as his cab, some authorities say —and ill-fed and weak. He has been a first-class once, but has been degraded to second-class for long and faithful service.

Still, he must take you as *far* for fifteen cents as the other horse takes you for twenty-five. If he can't do his fifteen-minute distance in fifteen minutes, he must still do the distance for the fifteen cents. Any stranger can check the distance off—by means of the most curious map I am acquainted with. It is issued by the city government and can be bought in any shop for a trifle. In it every street is sectioned off, like a string of long beads of different colours. Each long bead represents a minute's travel, and when you have covered fifteen of the beads you have got your money's worth. This map of Berlin is a gay-coloured maze, and looks like pictures of the circulation of the blood.

The streets are very clean. They are kept so—not by prayer and talk, and the other New York methods, but by daily and hourly work with scrapers and brooms ; and when an asphalted street has been tidily scraped after a rain or a light snowfall, they scatter clean sand over it. This saves some of the horses from falling down. In fact, this is a city government which seems to stop at no expense where the public convenience, comfort, and health are concerned—except in one detail. That is the naming of the streets and the numbering of the houses. Sometimes the name of a street will change in the middle of a block. You will not find it out till you get to the next corner and discover the new name on the wall, and of course you don't know just when the change happened.

The names are plainly marked on the corners—on all the corners—there are no exceptions. But the numbering of the houses—there has never been

anything like it since original chaos.   It is not possible that it was done by this wise city government.
At first one thinks it was done by an idiot; but
there is too much variety about it for that; an idiot
could not think of so many different ways of making
confusion and propagating blasphemy.   The numbers run up one side the street and down the other.
That is endurable, but the rest isn't.   They often
use one number for three or four houses—and sometimes they put the number on only one of the houses,
and let you guess at the others.   Sometimes they
put a number on a house— 4, for instance—then put
4*a*, 4*b*, 4*c*, on the succeeding houses, and one becomes old and decrepit before he finally arrives at
5.   A result of this systemless system is, that
when you are at No. 1 in a street, you haven't any
idea how far it may be to No. 150; it may be only
six or eight blocks, it may be a couple of miles.
Frederick Street is long, and is one of the great
thoroughfares.   The other day a man put up his
money behind the assertion that there were more
refreshment places in that street than numbers on
the houses—and he won.   There were 254 numbers
and 257 refreshment places.   Yet, as I have said, it
is a long street.

But the worst feature of all this complex business is, that in Berlin the numbers do not travel in any one direction; no, they travel along until they get to 50 or 60, perhaps, then suddenly you find yourself up in the hundreds—140, maybe; the next will be 139—then you perceive by that sign that the numbers are now travelling towards you from the opposite direction. They will keep that sort of insanity up as long as you travel that street; every now and then the numbers will turn and run the other way. As a rule there is an arrow under the number, to show by the direction of its flight which way the numbers are proceeding. There are a good many suicides in Berlin—I have seen six reported in a single day. There is always a deal of learned and laborious arguing and ciphering going on as to the cause of this state of things. If they will set to work and number their houses in a rational way, perhaps they will find out what was the matter.

More than a month ago Berlin began to prepare to celebrate Professor Virchow's seventieth birthday. When the birthday arrived, the middle of October, it seemed to me that all the world of science arrived with it; deputation after deputation came, bringing the homage and reverence of far cities and centres of learning, and during the whole of a long day the hero of it sat and received such witness of his greatness as has seldom been vouchsafed to any man in any walk of life in any time ancient or modern.  These demonstrations were continued in one form or another day after day, and were presently merged in similar demonstrations to his twin in science and achievement, Professor Helmholtz, whose seventieth birthday is separated from Virchow's by only about three weeks ; so nearly as this did these two extraordinary men come to being born together.  Two such births have seldom signalised a single year in human history.

But perhaps the final and closing demonstration was peculiarly grateful to them.  This was a Commers given in their honour the other night, by a thousand students.  It was held in a huge hall, very long and very lofty, which had five galleries, far above everybody's head, which were crowded with ladies—four or five hundred, I judged.

It was beautifully decorated with clustered flags and various ornamental devices, and was brilliantly lighted.  On the spacious floor of this place were ranged, in files, innumerable tables, seating twenty-four persons each, extending from one end of the great hall clear to the other, and with narrow aisles between the files. In the centre, on one side, was a high and tastefully decorated platform twenty or thirty feet long, with a long table on it behind which sat the half dozen chiefs of the givers of the Commers in the rich mediæval costumes of as many different college corps. Behind these youths a band of musicians was concealed. On the floor, directly in front of this platform, were half a dozen tables which were distinguished from the outlying continent of tables by being covered instead of left naked. Of these the central table was reserved for the two heroes of the occasion and twenty particularly eminent professors of the Berlin University, and the other covered tables were for the occupancy of a hundred less distinguished professors.

I was glad to be honoured with a place at the table of the two heroes of the occasion, although I was not really learned enough to deserve it. Indeed there was a pleasant strangeness in being in such company ; to be thus associated with twenty-three men who forget more every day than I ever knew. Yet there was nothing embarrassing about it, because loaded men and empty ones look about alike, and I knew that to that multitude there I was a professor. It required but little art to catch the ways and attitude of those men and imitate them, and I had no difficulty in looking as much like a professor as anybody there.

We arrived early ; so early that only Professors Virchow and Helmholtz and a dozen guests of the special tables were ahead of us, and three or four hundred students.  But people were arriving in floods, now, and within fifteen minutes all but the special tables were occupied, and the great house was crammed, the aisles included.  It was said that there were four thousand men present.  It was a most animated scene, there is no doubt about that ; it was a stupendous beehive.  At each end of each table stood a corps student in the uniform of his corps.  These quaint costumes are of brilliant-coloured silks and velvets, with sometimes a high plumed hat, sometimes a broad Scotch cap, with a great plume wound about it, sometimes—oftenest—a little shallow silk cap on the tip of the crown, like an inverted saucer ; sometimes the pantaloons are snow-white, sometimes of other colours ; the boots in all cases come up well above the knee ; and in all cases also white gauntlets are worn ; the sword is a rapier with a bowl-shaped guard for the hand, painted in several colours.  Each corps has a uniform of its own, and all are of rich material, brilliant in colour, and exceedingly picturesque ; for they are survivals of the vanished costumes of the Middle Ages, and they reproduce for us the time when men were beautiful to look at. The student who stood guard at our end of the table was of grave countenance and great frame and grace of form, and he was doubtless an accurate reproduction, clothes and all, of some ancestor of his of two or three centuries ago—a reproduction as far as the outside, the animal man, goes, I mean.

As I say, the place was now crowded. The nearest aisle was packed with students standing up, and they made a fence which shut off the rest of the house from view. As far down this fence as you could see, all these wholesome young faces were turned in one direction, all these intent and worshipping eyes were centred upon one spot—the place where Virchow and Helmholtz sat. The boys seemed lost to everything, unconscious of their own existence; they devoured these two intellectual giants with their eyes, they feasted upon them, and the worship that was in their hearts shone in their faces. It seemed to me that I would rather be flooded with a glory like that, instinct with sincerity, innocent of self-seeking, than win a hundred battles and break a million hearts.

There was a big mug of beer in front of each of

us, and more to come when wanted.  There was also a quarto pamphlet containing the words of the songs to be sung.  After the names of the officers of the feast were these words in large type :

*Während des Kommerses herrscht allgemeiner Burgfriede.*

I was not able to translate this to my satisfaction, but a professor helped me out.  This was his explanation : The students in uniform belong to different college corps; not all students belong to corps ; none join the corps except those who enjoy fighting.  The corps students fight duels with swords every week, one corps challenging another corps to furnish a certain number of duellists for the occasion, and it is only on this battle-field that students of different corps exchange courtesies.  In common life they do not drink with each other or speak.  The above line now translates itself: There is truce during the Commers, war is laid aside, and fellowship takes its place.

Now the performance began.  The concealed band played a piece of martial music ; then there was a pause.  The students on the platform rose to their feet, the middle one gave a toast to the Emperor, then all the house rose, mugs in hand.  At the call

' One—two—three ! ' all glasses were drained and then brought down with a slam on the tables in unison. The result was as good an imitation of thunder as I have ever heard. From now on, during an hour, there was singing, in mighty chorus. During each interval between songs a number of the special guests—the professors—arrived. There seemed to be some signal whereby the students on the platform were made aware that a professor had arrived at the remote door of entrance ; for you would see them suddenly rise to their feet, strike an erect military attitude, then draw their swords ; the swords of all their brethren standing guard at the innumerable tables would flash from the scabbards and be held aloft—a handsome spectacle. Three clear bugle notes would ring out, then all these swords would come down with a crash, twice repeated, on the tables, and be uplifted and held aloft again ; then in the distance you would see the gay uniforms and uplifted swords of a guard of honour, clearing the way and conducting the guest down to his place. The songs were stirring ; the immense outpour from young life and young lungs, the crash of swords and the thunder of the beer-mugs, gradually worked a body up to what seemed the last possible summit of excitement. It surely seemed to me that I had

T

reached that summit, that I had reached my limit, and that there was no higher lift desirable for me. When apparently the last eminent guest had long ago taken his place, again those three bugle blasts rang out, and once more the swords leaped from their scabbards.   Who might this late comer be ?   Nobody was interested to inquire.   Still, indolent eyes were turned towards the distant entrance; we saw the silken gleam and the lifted swords of a guard of honour ploughing through the remote crowds.   Then we saw that end of the house rising to its feet; saw it rise abreast the advancing guard all along, like a wave.   This supreme honour had been offered to no one before.   Then there was an excited whisper at our table—'MOMMSEN !' and the whole house rose. Rose and shouted and stamped and clapped, and banged the beer-mugs.   Just simply a storm.   Then the little man with his long hair and Emersonian face edged his way past us and took his seat.   I could have touched him with my hand—Mommsen ! —think of it !

This was one of those immense surprises that can happen only a few times in one's life.   I was not dreaming of him, he was to me only a giant myth, a world-shadowing spectre, not a reality.   The surprise of it all can be only comparable to a man's suddenly coming upon Mont Blanc, with its awful form towering into the sky, when he didn't suspect he was in its neighbourhood. I would have walked a great many miles to get a sight of him, and here he was, without trouble or tramp or cost of any kind. Here he was, clothed in a Titanic, deceptive modesty which made him look like other men. Here he was, carrying the Roman world and all the Cæsars in his hospitable skull, and doing it as easily as that other luminous vault, the skull of the universe, carries the Milky Way and the constellations.

One of the professors said that once upon a time an American young lady was introduced to Mommsen, and found herself badly scared and speechless. She dreaded to see his mouth unclose, for she was expecting him to choose a subject several miles above her comprehension, and didn't suppose he *could* get down to the world that other people lived in; but when his remark came, her terrors disappeared: 'Well, how do you do? Have you read Howells's last book? *I* think it's his best.'

The active ceremonies of the evening closed with the speeches of welcome, delivered by two students, and the replies made by Professors Virchow and Helmholtz.

Virchow has long been a member of the city

government of Berlin.  He works as hard for the city as does any other Berlin alderman, and gets the same pay—nothing.  I don't know that we in America could venture to ask our most illustrious citizen to serve in a board of aldermen, and if we might venture it I am not positively sure that we could elect him.  But here the municipal system is such that the best men in the city consider it an honour to serve gratis as aldermen, and the people have the good sense to prefer these men, and to elect them year after year.  As a result, Berlin is a thoroughly well-governed city.  It is a free city; its. affairs are not meddled with by the State; they are managed by its own citizens, and after methods of their own devising.

# *A PETITION TO THE QUEEN OF ENGLAND*

HARTFORD: *Nov. 6, 1887.*

MADAM,—You will remember that last May Mr. Edward Bright, the clerk of the Inland Revenue Office, wrote me about a tax which he said was due from me to the Government on books of mine published in London—that is to say, an income tax on the royalties. I do not know Mr. Bright, and it is embarrassing to me to correspond with strangers; for I was raised in the country and have always lived there, the early part in Marion county, Missouri, before the war, and this part in Hartford county, Connecticut, near Bloomfield, and about eight miles this side of Farmington, though some call it nine, which it is impossible to be, for I have walked it many and many a time in considerably under three hours, and General Hawley says he has done it in two and a quarter, which is not likely; so it has seemed best that I write your Majesty. It is true that I do not know your Majesty personally, but I have met the Lord Mayor, and if the rest of the family are like him, it is but just that it should be named royal ; and likewise plain that in a family matter like this, I cannot better forward my case than to frankly carry it to the head of the family itself. I have also met the Prince of Wales once, in the fall of 1873, but it was not in any familiar way, but in a quite informal way, being casual, and was, of course, a surprise to us both. It was in Oxford Street, just where you come out of Oxford into Regent Circus, and just as he turned up one side of the circle at the head of a procession, I went down the other side on the top of an omnibus. He will remember me on account of a grey coat with flap pockets that I wore, as I was the only person on the omnibus that had on that kind of a coat; I remember him, of course, as easy as I would a comet. He looked quite proud and satisfied, but that is not to be wondered at, he has a good situation. And once I called on your Majesty, but you were out.

But that is no matter, it happens with everybody. However, I have wandered a little away from what I started about. It was this way. Young Bright wrote my London publishers, Chatto and Windus—

their place is the one on the left as you come down
Piccadilly, about a block and a half above where
the minstrel show is—he wrote them that he wanted
them to pay income tax on the royalties of some
foreign authors, namely, 'Miss De La Ramé
(Ouida), Dr. Oliver Wendell Holmes, Mr. Francis
Bret Harte, and Mr. Mark Twain.' Well, Mr.
Chatto diverted him from the others, and tried to
divert him from me, but in this case he failed. So
then young Bright wrote me. And not only that,
but he sent me a printed document the size of a
newspaper, for me to sign, all over in different
places. Well, it was that kind of a document that
the more you study it the more it undermines you,
and makes everything seem uncertain to you ; and
so, while in that condition, and really not respon-
sible for my acts, I wrote Mr. Chatto to pay the tax,
and charge to me. Of course my idea was, that it
was for only one year, and that the tax would be
only about one per cent. or along there somewhere,
but last night I met Professor Sloane of Princeton
—you may not know him, but you have probably
seen him every now and then, for he goes to England a good deal ; a large man and very handsome,
and absorbed in thought, and if you have noticed
such a man on platforms after the train is gone,

that is the one, he generally gets left, like all those specialists and other scholars who know everything but how to apply it—and he said it was a back tax for *three* years, and not one per cent. but two and a half!

That gave what had seemed a little matter a new aspect. I then began to study the printed document again, to see if I could find anything in it that might modify my case, and I had what seems to be a quite promising success. For instance, it opens thus—polite and courteous, the way those English Government documents always are—I do not say that to hear myself talk, it is just the fact, and it is a credit:

'To Mr. Mark Twain: IN PURSUANCE of the Acts of Parliament for granting to Her Majesty Duties and Profits,' &c.

I had not noticed that before. My idea had been that it was for the Government, and so I wrote *to* the Government; but now I saw that it was a private matter, a family matter, and that the proceeds went to yourself, not the Government. I would always rather treat with principals, and I am glad I noticed that clause. With a principal one can always get at a fair and right understanding, whether it is about potatoes, or continents, or any of those things, or something entirely different; for the size or nature of the thing does not affect the fact; whereas, as a rule, a subordinate is more or less troublesome to satisfy. And yet this is not against them, but the other way. They have their duties to do, and must be harnessed to rules, and not allowed any discretion. Why, if your Majesty should equip young Bright with discretion—I mean his own discretion—it is an even guess that he would discretion you out of house and home in two or three years. He would not *mean* to get the family into straits, but that would be the usphot, just the same. Now then, with Bright out of the way, this is not going to be any Irish question; it is going to be settled pleasantly and satisfactorily for all of us, and when it is finished your Majesty is going to stand with the American people just as you have stood for fifty years, and surely no monarch can require better than that of an alien nation. They do not all pay a British income tax, but the most of them will in time, for we have shoals of new authors coming along every year; and of the population of your Canada, upwards of four-fifths are wealthy Americans, and more going there all the time.

Well, another thing which I noticed in the document was an item about 'Deductions.' I will come to that presently, your Majesty.   And another thing was this: that Authors are not mentioned in the document at all.   No, we have 'Quarries, Mines, Iron Works, Salt Springs, Alum Mines, Water Works, Canals, Docks, Drains, Levels, Fishings, Fairs, Tolls, Bridges, Ferries,' and so forth and so forth and so on—well, as much as a yard or a yard and a half of them, I should think—anyway a very large quantity or number.   I read along—down, and down, and down the list, further, and further, and further, and as I approached the bottom my hopes began to rise higher and higher, because I saw that everything in England, *that* far, was taxed by name and in detail, except, perhaps, the family, and may be Parliament, and yet still no mention of Authors. Apparently they were going to be overlooked.   And sure enough, they were!   My heart gave a great bound.   But I was too soon.   There was a footnote, in Mr. Bright's hand, which said: 'You are taxed under Schedule D, Section 14.'   I turned to that place, and found these three things: 'Trades, Offices, Gas Works.'

Of course, after a moment's reflection, hope came up again, and then certainty: Mr. Bright was in error, and clear off the track; for Authorship is not a Trade, it is an inspiration; Authorship does not keep an Office, its habitation is all out under the sky, and everywhere where the winds are blowing and the sun is shining and the creatures of God are free. Now then, since I have no Trade and keep no Office, I am not taxable under Schedule D, Section 14. Your Majesty sees that; so I will go on to that other thing that I spoke of, the 'Deductions' —deductions from my tax which I may get allowed, under conditions. Mr. Bright says all deductions to be claimed by me must be restricted to the provisions made in Paragraph No. 8, entitled 'Wear and Tear of Machinery or Plant.' This is curious, and shows how far he has gotten away on his wrong course after once he has got started wrong; for Offices and Trades do not have Plant, they do not have Machinery, such a thing was never heard of; and, moreover, they do not wear and tear. You see that, your Majesty, and that it is true. Here is the Paragraph No. 8:

'Amount claimed as a deduction for diminished value by reason of Wear and Tear, where the Machinery or Plant belongs to the Person or Company carrying on the Concern, or is let to such Person or Company so that the Lessee is bound to maintain and deliver over the same in good condition:—

*Amount £* ..............................................................'

There it is—the very words.

I could answer Mr. Bright thus :

It is my pride to say that my Brain is my Plant; and I do not claim any deduction for diminished value by reason of Wear and Tear, for the reason that it does not wear and tear, but stays sound and whole all the time. Yes, I could say to him, my Brain is my Plant, my Skull is my Workshop, my Hand is my Machinery, and I am the Person carrying on the Concern ; it is not leased to anybody, and so there is no Lessee bound to maintain and deliver over the same in good condition. There ! I do not wish to any way overrate this argument and answer, dashed off just so, and not a word of it altered from the way I first wrote it, your Majesty, but, indeed, it does seem to pulverise that young fellow, you can see that yourself. But that is all I say ; I stop there ; I never pursue a person after I have got him down.

Having thus shown your Majesty that I am not taxable, but am the victim of the error of a clerk who mistakes the nature of my commerce, it only remains for me to beg that you will of your justice annul my letter that I spoke of, so that my publisher can keep back that tax-money which, in the confusion and aberration caused by the document, I ordered him to pay.  You will not miss the sum, but this is a hard year for authors; and as for lectures, I do not suppose your Majesty ever saw such a dull season.

With always great, and ever increasing, respect, I beg to sign myself your Majesty's servant to command, MARK TWAIN.

HER MAJESTY THE QUEEN, LONDON.

# A MAJESTIC LITERARY FOSSIL

IF I were required to guess off-hand, and without collusion with higher minds, what is the bottom cause of the amazing material and intellectual advancement of the last fifty years, I should guess that it was the modern-born and previously non-existent disposition on the part of men to believe that a new idea can have value. With the long roll of the mighty names of history present in our minds, we are not privileged to doubt that for the past twenty or thirty centuries every conspicuous civilisation in the world has produced intellects able to invent and create the things which make our day a wonder; perhaps we may be justified in inferring, then, that the reason they did not do it was that the public reverence for old ideas and hostility to new ones always stood in their way, and was a wall they could not break down or climb over. The prevailing tone of old books regarding new ideas is one of suspicion and uneasiness at times, and at other times contempt. By contrast, our day is indifferent to old ideas, and even considers that their age makes their value questionable, but jumps at a new idea with enthusiasm and high hope—a hope which is high because it has not been accustomed to being disappointed. I make no guess as to just when this disposition was born to us, but it certainly is ours, was not possessed by any century before us, is our peculiar mark and badge, and is doubtless the bottom reason why we are a race of lightning-shod Mercuries, and proud of it—instead of being, like our ancestors, a race of plodding crabs, and proud of that.

So recent is this change from a three or four thousand year twilight to the flash and glare of open day that I have walked in both, and yet am not old. Nothing is to-day as it was when I was an urchin; but when I was an urchin, nothing was much different from what it had always been in this world. Take a single detail, for example—medicine. Galen could have come into my sick-room at any time during my first seven years—I mean any day when it wasn't fishing weather, and there wasn't any choice but school or sickness—and he could have sat down there and stood my doctor's watch without asking a question. He would have smelt around among the wilderness of cups and bottles and phials on the table and the shelves, and missed not a stench that used to glad him two thousand years before, nor discovered one that was of a later date. He would have examined me, and run across only one disappointment—I was already salivated; I would have him there; for I was always salivated, calomel was so cheap. He would get out his lancet then; but I would have him again; our family doctor didn't allow blood to accumulate in the system. However, he could take dipper and ladle, and freight me up with old familiar doses that had come down from Adam to his time and mine; and he could go out with a wheelbarrow and gather weeds and offal, and build some more, while those others were getting in their work. And if our reverend doctor came and found him there, he would be dumb with awe, and would get down and worship him. Whereas, if Galen should appear among us to-day, he could not stand anybody's watch; he would inspire no awe; he would be told he was a back number, and it would surprise him to see that that fact counted against him, instead of in his favour. He wouldn't know our medicines; he wouldn't know our practice; and the first time he tried to introduce his own, we would hang him.

This introduction brings me to my literary relic. It is a *Dictionary of Medicine*, by Dr. James, of London, assisted by Mr. Boswell's Doctor Samuel Johnson, and is a hundred and fifty years old, it having been published at the time of the rebellion of '45. If it had been sent against the Pretender's troops there probably wouldn't have been a survivor. In 1861 this deadly book was still working the cemeteries—down in Virginia. For three generations and a half it had been going quietly along, enriching the earth with its slain. Up to its last free day it was trusted and believed in, and its devastating advice taken, as was shown by notes inserted between its leaves. But our troops captured it and brought it home, and it has been out of business since. These remarks from its preface are in the true spirit of the olden time, sodden with worship of the old, disdain of the new:

'If we inquire into the Improvements which have been made by the Moderns, we shall be forced to confess that we have so little Reason to value ourselves beyond the Antients, or to be tempted to contemn them, that we cannot give stronger or more convincing Proofs of our own Ignorance, as well as our Pride.

'Among all the systematical Writers, I think there are very few who refuse the Preference to *Hieron, Fabricius ab Aquapendente*, as a Person of unquestion'd Learning and Judgment; and yet is he not asham'd to let his Readers know that *Celsus* among the Latins, *Paulus Aegineta* among the Greeks, and *Albucasis* among the Arabians, whom I am unwilling to place among the Moderns, tho' he liv'd but six hundred Years since, are the Triumvirate to whom he principally stands indebted, for the Assistance he had receiv'd from them in composing his excellent Book.

'[In a previous paragraph are puffs of Galen, Hippocrates, and other débris of the Old Silurian Period of Medicine.] How many Operations are there now in Use which were unknown to the Antients?'

That is true. The surest way for a nation's scientific men to prove that they were proud and ignorant was to claim to have found out something fresh in the course of a thousand years or so. Evidently the peoples of this book's day regarded themselves as children, and their remote ancestors as the only grown-up people that had existed. Con-

sider the contrast: without offence, without over-
egotism, our own scientific men may and do regard
themselves as grown people and their grandfathers
as children.  The change here presented is probably the most sweeping that has ever come over
mankind in the history of the race.  It is the utter
reversal, in a couple of generations, of an attitude
which had been maintained without challenge or
interruption from the earliest antiquity.  It
amounts to creating man over again on a new
plan; he was a canal boat before, he is an ocean
greyhound to-day.  The change from reptile to
bird was not more tremendous, and it took longer.

It is curious.  If you read between the lines
what this author says about Brer Albucasis, you
detect that in venturing to compliment him he has
to whistle a little to keep his courage up, because
Albucasis 'liv'd but six hundred Years since,' and
therefore came so uncomfortably near being a
'modern' that one couldn't respect him without
risk.

Phlebotomy, Venesection — terms to signify
bleeding—are not often heard in our day, because
we have ceased to believe that the best way to
make a bank or a body healthy is to squander its
capital; but in our author's time the physician

went around with a hatful of lancets on his person all the time, and took a hack at every patient whom he found still alive. He robbed his man of pounds and pounds of blood at a single operation. The details of this sort in this book make terrific reading. Apparently even the healthy did not escape, but were bled twelve times a year, on a particular day of the month, and exhaustively purged besides. Here is a specimen of the vigorous old-time practice ; it occurs in our author's adoring biography of a Doctor Aretæus, a licensed assassin of Homer's time, or thereabouts :

'In a Quinsey he used Venesection, and allow'd the Blood to flow till the Patient was ready to faint away.'

There is no harm in trying to cure a headache— in our day. You can't do it, but you get more or less entertainment out of trying, and that is something ; besides, you live to tell about it, and that is more. A century or so ago you could have had the first of these features in rich variety, but you might fail of the other once—and once would do. I quote :

'As Dissections of Persons who have died of severe Headachs, which have been related by Authors, are too numerous to be inserted in this

Place, we shall here abridge some of the most curious and important Observations relating to this Subject, collected by the celebrated *Bonetus*.'

The celebrated Bonetus's 'Observation No. 1' seems to me a sufficient sample, all by itself, of what people used to have to stand any time between the creation of the world and the birth of your father and mine when they had the disastrous luck to get a 'Head-ach':

'A certain Merchant, about forty Years of Age, of a Melancholic Habit, and deeply involved in the Cares of the World, was, during the Dog-days, seiz'd with a violent pain of his Head, which some time after oblig'd him to keep his Bed.

'I, being call'd, order'd Venesection in the Arms, the Application of Leeches to the Vessels of his Nostrils, Forehead, and Temples, as also to those behind his Ears; I likewise prescrib'd the Application of Cupping-glasses, with Scarification, to his Back: But, notwithstanding these Precautions, he dy'd. If any Surgeon, skill'd in Arteriotomy, had been present, I should have also order'd that Operation.'

I looked for 'Arteriotomy' in this same Dictionary, and found this definition, 'The opening of an Artery with a View of taking away Blood.'

Here was a person who was being bled in the arms, forehead, nostrils, back, temples, and behind the ears, yet the celebrated Bonetus was not satisfied, but wanted to open an artery, 'with a View' to inserting a pump, probably. 'Notwithstanding these Precautions'—he dy'd. No art of speech could more quaintly convey this butcher's innocent surprise. Now that we know what the celebrated Bonetus did when he wanted to relieve a Head-ach, it is no trouble to infer that if he wanted to comfort a man that had a Stomach-ach he disembowelled him.

I have given one 'Observation'—a single Head-ach case; but the celebrated Bonetus follows it with eleven more. Without enlarging upon the matter, I merely note this coincidence—they all 'dy'd.' Not one of these people got well; yet this obtuse hyena sets down every little gory detail of the several assassinations as complacently as if he imagined he was doing a useful and meritorious work in perpetuating the methods of his crimes. 'Observations,' indeed! They are confessions.

According to this book, 'the Ashes of an Ass's hoof mix'd with Woman's milk cures chilblains.' Length of time required not stated. Another item: 'The constant Use of Milk is bad for the

Teeth, and causes them to rot, and loosens the Gums.' Yet in our day babies use it constantly without hurtful results. This author thinks you ought to wash out your mouth with wine before venturing to drink milk. Presently, when we come to notice what fiendish decoctions those people introduced into their stomachs by way of medicine, we shall wonder that they could have been afraid of milk.

It appears that they had false teeth in those days. They were made of ivory sometimes, sometimes of bone, and were thrust into the natural sockets, and lashed to each other and to the neighbouring teeth with wires or with silk threads. They were not to eat with, nor to laugh with, because they dropped out when not in repose. You could smile with them, but you had to practise first, or you would overdo it. They were not for business, but just decoration. They filled the bill according to their lights.

This author says 'the Flesh of Swine nourishes above all other eatables.' In another place he mentions a number of things, and says 'these are very easy to be digested; so is Pork.' This is probably a lie. But he is pretty handy in that line; and when he hasn't anything of the sort in stock himself he gives some other expert an opening. For instance, under the head of 'Attractives' he introduces Paracelsus, who tells of a nameless 'Specific'—quantity of it not set down—which is able to draw a hundred pounds of flesh to itself—distance not stated—and then proceeds, 'It happened in our own Days that an Attractive of this Kind drew a certain Man's Lungs up into his Mouth, by which he had the Misfortune to be suffocated.' This is more than doubtful. In the first place, his Mouth couldn't accommodate his Lungs—in fact, his Hat couldn't; secondly, his Heart being more eligibly Situated, it would have got the Start of his Lungs, and being a lighter Body, it would have Sail'd in ahead and Occupied the Premises; thirdly, you will Take Notice, a Man with his Heart in his Mouth hasn't any Room left for his Lungs—he has got all he can Attend to; and, finally, the Man must have had the Attractive in his Hat, and when he saw what was going to Happen he would have Remov'd it and Sat Down on it. Indeed he would; and then how could it Choke him to Death? I don't believe the thing ever happened at all.

Paracelsus adds this effort: 'I myself saw a Plaister which attracted as much Water as was sufficient to fill a Cistern; and by these very

Attractives Branches may be torn from Trees; and, which is still more surprising, a Cow may be carried up into the Air.' Paracelsus is dead now; he was always straining himself that way.

They liked a touch of mystery along with their medicine in the olden time; and the medicine-man of that day, like the medicine-man of our Indian tribes, did what he could to meet the requirement:

'*Arcanum.* A Kind of Remedy whose Manner of Preparation, or singular Efficacy, is industriously concealed, in order to enhance its Value. By the Chymists it is generally defined a thing secret, incorporeal, and immortal, which cannot be Known by Man, unless by Experience; for it is the Virtue of every thing, which operates a thousand times more than the thing itself.'

To me the butt end of this explanation is not altogether clear. A little of what they knew about natural history in the early times is exposed here and there in the *Dictionary.*

'*The Spider.* It is more common than welcome in Houses. Both the Spider and its Web are used in Medicine: The Spider is said to avert the Paroxysms of Fevers, if it be apply'd to the Pulse of the Wrist, or the Temples; but it is peculiarly recommended against a Quartan, being enclosed in the Shell of a Hazlenut.

'Among approved Remedies, I find that the distill'd Water of Black Spiders is an excellent Cure for Wounds, and that this was one of the choice Secrets of Sir Walter Raleigh.

'The Spider which some call the Catcher, or Wolf, being beaten into a Plaister, then sew'd up in Linen, and apply'd to the Forehead or Temples, prevents the Returns of a Tertian.

'There is another Kind of Spider, which spins a white, fine, and thick Web. One of this Sort, wrapp'd in Leather, and hung about the Arm, will avert the Fit of a Quartan. Boil'd in Oil of Roses, and instilled into the Ears, it eases Pains in those Parts. *Dioscorides, Lib.* 2, *Cap.* 68.

'Thus we find that Spiders have in all Ages been celebrated for their febrifuge Virtues; and it is worthy of Remark, that a Spider is usually given to Monkeys, and is esteem'd a sovereign Remedy for the Disorders those Animals are principally subject to.'

Then follows a long account of how a dying woman, who had suffered nine hours a day with an ague during eight weeks, and who had been bled dry some dozens of times meantime without apparent benefit, was at last forced to swallow several wads of 'Spiders-web,' whereupon she straightway mended, and promptly got well. So the sage is full of enthusiasm over the spider-webs, and mentions only in the most casual way the discontinuance of the daily bleedings, plainly never suspecting that this had anything to do with the cure.

'As concerning the venomous Nature of Spiders, *Scaliger* takes notice of a certain Species of them (which he had forgotten), whose Poison was of so great Force as to affect one *Vincentinus* thro' the Sole of his Shoe, by only treading on it.'

The sage takes that in without a strain, but the following case was a trifle too bulky for him, as his comment reveals :

'In Gascony, observes *Scaliger*, there is a very small Spider, which, running over a Looking-glass, will crack the same by the Force of her Poison. (*A mere Fable.*)'

But he finds no fault with the following facts :

'Remarkable is the Enmity recorded between this Creature and the Serpent, as also the Toad : Of the former it is reported, That, lying (as he thinks securely) under the Shadow of some Tree, the Spider lets herself down by her Thread, and, striking her Proboscis or Sting into the Head, with that Force and Efficacy, injecting likewise her venomous Juice, that, wringing himself about, he immediately grows giddy, and quickly after dies.

'When the Toad is bit or stung in Fight with this Creature, the Lizard, Adder, or other that is poisonous, she finds relief from Plantain, to which she resorts. In her Combat with the Toad, the Spider useth the same Stratagem, as with the Serpent, hanging by her own Thread from the Bough of some Tree, and striking her Sting into her enemy's Head, upon which the other, enraged, swells up, and sometimes bursts.

'To this Effect is the Relation of *Erasmus*, which he saith he had from one of the Spectators, of a Person lying along upon the Floor of his Chamber, in the Summer-time, to sleep in a supine Posture, when a Toad, creeping out of some green Rushes, brought just before in, to adorn the Chimney, gets upon his Face, and with his Feet sits across his Lips. To force off the Toad, says the Historian, would have been accounted sudden Death to the Sleeper ; and to leave her there, very cruel and dangerous ; so that upon Consultation it was concluded to find out a Spider, which, together with her Web, and the Window she was fasten'd to, was brought carefully, and so contrived as to be held perpendicularly to the Man's Face; which was no sooner done, but the Spider, discovering his Enemy, let himself down, and struck in his Dart, afterwards betaking himself up again to his Web; the Toad swell'd, but as yet kept his Station: The second Wound is given quickly after by the Spider, upon which he swells yet more, but remain'd alive still.—The Spider, coming down again by his Thread, gives the third Blow; and the Toad, taking off his Feet from over the Man's Mouth, fell off dead.'

To which the sage appends this grave remark, 'And so much for the historical Part.'   Then he passes on to a consideration of 'the Effects and Cure of the Poison.'

One of the most interesting things about this tragedy is the double sex of the Toad, and also of the Spider.

Now the sage quotes from one Turner:

'I remember, when a very young Practitioner, being sent for to a certain Woman, whose Custom was usually, when she went to the Cellar by Candle-light, to go also a Spider-hunting, setting Fire to their Webs, and burning them with the Flame of the Candle still as she pursued them.  It happen'd

at length, after this Whimsy had been follow'd a
long time, one of them sold his Life much dearer
than those Hundreds she had destroy'd; for, light-
ing upon the melting Tallow of her Candle, near the
Flame, and his legs being entangled therein, so that
he could not extricate himself, the Flame or Heat
coming on, he was made a Sacrifice to his cruel
Persecutor, who, delighting her Eyes with the
Spectacle, still waiting for the Flame to take hold
of him, he presently burst with a great Crack, and
threw his Liquor, some into her Eyes, but mostly
upon her Lips; by means of which, flinging away
her Candle, she cry'd out for Help, as fansying herself kill'd already with the Poison. However, in
the Night, her Lips swell'd up excessively, and one
of her Eyes was much inflam'd; also her Tongue
and Gums were somewhat affected; and, whether
from the Nausea excited by the Thoughts of the
Liquor getting into her Mouth, or from the poisonous Impressions communicated by the Nervous
*Fibrillæ* of those Parts to those of the Ventricle, a
continual Vomiting attended: To take off which,
when I was call'd, I order'd a Glass of mull'd Sack,
with a Scruple of Salt of Wormwood, and some
hours after a Theriacal Bolus, which she flung up
again. I embrocated the Lips with the Oil of

Scorpions mix'd with the Oil of Roses; and, in
Consideration of the Ophthalmy, tho' I was not
certain but the Heat of the Liquor, rais'd by the
Flame of the Candle before the Body of the Creature burst, might, as well as the Venom, excite the
Disturbance, (altho' Mr. *Boyle's* Case of a Person
blinded by this Liquor dropping from the living
Spider, makes the latter sufficient;) yet observing
the great Tumefaction of the Lips, together with
the other Symptoms not likely to arise from simple
Heat, I was inclin'd to believe a real Poison in the
Case; and therefore not daring to let her Blood in
the Arm [If a man's throat were cut in those old
days, the doctor would come and bleed the other
end of him].  I did, however, with good Success,
set Leeches to her Temples, which took off much
of the Inflammation; and her Pain was likewise
abated, by instilling into her Eyes a thin Mucilage
of the Seeds of Quinces and white Poppies extracted
with Rose-water; yet the Swelling on the Lips
increased; upon which, in the Night, she wore a
Cataplasm prepared by boiling the Leaves of Scordium, Rue, and Elderflowers, and afterwards
thicken'd with the Meal of Vetches.  In the mean
time, her Vomiting having left her, she had given
her, between whiles, a little Draught of distill'd

Water of Carduus Benedictus and Scordium, with some of the Theriaca dissolved; and upon going off of the Symptoms, an old Woman came luckily in, who, with Assurance suitable to those People (whose Ignorance and Poverty is their Safety and Protection), took off the Dressings, promising to cure her in two Days' time, altho' she made it as many Weeks, yet had the Reputation of the Cure; applying only Plantain Leaves bruis'd and mixed with Cobwebs, dropping the Juice into her Eye, and giving some Spoonfuls of the same inwardly, two or three times a day.'

So ends the wonderful affair. Whereupon the sage gives Mr. Turner the following shot—strengthening it with italics—and passes calmly on:

'*I must remark upon this History, that the Plantain, as a Cooler, was much more likely to cure this Disorder than warmer Applications and Medicines.*'

How strange that narrative sounds to-day, and how grotesque, when one reflects that it was a grave contribution to medical 'science' by an old and reputable physician! Here was all this to-do—two weeks of it—over a woman who had scorched her eye and her lips with candle grease. The poor wench is as elaborately dosed, bled, embrocated,

and otherwise harried and bedevilled, as if there
had been really something the matter with her;
and when a sensible old woman comes along at last,
and treats the trivial case in a sensible way, the
educated ignoramus rails at her ignorance, serenely
unconscious of his own.  It is pretty suggestive of
the former snail pace of medical progress that the
spider retained his terrors during three thousand
years, and only lost them within the last thirty or
forty.

Observe what imagination can do.  'This same
young Woman' used to be so affected by the strong
(imaginary) smell which emanated from the burning
spiders that 'the Objects about her seem'd to turn
round; she grew faint also with cold Sweats, and
sometimes a light Vomiting.'  There could have
been Beer in that cellar as well as Spiders.

Here are some more of the effects of imagination: '*Sennertus* takes Notice of the Signs of the
Bite or Sting of this Insect to be a Stupor or Numb-
ness upon the Part, with a sense of Cold, Horror,
or Swelling of the Abdomen, Paleness of the Face,
involuntary Tears, Trembling, Contractions, a
(****), Convulsions, cold Sweats; but these latter
chiefly when the Poison has been received inwardly;'
whereas the modern physician holds that a few

spiders taken inwardly, by a bird or a man, will do neither party any harm.

The above 'Signs' are not restricted to spider bites—often they merely indicate fright. I have seen a person with a hornet in his pantaloons exhibit them all.

'As to the Cure, not slighting the usual Alexipharmics taken internally, the Place bitten must be immediately washed with Salt Water, or a Sponge dipped in hot Vinegar, or fomented with a Decoction of Mallows, Origanum, and Mother of Thyme; after which a Cataplasm must be laid on of the Leaves of Bay, Rue, Leeks, and the Meal of Barley, boiled with Vinegar, or of Garlick and Onions, contused with Goat's Dung and fat Figs. Mean time the Patient should eat Garlick and drink Wine freely.'

As for me, I should prefer the spider bite. Let us close this review with a sample or two of the earthquakes which the old-time doctor used to introduce into his patient when he could find room. Under this head we have 'Alexander's Golden Antidote,' which is good for—well, pretty much everything. It is probably the old original first patent-medicine. It is built as follows:

'Take of Afarabocca, Henbane, Carpobalsamum,

each two Drams and a half; of Cloves, Opium, Myrrh, Cyperus, each two Drams; of Opobalsamum, Indian Leaf, Cinnamon, Zedoary, Ginger, Coftus, Coral, Cassia, Euphorbium, Gum Tragacanth, Frankincense, Styrax Calamita, Celtic, Nard, Spignel, Hartwort, Mustard, Saxifrage, Dill, Anise, each one Dram; of Xylaloes, Rheum, Ponticum, Alipta Moschata, Castor, Spikenard, Galangals, Opoponax, Anacardium, Mastich, Brimstone, Peony, Eringo, Pulp of Dates, red and white Hermodactyls, Roses, Thyme, Acorns, Pennyroyal, Gentian, the Bark of the Root of Mandrake, Germander, Valerian, Bishops Weed, Bay-Berries, long and white Pepper, Xylobalsamum, Carnabadium, Macodonian, Parsley-seeds, Lovage, the Seeds of Rue, and Sinon, of each a Dram and a half; of pure Gold, pure Silver, Pearls not perforated, the Blatta Byzantina, the Bone of the Stag's Heart, of each the Quantity of fourteen Grains of Wheat; of Sapphire, Emerald, and Jasper Stones, each one Dram; of Hasle-nut, two Drams; of Pellitory of Spain, Shavings of Ivory, Calamus Odoratus, each the Quantity of twenty-nine Grains of Wheat; of Honey or Sugar a sufficient Quantity.'

Serve with a shovel. No; one might expect

such an injunction after such formidable preparation; but it is not so.  The dose recommended is
' the Quantity of an Hasle-nut.'  Only that; it is
because there is so much jewellery in it, no doubt.

' *Aqua Limacum.* Take a great Peck of Garden-
snails, and wash them in a great deal of Beer, and
make your Chimney very clean, and set a Bushel
of Charcoal on Fire; and when they are thoroughly kindled, make a Hole in the Middle of the
Fire, and put the Snails in, and scatter more
Fire amongst them, and let them roast till they
make a Noise; then take them out, and, with a
Knife and coarse Cloth, pick and wipe away all the
green Froth : Then break them, Shells and all, in a
Stone Mortar.  Take also a Quart of Earth-worms,
and scour them with Salt, divers times over.  Then
take two Handfuls of Angelica and lay them in the
Bottom of the Still; next lay two Handfuls of
Celandine; next a Quart of Rosemary-flowers;
then two Handfuls of Bears-foot and Agrimony;
then Fenugreek; then Turmerick; of each one
Ounce : Red Dock-root, Bark of Barberry-trees,
Wood-sorrel, Betony, of each two Handfuls.—Then
lay the Snails and Worms on the Top of the Herbs;
and then two Handfuls of Goose-dung, and two
Handfuls of Sheep-dung.  Then put in three

Gallons of Strong Ale, and place the pot where you mean to set Fire under it : Let it stand all Night, or longer ; in the Morning put in three Ounces of Cloves well beaten, and a small Quantity of Saffron, dry'd to Powder ; then six Ounces of Shavings of Hartshorn, which must be uppermost.  Fix on the Head and Refrigeratory, and distil according to Art.'

There !  The book does not say whether this is all one dose, or whether you have a right to split it and take a second chance at it, in case you live.  Also, the book does not seem to specify what ailment it was for ; but it is of no consequence, for of course that would come out on the inquest.

Upon looking further, I find that this formidable nostrum is 'good for raising Flatulencies in the Stomach '—meaning *from* the stomach, no doubt. So it would appear that when our progenitors chanced to swallow a sigh, they emptied a sewer down their throats to expel it.  It is like dislodging skippers from cheese with artillery.

When you reflect that your own father had to take such medicines as the above, and that you would be taking them to-day yourself but for the introduction of homœopathy, which forced the old-school doctor to stir around and learn something of a rational nature about his business, you may honestly feel grateful that homœopathy survived the attempts of the allopathists to destroy it, even though you may never employ any physician but an allopathist while you live.

PRINTED BY
SPOTTISWOODE AND CO., NEW-STREET SQUARE
LONDON

# A List of Books

PUBLISHED BY

# CHATTO & WINDUS

214, Piccadilly, London, W.

*Sold by all Booksellers, or sent post-free for the published price by the Publishers.*

---

**ABOUT.—THE FELLAH:** An Egyptian Novel. By EDMOND ABOUT. Translated by Sir RANDAL ROBERTS. Post 8vo, illustrated boards, **2s.**

**ADAMS (W. DAVENPORT), WORKS BY.**
A DICTIONARY OF THE DRAMA. Being a comprehensive Guide to the Plays, Playwrights, Players, and Playhouses of the United Kingdom and America. Crown 8vo half-bound, **12s. 6d.** [*Preparing.*
QUIPS AND QUIDDITIES. Selected by W. D. ADAMS. Post 8vo, cloth limp, **2s. 6d.**

**AGONY COLUMN (THE) OF "THE TIMES,"** from 1800 to 1870. Edited, with an Introduction, by ALICE CLAY. Post 8vo, cloth limp, **2s. 6d.**

**AIDE (HAMILTON), WORKS BY.** Post 8vo, illustrated boards, **2s.** each.
CARR OF CARRLYON. | CONFIDENCES.

**ALBERT.—BROOKE FINCHLEY'S DAUGHTER.** By MARY ALBERT. Post 8vo, picture boards, **2s.**; cloth limp, **2s. 6d.**

**ALDEN.—A LOST SOUL.** By W. L. ALDEN. Fcap. 8vo, cl. bds., **1s. 6d.**

**ALEXANDER (MRS.), NOVELS BY.** Post 8vo, illustrated boards, **2s.** each.
MAID, WIFE, OR WIDOW? | VALERIE'S FATE.

**ALLEN (F. M.).—GREEN AS GRASS.** By F. M. ALLEN, Author of "Through Green Glasses." Frontispiece by J. SMYTH. Cr. 8vo, cloth ex., **3s. 6d.**

**ALLEN (GRANT), WORKS BY.** Crown 8vo, cloth extra, **6s.** each.
THE EVOLUTIONIST AT LARGE. | COLIN CLOUT'S CALENDAR.

Crown 8vo, cloth extra, **3s. 6d.** each; post 8vo, illustrated boards, **2s.** each.
| PHILISTIA. | FOR MAIMIE'S SAKE. | THE TENTS OF SHEM. |
| BABYLON. | IN ALL SHADES. | THE GREAT TABOO. |
| STRANGE STORIES. | THE DEVIL'S DIE. | DUMARESQ'S DAUGHTER. |
| BECKONING HAND. | THIS MORTAL COIL. | |

Crown 8vo, cloth extra, **3s. 6d.** each.
THE DUCHESS OF POWYSLAND. | BLOOD ROYAL.
IVAN GREET'S MASTERPIECE, &c. With a Frontispiece. [*Shortly.*

**AMERICAN LITERATURE, A LIBRARY OF,** from the Earliest Settlement to the Present Time. Compiled and Edited by EDMUND CLARENCE STEDMAN and ELLEN MACKAY HUTCHINSON. Eleven Vols., royal 8vo, cloth extra, **£6 12s.**

**ARCHITECTURAL STYLES, A HANDBOOK OF.** By A. ROSENGARTEN. Translated by W. COLLETT-SANDARS. With 639 Illusts. Cr. 8vo, cl. ex., **7s. 6d.**

**ART (THE) OF AMUSING:** A Collection of Graceful Arts, Games, Tricks, Puzzles, and Charades. By FRANK BELLEW. 300 Illusts. Cr. 8vo, cl. ex., **4s. 6d.**

**ARNOLD (EDWIN LESTER), WORKS BY.**
THE WONDERFUL ADVENTURES OF PHRA THE PHŒNICIAN. With Introduction by Sir EDWIN ARNOLD, and 12 Illustrations by H. M. PAGET. Crown 8vo, cloth extra, **3s. 6d.**; post 8vo, illustrated boards, **2s.**
THE CONSTABLE OF ST. NICHOLAS. Crown 8vo, cloth, **3s. 6d.** [*Shortly.*
BIRD LIFE IN ENGLAND. Crown 8vo, cloth extra, **6s.**

**ARTEMUS WARD'S WORKS.** With Portrait and Facsimile. Crown 8vo, cloth extra, **7s. 6d.**—Also a POPULAR EDITION, post 8vo, picture boards, **2s.**
THE GENIAL SHOWMAN: Life and Adventures of ARTEMUS WARD. By EDWARD P. HINGSTON. With a Frontispiece. Crown 8vo, cloth extra, **3s. 6d.**

**ASHTON (JOHN), WORKS BY.** Crown 8vo, cloth extra, **7s. 6d.** each.
HISTORY OF THE CHAP-BOOKS OF THE 18th CENTURY. With 334 Illusts.
SOCIAL LIFE IN THE REIGN OF QUEEN ANNE. With 85 Illustrations.
HUMOUR, WIT, AND SATIRE OF SEVENTEENTH CENTURY. With 82 Illusts.
ENGLISH CARICATURE AND SATIRE ON NAPOLEON THE FIRST. 115 Illusts.
MODERN STREET BALLADS. With 57 Illustrations.

**BACTERIA.—A SYNOPSIS OF THE BACTERIA AND YEAST** FUNGI AND ALLIED SPECIES. By W. B. GROVE, B.A. With 87 Illustrations. Crown 8vo, cloth extra, **3s. 6d.**

**BARDSLEY (REV. C. W.), WORKS BY.**
ENGLISH SURNAMES: Their Sources and Significations. Cr. 8vo, cloth, **7s. 6d.**
CURIOSITIES OF PURITAN NOMENCLATURE. Crown 8vo, cloth extra, **6s.**

**BARING GOULD (S.,** Author of "John Herring," &c.), **NOVELS BY.**
Crown 8vo, cloth extra, **3s. 6d.** each; post 8vo, illustrated boards, **2s.** each.
RED SPIDER. | EVE.

**BARRETT (FRANK,** Author of "Lady Biddy Fane,") **NOVELS BY.**
Post 8vo, illustrated boards, **2s.** each; cloth, **2s. 6d.** each.

| | |
|---|---|
| FETTERED FOR LIFE. | A PRODIGAL'S PROGRESS. |
| THE SIN OF OLGA ZASSOULICH. | JOHN FORD; and HIS HELPMATE. |
| BETWEEN LIFE AND DEATH. | A RECOILING VENGEANCE. |
| FOLLY MORRISON. \| HONEST DAVIE. | FOUND GUILTY. |
| LIEUT. BARNABAS. | FOR LOVE AND HONOUR. |
| LITTLE LADY LINTON. | |

**BEACONSFIELD, LORD:** A Biography. By T. P. O'CONNOR, M.P. Sixth Edition, with an Introduction. Crown 8vo, cloth extra, **5s.**

**BEAUCHAMP.—GRANTLEY GRANGE:** A Novel. By SHELSLEY BEAUCHAMP. Post 8vo, illustrated boards, **2s.**

**BEAUTIFUL PICTURES BY BRITISH ARTISTS:** A Gathering of Favourites from our Picture Galleries, beautifully engraved on Steel. With Notices of the Artists by SYDNEY ARMYTAGE, M.A. Imperial 4to, cloth extra, gilt edges, **21s.**

**BECHSTEIN.—AS PRETTY AS SEVEN,** and other German Stories. Collected by LUDWIG BECHSTEIN. With Additional Tales by the Brothers GRIMM, and 98 Illustrations by RICHTER. Square 8vo, cloth extra, **6s. 6d.**; gilt edges, **7s. 6d.**

**BEERBOHM.—WANDERINGS IN PATAGONIA;** or, Life among the Ostrich Hunters. By JULIUS BEERBOHM. With Illusts. Cr. 8vo, cl. extra, **3s. 6d.**

**BENNETT (W. C., LL.D.), WORKS BY.** Post 8vo, cloth limp, **2s.** each.
A BALLAD HISTORY OF ENGLAND. | SONGS FOR SAILORS.

**BESANT (WALTER), NOVELS BY.**
Cr. 8vo, cl. ex., **3s. 6d.** each; post 8vo, illust. bds., **2s.** each; cl. limp, **2s. 6d.** each.
ALL SORTS AND CONDITIONS OF MEN. With Illustrations by FRED. BARNARD.
THE CAPTAINS' ROOM, &c. With Frontispiece by E. J. WHEELER.
ALL IN A GARDEN FAIR. With 6 Illustrations by HARRY FURNISS.
DOROTHY FORSTER. With Frontispiece by CHARLES GREEN.
UNCLE JACK, and other Stories. | CHILDREN OF GIBEON.
THE WORLD WENT VERY WELL THEN. With 12 Illustrations by A. FORESTIER.
HERR PAULUS: His Rise, his Greatness, and his Fall.
FOR FAITH AND FREEDOM. With Illustrations by A. FORESTIER and F. WADDY.
TO CALL HER MINE, &c. With 9 Illustrations by A. FORESTIER.
THE BELL OF ST. PAUL'S.
THE HOLY ROSE, &c. With Frontispiece by F. BARNARD.
ARMOREL OF LYONESSE: A Romance of To-day. With 12 Illusts. by F. BARNARD.
ST. KATHERINE'S BY THE TOWER. With 12 page Illustrations by C. GREEN.

Crown 8vo, cloth extra, **3s. 6d.** each.
VERBENA CAMELLIA STEPHANOTIS, &c. Frontispiece by GORDON BROWNE.
THE IVORY GATE: A Novel. *[Shortly.*
FIFTY YEARS AGO. With 144 Plates and Woodcuts. Crown 8vo, cloth extra, **5s.**
THE EULOGY OF RICHARD JEFFERIES. With Portrait. Cr. 8vo, cl. extra, **6s.**
THE ART OF FICTION. Demy 8vo, **1s.**
LONDON. With 124 Illustrations. Demy 8vo, cloth extra, **18s.**
THE REBEL QUEEN: A Novel. Three Vols., crown 8vo. *[Shortly.*

**BESANT (WALTER) AND JAMES RICE, NOVELS BY.**
Cr. 8vo, cl. ex., **3s. 6d.** each ; post 8vo, illust. bds., **2s.** each; cl. limp, **2s. 6d.** each.

READY-MONEY MORTIBOY. | BY CELIA'S ARBOUR.
MY LITTLE GIRL. | THE CHAPLAIN OF THE FLEET.
WITH HARP AND CROWN. | THE SEAMY SIDE.
THIS SON OF VULCAN. | THE CASE OF MR. LUCRAFT, &c.
THE GOLDEN BUTTERFLY. | 'TWAS IN TRAFALGAR'S BAY, &c.
THE MONKS OF THELEMA. | THE TEN YEARS' TENANT, &c.

*.* There is also a LIBRARY EDITION of the above Twelve Volumes, handsomely set in new type, on a large crown 8vo page, and bound in cloth extra. **6s.** each.

**BEWICK (THOMAS) AND HIS PUPILS.** By AUSTIN DOBSON. With 95 Illustrations. Square 8vo, cloth extra, **6s.**

**BIERCE.—IN THE MIDST OF LIFE :** Tales of Soldiers and Civilians. By AMBROSE BIERCE. Crown 8vo, cloth extra, **6s.;** post 8vo, illustrated boards, **2s.**

**BLACKBURN'S (HENRY) ART HANDBOOKS.**
ACADEMY NOTES, separate years, from 1875–1887, 1889–1892, each **1s.**
ACADEMY NOTES, 1893. With Illustrations. **1s.**
ACADEMY NOTES, 1875–79. Complete in One Vol., with 600 Illusts. Cloth limp, **6s.**
ACADEMY NOTES, 1880–84. Complete in One Vol. with 700 Illusts. Cloth limp, **6s.**
GROSVENOR NOTES, 1877. **6d.**
GROSVENOR NOTES, separate years, from 1878 to 1890, each **1s.**
GROSVENOR NOTES, Vol. I., 1877–82. With 300 Illusts. Demy 8vo, cloth limp, **6s.**
GROSVENOR NOTES, Vol. II., 1883–87. With 300 Illusts. Demy 8vo, cloth limp, **6s.**
THE NEW GALLERY, 1888–1892. With numerous Illustrations, each **1s.**
THE NEW GALLERY, 1893. With Illustrations. **1s.**
THE NEW GALLERY, Vol. I., 1888–1892. With 250 Illusts. Demy 8vo, cloth, **6s.**
ENGLISH PICTURES AT THE NATIONAL GALLERY. 114 Illustrations. **1s.**
OLD MASTERS AT THE NATIONAL GALLERY. 128 Illustrations. **1s. 6d.**
ILLUSTRATED CATALOGUE TO THE NATIONAL GALLERY. 242 Illusts. cl., **3s.**
THE PARIS SALON, 1893. With Facsimile Sketches. **3s.**
THE PARIS SOCIETY OF FINE ARTS, 1893. With Sketches. **3s. 6d.** [Shortly.

**BLAKE (WILLIAM) :** India-proof Etchings from his Works by WILLIAM BELL SCOTT. With descriptive Text. Folio, half-bound boards, **21s.**

**BLIND (MATHILDE).** Poems by. Crown 8vo, cloth extra, **5s.** each.
THE ASCENT OF MAN.
DRAMAS IN MINIATURE. With a Frontispiece by FORD MADOX BROWN.
SONGS AND SONNETS. Fcap. 8vo, vellum and gold.

**BOURNE (H. R. FOX), WORKS BY.**
ENGLISH MERCHANTS : Memoirs in Illustration of the Progress of British Commerce. With numerous Illustrations. Crown 8vo, cloth extra, **7s. 6d.**
ENGLISH NEWSPAPERS: The History of Journalism. Two Vols., demy 8vo, cl., **25s.**
THE OTHER SIDE OF THE EMIN PASHA RELIEF EXPEDITION. Crown 8vo, cloth extra, **6s.**

**BOWERS.—LEAVES FROM A HUNTING JOURNAL.** By GEORGE BOWERS. Oblong folio, half-bound, **21s.**

**BOYLE (FREDERICK), WORKS BY.** Post 8vo, illustrated boards, **2s.** each.
CHRONICLES OF NO-MAN'S LAND. | CAMP NOTES.
SAVAGE LIFE. Crown 8vo, cloth extra, **3s. 6d.;** post 8vo, picture boards, **2s.**

**BRAND'S OBSERVATIONS ON POPULAR ANTIQUITIES ;** chiefly illustrating the Origin of our Vulgar Customs, Ceremonies, and Superstitions. With the Additions of Sir HENRY ELLIS, and Illustrations. Cr. 8vo. cloth extra, **7s. 6d.**

**BREWER (REV. DR.), WORKS BY.**
THE READER'S HANDBOOK OF ALLUSIONS, REFERENCES, PLOTS, AND STORIES. Fifteenth Thousand. Crown 8vo. cloth extra, **7s. 6d.**
AUTHORS AND THEIR WORKS, WITH THE DATES: Being the Appendices to "The Reader's Handbook," separately printed. Crown 8vo. cloth limp, **2s.**
A DICTIONARY OF MIRACLES. Crown 8vo. cloth extra, **7s. 6d.**

**BREWSTER (SIR DAVID), WORKS BY.** Post 8vo cl. ex. **4s. 6d.** each.
MORE WORLDS THAN ONE: Creed of Philosopher and Hope of Christian. Plates.
THE MARTYRS OF SCIENCE: GALILEO, TYCHO BRAHE, and KEPLER. With Portraits.
LETTERS ON NATURAL MAGIC. With numerous Illustrations.

**BRILLAT-SAVARIN.—GASTRONOMY AS A FINE ART.** By BRILLAT-SAVARIN. Translated by R. E. ANDERSON, M.A. Post 8vo, half-bound, **2s.**

## BRET HARTE, WORKS BY.

LIBRARY EDITION. In Seven Volumes, crown 8vo, cloth extra, **6s.** each.
BRET HARTE'S COLLECTED WORKS. Arranged and Revised by the Author.
Vol.   I. COMPLETE POETICAL AND DRAMATIC WORKS. With Steel Portrait.
Vol.  II. LUCK OF ROARING CAMP—BOHEMIAN PAPERS—AMERICAN LEGENDS.
Vol. III. TALES OF THE ARGONAUTS—EASTERN SKETCHES.
Vol. IV. GABRIEL CONROY. | Vol. V. STORIES—CONDENSED NOVELS, &c.
Vol. VI. TALES OF THE PACIFIC SLOPE.
Vol.VII. TALES OF THE PACIFIC SLOPE—II. With Portrait by JOHN PETTIE, R.A.

THE SELECT WORKS OF BRET HARTE, in Prose and Poetry  With Introductory
Essay by J. M. BELLEW, Portrait of Author, and 50 Illusts. Cr. 8vo, cl. ex., **7s. 6d.**
BRET HARTE'S POETICAL WORKS. Hand-made paper & buckram. Cr.8vo, **4s.6d.**
THE QUEEN OF THE PIRATE ISLE. With 28 original Drawings by KATE
GREENAWAY, reproduced in Colours by EDMUND EVANS. Small 4to, cloth, **5s.**

Crown 8vo, cloth extra, **3s. 6d.** each.
A WAIF OF THE PLAINS. With 60 Illustrations by STANLEY L. WOOD.
A WARD OF THE GOLDEN GATE. With 59 Illustrations by STANLEY L. WOOD
A SAPPHO OF GREEN SPRINGS, &c. With Two Illustrations by HUME NISBET
COLONEL STARBOTTLE'S CLIENT, AND SOME OTHER PEOPLE. With a
Frontispiece by FRED. BARNARD.
SUSY: A Novel. With Frontispiece and Vignette by J. A. CHRISTIE.
SALLY DOWS, &c. With 47 Illustrations by W. D. ALMOND, &c.

Post 8vo, illustrated boards, **2s.** each.

| | |
|---|---|
| GABRIEL CONROY. | THE LUCK OF ROARING CAMP, &c. |
| AN HEIRESS OF RED DOG, &c. | CALIFORNIAN STORIES. |

Post 8vo, illustrated boards, **2s.** each; cloth limp, **2s. 6d.** each.

| | | |
|---|---|---|
| FLIP. | MARUJA. | A PHYLLIS OF THE SIERRAS. |

Fcap. 8vo, picture cover, **1s.** each.

| | |
|---|---|
| THE TWINS OF TABLE MOUNTAIN. | JEFF BRIGGS'S LOVE STORY. |
| SNOW-BOUND AT EAGLE'S. | |

## BRYDGES.—UNCLE SAM AT HOME. By HAROLD BRYDGES. Post
8vo, illustrated boards, **2s.**; cloth limp, **2s. 6d.**

## BUCHANAN'S (ROBERT) WORKS. Crown 8vo, cloth extra, **6s.** each.

SELECTED POEMS OF ROBERT BUCHANAN. With Frontispiece by T. DALZIEL
THE EARTHQUAKE; or, Six Days and a Sabbath.
THE CITY OF DREAM: An Epic Poem. With Two Illustrations by P. MACNAB.
THE WANDERING JEW: A Christmas Carol. Second Edition.
THE OUTCAST: A Rhyme for the Time. With 15 Illustrations by RUDOLF BLIND,
PETER MACNAB, and HUME NISBET. Small demy 8vo, cloth extra, **8s.**
ROBERT BUCHANAN'S COMPLETE POETICAL WORKS. With Steel-plate Por-
trait. Crown 8vo, cloth extra, **7s. 6d.**

Crown 8vo, cloth extra, **3s. 6d.** each; post 8vo, illustrated boards, **2s.** each.

| | |
|---|---|
| THE SHADOW OF THE SWORD. | LOVE ME FOR EVER. Frontispiece. |
| A CHILD OF NATURE. Frontispiece. | ANNAN WATER. \| FOXGLOVE MANOR. |
| GOD AND THE MAN. With 11 Illus- | THE NEW ABELARD. |
| trations by FRED. BARNARD. | MATT: A Story of a Caravan. Front. |
| THE MARTYRDOM OF MADELINE. | THE MASTER OF THE MINE. Front. |
| With Frontispiece by A. W. COOPER. | THE HEIR OF LINNE. |

## BURTON (CAPTAIN).—THE BOOK OF THE SWORD: Being a
History of the Sword and its Use in all Countries, from the Earliest Times. By
RICHARD F. BURTON. With over 400 Illustrations. Square 8vo, cloth extra. **32s.**

## BURTON (ROBERT).

THE ANATOMY OF MELANCHOLY: A New Edition, with translations of the
Classical Extracts. Demy 8vo, cloth extra, **7s. 6d.**
MELANCHOLY ANATOMISED  Being an Abridgment, for popular use, of BURTON'S
ANATOMY OF MELANCHOLY. Post 8vo, cloth limp, **2s. 6d.**

## CAINE (T. HALL), NOVELS BY. Crown 8vo, cloth extra, **3s. 6d.** each;
post 8vo, illustrated boards, **2s.** each; cloth limp, **2s. 6d.** each.
SHADOW OF A CRIME. | A SON OF HAGAR. | THE DEEMSTER.

## CAMERON (COMMANDER).—THE CRUISE OF THE "BLACK
PRINCE" PRIVATEER. By V. LOVETT CAMERON, R.N., C.B. With Two Illustrations by P. MACNAB. Crown 8vo, cloth extra, **5s.**; post 8vo, illustrated boards, **2s.**

## CAMERON (MRS. H. LOVETT), NOVELS BY. Post 8vo, illust. bds., **2s.** each.
JULIET'S GUARDIAN. | DECEIVERS EVER.

**CARLYLE (THOMAS) ON THE CHOICE OF BOOKS.** With Life by R. H. Shepherd, and Three Illustrations. Post 8vo, cloth extra, **1s. 6d.**
**CORRESPONDENCE OF THOMAS CARLYLE AND R. W. EMERSON, 1834 to 1872.** Edited by C. E. Norton. With Portraits. Two Vols., crown 8vo, cloth, **24s.**

**CARLYLE (JANE WELSH), LIFE OF.** By Mrs. Alexander Ireland. With Portrait and Facsimile Letter. Small demy 8vo, cloth extra, **7s. 6d.**

**CHAPMAN'S (GEORGE) WORKS.** Vol. I. contains the Plays complete, including the doubtful ones. Vol. II., the Poems and Minor Translations, with an Introductory Essay by Algernon Charles Swinburne. Vol. III., the Translations of the Iliad and Odyssey. Three Vols., crown 8vo, cloth extra, **6s.** each.

**CHATTO AND JACKSON.—A TREATISE ON WOOD ENGRAVING,** Historical and Practical. By William Andrew Chatto and John Jackson. With an Additional Chapter by Henry G. Bohn, and 450 fine Illusts. Large 4to, hf.-bd., **28s.**

**CHAUCER FOR CHILDREN: A Golden Key.** By Mrs. H. R. Haweis. With 8 Coloured Plates and 30 Woodcuts. Small 4to, cloth extra, **6s.**
**CHAUCER FOR SCHOOLS.** By Mrs. H. R. Haweis. Demy 8vo, cloth limp, **2s. 6d.**

**CLARE.—FOR THE LOVE OF A LASS: A Tale of Tynedale.** By Austin Clare. Post 8vo, picture boards, **2s.**; cloth limp, **2s. 6d.**

**CLIVE (MRS. ARCHER), NOVELS BY.** Post 8vo, illust. boards, **2s.** each.
**PAUL FERROLL.**  |  **WHY PAUL FERROLL KILLED HIS WIFE.**

**CLODD.—MYTHS AND DREAMS.** By Edward Clodd, F.R.A.S. Second Edition, Revised. Crown 8vo, cloth extra, **3s. 6d.**

**COBBAN (J. MACLAREN), NOVELS BY.**
**THE CURE OF SOULS.** Post 8vo, illustrated boards, **2s.**
**THE RED SULTAN.** Three Vols., crown 8vo.                          [*Shortly*.

**COLEMAN (JOHN), WORKS BY.**
**PLAYERS AND PLAYWRIGHTS I HAVE KNOWN.** Two Vols., 8vo, cloth, **24s.**
**CURLY: An Actor's Story.** With 21 Illusts. by J. C. Dollman. Cr. 8vo, cl., **1s. 6d.**

**COLERIDGE.—THE SEVEN SLEEPERS OF EPHESUS.** By M. E. Coleridge. Fcap. 8vo, cloth, **1s. 6d.**

**COLLINS (C. ALLSTON).—THE BAR SINISTER.** Post 8vo, 2s.

**COLLINS (MORTIMER AND FRANCES), NOVELS BY.**
Crown 8vo, cloth extra, **3s. 6d.** each; post 8vo, illustrated boards, **2s.** each.
**FROM MIDNIGHT TO MIDNIGHT.**  |  **BLACKSMITH AND SCHOLAR.**
**TRANSMIGRATION.**  |  **YOU PLAY ME FALSE.**  |  **A VILLAGE COMEDY.**
Post 8vo, illustrated boards, **2s.** each.
**SWEET ANNE PAGE.** | **FIGHT WITH FORTUNE.** | **SWEET & TWENTY.** | **FRANCES**

**COLLINS (WILKIE), NOVELS BY.**
Cr. 8vo, cl. ex., **3s. 6d.** each; post 8vo, illust. bds., **2s.** each; cl. limp, **2s. 6d.** each.
**ANTONINA.** With a Frontispiece by Sir John Gilbert, R.A.
**BASIL.** Illustrated by Sir John Gilbert, R.A., and J. Mahoney.
**HIDE AND SEEK.** Illustrated by Sir John Gilbert, R.A., and J. Mahoney.
**AFTER DARK.** Illustrations by A. B. Houghton. | **THE TWO DESTINIES.**
**THE DEAD SECRET.** With a Frontispiece by Sir John Gilbert, R.A.
**QUEEN OF HEARTS.** With a Frontispiece by Sir John Gilbert, R.A.
**THE WOMAN IN WHITE.** With Illusts. by Sir J. Gilbert, R.A., and F. A. Fraser.
**NO NAME.** With Illustrations by Sir J. E. Millais, R.A., and A. W. Cooper.
**MY MISCELLANIES.** With a Steel-plate Portrait of Wilkie Collins.
**ARMADALE.** With Illustrations by G. H. Thomas.
**THE MOONSTONE.** With Illustrations by G. Du Maurier and F. A. Fraser.
**MAN AND WIFE.** With Illustrations by William Small.
**POOR MISS FINCH.** Illustrated by G. Du Maurier and Edward Hughes.
**MISS OR MRS.?** With Illusts. by S. L. Fildes, R.A., and Henry Woods, A.R.A.
**THE NEW MAGDALEN.** Illustrated by G. Du Maurier and C. S. Reinhardt.
**THE FROZEN DEEP.** Illustrated by G. Du Maurier and J. Mahoney.
**THE LAW AND THE LADY.** Illusts. by S. L. Fildes, R.A., and Sydney Hall.
**THE HAUNTED HOTEL.** Illustrated by Arthur Hopkins.
**THE FALLEN LEAVES.** | **HEART AND SCIENCE.** | **THE EVIL GENIUS.**
**JEZEBEL'S DAUGHTER.** | **"I SAY NO."** | **LITTLE NOVELS.**
**THE BLACK ROBE.** | **A ROGUE'S LIFE.** | **THE LEGACY OF CAIN.**
**BLIND LOVE.** With Preface by Walter Besant, and Illusts. by A. Forestier.

**COLLINS (JOHN CHURTON, M.A.), BOOKS BY.**
**ILLUSTRATIONS OF TENNYSON.** Crown 8vo, cloth extra, **6s.**
**JONATHAN SWIFT: A Biographical and Critical Study.** Cr. 8vo, cl. ex., **8s.** [*Shortly*

**COLMAN'S HUMOROUS WORKS:** "Broad Grins," "My Nightgown and Slippers," and other Humorous Works of GEORGE COLMAN. With Life by G. B. BUCKSTONE, and Frontispiece by HOGARTH. Crown 8vo, cloth extra, **7s. 6d.**

**COLMORE.—A VALLEY OF SHADOWS.** By G. COLMORE, Author of "A Conspiracy of Silence." Two Vols., crown 8vo.

**COLQUHOUN.—EVERY INCH A SOLDIER:** A Novel. By M. J. COLQUHOUN. Post 8vo, illustrated boards, **2s.**

**CONVALESCENT COOKERY:** A Family Handbook. By CATHERINE RYAN. Crown 8vo, **1s.;** cloth limp, **1s. 6d.**

**CONWAY (MONCURE D.), WORKS BY.**
DEMONOLOGY AND DEVIL-LORE. 65 Illustrations. Two Vols., 8vo, cloth **28s.**
A NECKLACE OF STORIES. 25 Illusts. by W. J. HENNESSY. Sq. 8vo, cloth, **6s.**
PINE AND PALM: A Novel. Two Vols., crown 8vo, cloth extra, **21s.**
GEORGE WASHINGTON'S RULES OF CIVILITY. Fcap. 8vo, Jap. vellum, **2s. 6d.**

**COOK (DUTTON), NOVELS BY.**
PAUL FOSTER'S DAUGHTER. Cr. 8vo, cl. ex., **3s. 6d.**; post 8vo, illust. boards, **2s.**
LEO. Post 8vo, illustrated boards, **2s.**

**COOPER (EDWARD H.)—GEOFFORY HAMILTON.** Two Vols.

**CORNWALL.—POPULAR ROMANCES OF THE WEST OF ENGLAND;** or, The Drolls, Traditions, and Superstitions of Old Cornwall. Collected by ROBERT HUNT, F.R.S. Two Steel-plates by GEO. CRUIKSHANK. Cr. 8vo. cl., **7s. 6d.**

**COTES.—TWO GIRLS ON A BARGE.** By V. CECIL COTES. With 44 Illustrations by F. H. TOWNSEND. Crown 8vo, cloth extra, **3s. 6d.**

**CRADDOCK.—THE PROPHET OF THE GREAT SMOKY MOUNTAINS.** By CHARLES EGBERT CRADDOCK. Post 8vo, illust. bds., **2s.**; cl. limp, **2s. 6d.**

**CRIM.—ADVENTURES OF A FAIR REBEL.** By MATT CRIM. With a Frontispiece. Crown 8vo, cloth extra, **3s. 6d.**; post 8vo, illustrated boards, **2s.**

**CROKER (B.M.), NOVELS BY.** Crown 8vo, cloth extra, **3s. 6d.** each; post 8vo, illustrated boards, **2s.** each; cloth limp, **2s. 6d.** each.
PRETTY MISS NEVILLE.
A BIRD OF PASSAGE.
DIANA BARRINGTON.
PROPER PRIDE.
A FAMILY LIKENESS. Three Vols., crown 8vo.

**CRUIKSHANK'S COMIC ALMANACK.** Complete in TWO SERIES: The FIRST from 1835 to 1843; the SECOND from 1844 to 1853. A Gathering of the BEST HUMOUR of THACKERAY, HOOD, MAYHEW, ALBERT SMITH, A'BECKETT, ROBERT BROUGH, &c. With numerous Steel Engravings and Woodcuts by CRUIKSHANK, HINE, LANDELLS, &c. Two Vols., crown 8vo, cloth gilt, **7s. 6d.** each.
THE LIFE OF GEORGE CRUIKSHANK. By BLANCHARD JERROLD. With 84 Illustrations and a Bibliography. Crown 8vo, cloth extra, **7s. 6d.**

**CUMMING (C. F. GORDON), WORKS BY.** Demy 8vo, cl. ex., **8s. 6d.** each.
IN THE HEBRIDES. With Autotype Facsimile and 23 Illustrations.
IN THE HIMALAYAS AND ON THE INDIAN PLAINS. With 42 Illustrations.
TWO HAPPY YEARS IN CEYLON. With 28 Illustrations.
VIA CORNWALL TO EGYPT. With Photogravure Frontis. Demy 8vo, cl., **7s. 6d.**

**CUSSANS.—A HANDBOOK OF HERALDRY;** with Instructions for Tracing Pedigrees and Deciphering Ancient MSS., &c. By JOHN E. CUSSANS. With 408 Woodcuts and 2 Coloured Plates. New edition, revised, crown 8vo, cloth, **6s.**

**CYPLES (W.)—HEARTS of GOLD.** Cr. 8vo, cl., **3s. 6d.**; post 8vo, bds., **2s.**

**DANIEL.—MERRIE ENGLAND IN THE OLDEN TIME.** By GEORGE DANIEL. With Illustrations by ROBERT CRUIKSHANK. Crown 8vo, cloth extra, **3s. 6d.**

**DAUDET.—THE EVANGELIST;** or, Port Salvation. By ALPHONSE DAUDET. Crown 8vo, cloth extra, **3s. 6d.**; post 8vo, illustrated boards, **2s.**

**DAVENANT.—HINTS FOR PARENTS ON THE CHOICE OF A PROFESSION FOR THEIR SONS.** By F. DAVENANT, M.A. Post 8vo, **1s.**; cl., **1s. 6d.**

**DAVIES (DR. N. E. YORKE-), WORKS BY.**
Crown 8vo, **1s.** each; cloth limp, **1s. 6d.** each.
ONE THOUSAND MEDICAL MAXIMS AND SURGICAL HINTS.
NURSERY HINTS: A Mother's Guide in Health and Disease.
FOODS FOR THE FAT: A Treatise on Corpulency, and a Dietary for its Cure.
AIDS TO LONG LIFE. Crown 8vo, **2s.**; cloth limp, **2s. 6d.**

**DAVIES' (SIR JOHN) COMPLETE POETICAL WORKS,** for the first time Collected and Edited, with Memorial-Introduction and Notes, by the Rev. A. B. GROSART, D.D.  Two Vols., crown 8vo, cloth boards. 12s.

**DAWSON.—THE FOUNTAIN OF YOUTH:** A Novel of Adventure. By ERASMUS DAWSON, M.B.  Edited by PAUL DEVON.  With Two Illustrations by HUME NISBET.  Crown 8vo, cloth extra, 3s. 6d.; post 8vo, illustrated boards, 2s.

**DE GUERIN.—THE JOURNAL OF MAURICE DE GUERIN.**  Edited by G. S. TREBUTIEN.  With a Memoir by SAINTE-BEUVE.  Translated from the 20th French Edition by JESSIE P. FROTHINGHAM.  Fcap. 8vo, half-bound, 2s. 6d.

**DE MAISTRE.—A JOURNEY ROUND MY ROOM.**  By XAVIER DE MAISTRE.  Translated by HENRY ATTWELL.  Post 8vo, cloth limp, 2s. 6d.

**DE MILLE.—A CASTLE IN SPAIN.**  By JAMES DE MILLE.  With a Frontispiece.  Crown 8vo, cloth extra, 3s. 6d.; post 8vo, illustrated boards, 2s.

**DERBY (THE).—THE BLUE RIBBON OF THE TURF:** A Chronicle of the RACE FOR THE DERBY, from Diomed to Donovan.  With Brief Accounts of THE OAKS.  By LOUIS HENRY CURZON.  Crown 8vo, cloth limp, 2s. 6d.

**DERWENT (LEITH), NOVELS BY.**  Cr. 8vo, cl., 3s. 6d. ea.; post 8vo, bds., 2s. ea.
| | |
|---|---|
| OUR LADY OF TEARS. | CIRCE'S LOVERS. |

**DICKENS (CHARLES), NOVELS BY.**  Post 8vo, illustrated boards, 2s. each.
| | |
|---|---|
| SKETCHES BY BOZ. | NICHOLAS NICKLEBY. |
| THE PICKWICK PAPERS. | OLIVER TWIST. |

THE SPEECHES OF CHARLES DICKENS, 1841-1870.  With a New Bibliography. Edited by RICHARD HERNE SHEPHERD.  Crown 8vo, cloth extra, 6s.—Also a SMALLER EDITION, in the *Mayfair Library*, post 8vo, cloth limp, 2s. 6d.
ABOUT ENGLAND WITH DICKENS.  By ALFRED RIMMER.  With 57 Illustrations by C. A. VANDERHOOF, ALFRED RIMMER, and others.  Sq. 8vo, cloth extra, 7s. 6d.

**DICTIONARIES.**
A DICTIONARY OF MIRACLES: Imitative, Realistic, and Dogmatic.  By the Rev. E. C. BREWER, LL.D.  Crown 8vo, cloth extra, 7s. 6d.
THE READER'S HANDBOOK OF ALLUSIONS, REFERENCES, PLOTS, AND STORIES.  By the Rev. E. C. BREWER, LL.D.  With an ENGLISH BIBLIOGRAPHY. Fifteenth Thousand.  Crown 8vo, cloth extra, 7s. 6d.
AUTHORS AND THEIR WORKS, WITH THE DATES.  Cr. 8vo, cloth limp, 2s.
FAMILIAR SHORT SAYINGS OF GREAT MEN.  With Historical and Explanatory Notes.  By SAMUEL A. BENT, A.M.  Crown 8vo, cloth extra, 7s. 6d.
SLANG DICTIONARY: Etymological, Historical, and Anecdotal.  Cr. 8vo, cl., 6s. 6d.
WOMEN OF THE DAY: A Biographical Dictionary.  By F. HAYS.  Cr. 8vo, cl., 5s.
WORDS, FACTS, AND PHRASES: A Dictionary of Curious, Quaint, and Out-of-the-Way Matters.  By ELIEZER EDWARDS.  Crown 8vo, cloth extra, 7s. 6d.

**DIDEROT.—THE PARADOX OF ACTING.**  Translated, with Annotations, from Diderot's "Le Paradoxe sur le Comédien," by WALTER HERRIES POLLOCK. With a Preface by HENRY IRVING.  Crown 8vo, parchment, 4s. 6d.

**DOBSON (AUSTIN), WORKS BY.**
THOMAS BEWICK & HIS PUPILS.  With 95 Illustrations.  Square 8vo, cloth, 6s.
FOUR FRENCHWOMEN.  Fcap. 8vo, hf.-roxburghe, with a Portrait, 2s. 6d.— Also, a Library Edition, with 4 Portraits, crown 8vo, buckram, gilt top, 6s.
EIGHTEENTH CENTURY VIGNETTES.  Crown 8vo, buckram, gilt top, 6s.

**DOBSON (W. T.)—POETICAL INGENUITIES AND ECCENTRICITIES.**  Post 8vo, cloth limp, 2s. 6d.

**DONOVAN (DICK), DETECTIVE STORIES BY.**
Post 8vo, illustrated boards, 2s. each; cloth limp, 2s. 6d. each.
| | |
|---|---|
| THE MAN-HUNTER. \| WANTED! | A DETECTIVE'S TRIUMPHS. |
| CAUGHT AT LAST! | IN THE GRIP OF THE LAW. |
| TRACKED AND TAKEN. | FROM INFORMATION RECEIVED. |
| WHO POISONED HETTY DUNCAN? | |

Crown 8vo, cloth extra, 3s. 6d. each; post 8vo, illustrated boards, 2s. each; cloth limp, 2s. 6d. each.
THE MAN FROM MANCHESTER.  With 23 Illustrations.
TRACKED TO DOOM.  With 6 full-page Illustrations by GORDON BROWNE.

**DOYLE (CONAN).—THE FIRM OF GIRDLESTONE.**  By A. CONAN DOYLE, Author of "Micah Clarke."  Crown 8vo, cloth extra, 3s. 6d.

**DRAMATISTS, THE OLD.** With Vignette Portraits. Cr. 8vo, cl. ex., **6s.** per Vol.
   **BEN JONSON'S WORKS.** With Notes Critical and Explanatory, and a Biographical Memoir by WM. GIFFORD. Edited by Col. CUNNINGHAM. Three Vols.
   **CHAPMAN'S WORKS.** Complete in Three Vols. Vol. I. contains the Plays complete; Vol. II., Poems and Minor Translations, with an Introductory Essay by A. C. SWINBURNE; Vol. III., Translations of the Iliad and Odyssey.
   **MARLOWE'S WORKS.** Edited, with Notes, by Col. CUNNINGHAM. One Vol.
   **MASSINGER'S PLAYS.** From GIFFORD'S Text. Edit by Col. CUNNINGHAM. OneVol.

**DUNCAN (SARA JEANNETTE), WORKS BY.**
Crown 8vo, cloth extra, **7s. 6d.** each.
   **A SOCIAL DEPARTURE:** How Orthodocia and I Went round the World by Ourselves. With 111 Illustrations by F. H. TOWNSEND.
   **AN AMERICAN GIRL IN LONDON.** With 80 Illustrations by F. H. TOWNSEND.
   **THE SIMPLE ADVENTURES OF A MEMSAHIB.** Numerous Illusts. [*Preparing.*

**DYER.—THE FOLK-LORE OF PLANTS.** By Rev. T. F. THISELTON DYER, M.A. Crown 8vo, cloth extra, **6s.**

**EARLY ENGLISH POETS.** Edited, with Introductions and Annotations, by Rev. A. B. GROSART, D.D. Crown 8vo, cloth boards, **6s.** per Volume.
   **FLETCHER'S (GILES) COMPLETE POEMS.** One Vol.
   **DAVIES' (SIR JOHN) COMPLETE POETICAL WORKS.** Two Vols.
   **HERRICK'S (ROBERT) COMPLETE COLLECTED POEMS.** Three Vols.
   **SIDNEY'S (SIR PHILIP) COMPLETE POETICAL WORKS.** Three Vols.

**EDGCUMBE.—ZEPHYRUS :** A Holiday in Brazil and on the River Plate. By E. R. PEARCE EDGCUMBE. With 41 Illustrations. Crown 8vo, cloth extra, **5s.**

**EDWARDES (MRS. ANNIE), NOVELS BY:**
   **A POINT OF HONOUR.** Post 8vo, illustrated boards, **2s.**
   **ARCHIE LOVELL.** Crown 8vo, cloth extra, **3s. 6d.**; post 8vo, illust. boards, **2s.**

**EDWARDS (ELIEZER).—WORDS, FACTS, AND PHRASES:** A Dictionary of Curious, Quaint, and Out-of-the-Way Matters. By ELIEZER EDWARDS. Crown 8vo, cloth extra, **7s. 6d.**

**EDWARDS (M. BETHAM-), NOVELS BY.**
   **KITTY.** Post 8vo, illustrated boards, **2s.**; cloth limp, **2s. 6d.**
   **FELICIA.** Post 8vo, illustrated boards, **2s.**

**EGERTON.—SUSSEX FOLK & SUSSEX WAYS.** By Rev. J. C. EGERTON. With Introduction by Rev. Dr. H. WACE, and 4 Illustrations. Cr. 8vo, cloth ex., **5s.**

**EGGLESTON (EDWARD).—ROXY :** A Novel. Post 8vo, illust. bds., **2s.**

**ENGLISHMAN'S HOUSE, THE :** A Practical Guide to all interested in Selecting or Building a House; with Estimates of Cost, Quantities, &c. By C. J. RICHARDSON. With Coloured Frontispiece and 600 Illusts. Crown 8vo, cloth, **7s. 6d.**

**EWALD (ALEX. CHARLES, F.S.A.), WORKS BY.**
   **THE LIFE AND TIMES OF PRINCE CHARLES STUART,** Count of Albany (THE YOUNG PRETENDER). With a Portrait. Crown 8vo, cloth extra, **7s. 6d.**
   **STORIES FROM THE STATE PAPERS.** With an Autotype. Crown 8vo, cloth, **6s.**

**EYES, OUR :** How to Preserve Them from Infancy to Old Age. By JOHN BROWNING, F.R.A.S. With 70 Illusts. Eighteenth Thousand. Crown 8vo, **1s.**

**FAMILIAR SHORT SAYINGS OF GREAT MEN.** By SAMUEL ARTHUR BENT, A.M. Fifth Edition, Revised and Enlarged. Crown 8vo, cloth extra, **7s. 6d.**

**FARADAY (MICHAEL), WORKS BY.** Post 8vo, cloth extra, **4s. 6d.** each.
   **THE CHEMICAL HISTORY OF A CANDLE:** Lectures delivered before a Juvenile Audience. Edited by WILLIAM CROOKES, F.C.S. With numerous Illustrations.
   **ON THE VARIOUS FORCES OF NATURE, AND THEIR RELATIONS TO EACH OTHER.** Edited by WILLIAM CROOKES, F.C.S. With Illustrations.

**FARRER (J. ANSON), WORKS BY.**
   **MILITARY MANNERS AND CUSTOMS.** Crown 8vo, cloth extra, **6s.**
   **WAR:** Three Essays, reprinted from "Military Manners." Cr. 8vo, **1s.**; cl., **1s. 6d.**

**FENN (G. MANVILLE), NOVELS BY.**
   **THE NEW MISTRESS.** Cr. 8vo, cloth extra, **3s. 6d.**; post 8vo, illust. boards, **2s.**
   **WITNESS TO THE DEED.** Three Vols., crown 8vo.

**FIN-BEC.—THE CUPBOARD PAPERS:** Observations on the Art of Living and Dining. By FIN-BEC. Post 8vo, cloth limp, **2s. 6d.**

**FIREWORKS, THE COMPLETE ART OF MAKING;** or, The Pyrotechnist's Treasury. By THOMAS KENTISH. With 267 Illustrations. Cr. 8vo, cl., **5s.**

**FITZGERALD (PERCY, M.A., F.S.A.), WORKS BY.**
THE WORLD BEHIND THE SCENES. Crown 8vo, cloth extra, **3s. 6d.**
LITTLE ESSAYS: Passages from Letters of CHARLES LAMB. Post 8vo, cl., **2s. 6d.**
A DAY'S TOUR: Journey through France and Belgium. With Sketches. Cr. 4to, **1s.**
FATAL ZERO. Crown 8vo, cloth extra, **3s. 6d.**: post 8vo, illustrated boards, **2s.**
Post 8vo, illustrated boards, **2s.** each.

| | | |
|---|---|---|
| BELLA DONNA. | LADY OF BRANTOME. | THE SECOND MRS. TILLOTSON. |
| POLLY. | NEVER FORGOTTEN. | SEVENTY-FIVE BROOKE STREET. |

LIFE OF JAMES BOSWELL (of Auchinleck). With an Account of his Sayings, Doings, and Writings; and Four Portraits. Two Vols., demy 8vo, cloth, **24s.**

**FLAMMARION.—URANIA:** A Romance. By CAMILLE FLAMMARION. Translated by AUGUSTA RICE STETSON. With 87 Illustrations by DE BIELER, MYRBACH, and GAMBARD. Crown 8vo, cloth extra, **5s.**

**FLETCHER'S (GILES, B.D.) COMPLETE POEMS:** Christ's Victorie in Heaven, Christ's Victorie on Earth, Christ's Triumph over Death, and Minor Poems. With Notes by Rev. A. B. GROSART, D.D. Crown 8vo, cloth boards, **6s.**

**FLUDYER (HARRY) AT CAMBRIDGE:** A Series of Family Letters. Post 8vo, picture cover, **1s.**; cloth limp, **1s. 6d.**

**FONBLANQUE (ALBANY).—FILTHY LUCRE.** Post 8vo, illust. bds., 2s.

**FRANCILLON (R. E.), NOVELS BY.**
Crown 8vo, cloth extra, **3s. 6d.** each: post 8vo, illustrated boards, **2s.** each.
ONE BY ONE. | QUEEN COPHETUA. | A REAL QUEEN. | KING OR KNAVE?
OLYMPIA. Post 8vo, illust. bds., **2s.** | ESTHER'S GLOVE. Fcap. 8vo, pict. cover, **1s.**
ROMANCES OF THE LAW. Crown 8vo, cloth, **6s.**; post 8vo, illust. boards, **2s.**
ROPES OF SAND. 3 vols., crown 8vo.

**FREDERIC (HAROLD), NOVELS BY.**
SETH'S BROTHER'S WIFE. Post 8vo, illustrated boards, **2s.**
THE LAWTON GIRL. Cr. 8vo, cloth ex., **6s.**: post 8vo, illustrated boards, **2s.**

**FRENCH LITERATURE, A HISTORY OF.** By HENRY VAN LAUN. Three Vols., demy 8vo, cloth boards, **7s. 6d.** each.

**FRERE.—PANDURANG HARI;** or, Memoirs of a Hindoo. With Preface by Sir BARTLE FRERE. Crown 8vo, cloth, **3s. 6d.**; post 8vo, illust. bds., **2s.**

**FRISWELL (HAIN).—ONE OF TWO:** A Novel. Post 8vo, illust. bds., 2s.

**FROST (THOMAS), WORKS BY.** Crown 8vo, cloth extra, **3s. 6d.** each.
CIRCUS LIFE AND CIRCUS CELEBRITIES. | LIVES OF THE CONJURERS.
THE OLD SHOWMEN AND THE OLD LONDON FAIRS.

**FRY'S (HERBERT) ROYAL GUIDE TO THE LONDON CHARITIES.** Showing their Name, Date of Foundation, Objects, Income, Officials, &c. Edited by JOHN LANE. Published Annually. Crown 8vo, cloth, **1s. 6d.**

**GARDENING BOOKS.** Post 8vo, **1s.** each; cloth limp, **1s. 6d.** each.
A YEAR'S WORK IN GARDEN AND GREENHOUSE: Practical Advice as to the Management of the Flower, Fruit, and Frame Garden. By GEORGE GLENNY.
HOUSEHOLD HORTICULTURE. By TOM and JANE JERROLD. Illustrated.
THE GARDEN THAT PAID THE RENT. By TOM JERROLD.
OUR KITCHEN GARDEN: The Plants we Grow, and How we Cook Them. By TOM JERROLD. Crown 8vo, cloth, 1s. 6d.
MY GARDEN WILD, AND WHAT I GREW THERE. By FRANCIS G. HEATH Crown 8vo, cloth extra, gilt edges, **6s.**

**GARRETT.—THE CAPEL GIRLS:** A Novel. By EDWARD GARRETT. Crown 8vo, cloth extra, **3s. 6d.**; post 8vo, illustrated boards, **2s.**

**GENTLEMAN'S MAGAZINE, THE. 1s.** Monthly. In addition to Articles upon subjects in Literature, Science, and Art, "TABLE TALK" by SYLVANUS URBAN, and "PAGES ON PLAYS" by JUSTIN H. McCARTHY, appear monthly.
*.* Bound Volumes for recent years kept in stock, **8s. 6d.** each; Cases for binding, **2s.**

**GENTLEMAN'S ANNUAL, THE.** Published Annually in November. 1s.
The 1892 Annual, written by T. W. SPEIGHT, is entitled "**THE LOUDWATER TRAGEDY.**"

**GERMAN POPULAR STORIES.** Collected by the Brothers GRIMM
and Translated by EDGAR TAYLOR. With Introduction by JOHN RUSKIN, and 22 Steel
Plates after GEORGE CRUIKSHANK. Square 8vo. cloth, 6s. 6d.; gilt edges, 7s. 6d.

**GIBBON (CHARLES), NOVELS BY.**
Crown 8vo, cloth extra, 3s. 6d. each; post 8vo, illustrated boards, 2s. each.

| | |
|---|---|
| ROBIN GRAY.   LOVING A DREAM. | THE GOLDEN SHAFT. |
| THE FLOWER OF THE FOREST. | OF HIGH DEGREE. |

Post 8vo, illustrated boards, 2s. each.

| | |
|---|---|
| THE DEAD HEART. | IN LOVE AND WAR. |
| FOR LACK OF GOLD. | A HEART'S PROBLEM. |
| WHAT WILL THE WORLD SAY? | BY MEAD AND STREAM. |
| FOR THE KING.   A HARD KNOT. | THE BRAES OF YARROW. |
| QUEEN OF THE MEADOW. | FANCY FREE.   IN HONOUR BOUND. |
| IN PASTURES GREEN. | HEART'S DELIGHT.   BLOOD-MONEY. |

**GIBNEY (SOMERVILLE).—SENTENCED!** Cr. 8vo, 1s.; cl., 1s. 6d.

**GILBERT (WILLIAM), NOVELS BY.** Post 8vo, illustrated boards, 2s. each.

| | |
|---|---|
| DR. AUSTIN'S GUESTS. | JAMES DUKE, COSTERMONGER. |
| THE WIZARD OF THE MOUNTAIN. | |

**GILBERT (W. S.), ORIGINAL PLAYS BY.** Two Series, 2s. 6d. each.
The FIRST SERIES contains: The Wicked World—Pygmalion and Galatea—
Charity—The Princess—The Palace of Truth—Trial by Jury.
The SECOND SERIES: Broken Hearts—Engaged—Sweethearts—Gretchen—Dan'l
Druce—Tom Cobb—H.M.S. "Pinafore"—The Sorcerer—Pirates of Penzance.

**EIGHT ORIGINAL COMIC OPERAS** written by W. S. GILBERT. Containing:
The Sorcerer—H.M.S. "Pinafore"—Pirates of Penzance—Iolanthe—Patience—
Princess Ida—The Mikado—Trial by Jury. Demy 8vo, cloth limp, 2s. 6d.
**THE "GILBERT AND SULLIVAN" BIRTHDAY BOOK:** Quotations for Every
Day in the Year, Selected from Plays by W. S. GILBERT set to Music by Sir A.
SULLIVAN. Compiled by ALEX. WATSON. Royal 16mo, Jap. leather, 2s. 6d.

**GLANVILLE (ERNEST), NOVELS BY.**
Crown 8vo, cloth extra, 3s. 6d. each; post 8vo, illustrated boards, 2s. each.
**THE LOST HEIRESS:** A Tale of Love, Battle, and Adventure. With 2 Illusts.
**THE FOSSICKER:** A Romance of Mashonaland. With 2 Illusts. by HUME NISBET.

**GLENNY.—A YEAR'S WORK IN GARDEN AND GREENHOUSE:**
Practical Advice to Amateur Gardeners as to the Management of the Flower, Fruit,
and Frame Garden. By GEORGE GLENNY. Post 8vo, 1s.; cloth limp, 1s. 6d.

**GODWIN.—LIVES OF THE NECROMANCERS.** By WILLIAM GOD-
WIN. Post 8vo, cloth limp, 2s.

**GOLDEN TREASURY OF THOUGHT, THE:** An Encyclopædia of
QUOTATIONS. Edited by THEODORE TAYLOR. Crown 8vo, cloth gilt, 7s. 6d.

**GOODMAN.—THE FATE OF HERBERT WAYNE.** By E. J. GOOD-
MAN, Author of "Too Curious." Crown 8vo, cloth, 3s. 6d.

**GOWING.—FIVE THOUSAND MILES IN A SLEDGE:** A Midwinter
Journey Across Siberia. By LIONEL F. GOWING. With 30 Illustrations by C. J.
UREN, and a Map by E. WELLER. Large crown 8vo, cloth extra. 8s.

**GRAHAM. — THE PROFESSOR'S WIFE:** A Story By LEONARD
GRAHAM. Fcap. 8vo, picture cover, 1s.

**GREEKS AND ROMANS, THE LIFE OF THE,** described from
Antique Monuments. By ERNST GUHL and W. KONER. Edited by Dr. F. HUEFFER.
With 545 Illustrations. Large crown 8vo, cloth extra. 7s. 6d.

**GREENWOOD (JAMES), WORKS BY.** Cr. 8vo, cloth extra, 3s. 6d. each.

| | |
|---|---|
| THE WILDS OF LONDON. | LOW-LIFE DEEPS. |

**GREVILLE (HENRY), NOVELS BY:**
**NIKANOR.** Translated by ELIZA E. CHASE. With 8 Illustrations. Crown 8vo,
cloth extra, 6s.; post 8vo, illustrated boards, 2s.
**A NOBLE WOMAN.** Crown 8vo, cloth extra, 5s.; post 8vo, illustrated boards, 2s.

**GRIFFITH.—CORINTHIA MARAZION:** A Novel. By CECIL GRIF-
FITH, Author of "Victory Deane," &c. Crown 8vo, cloth extra, 3s. 6d.

**H**ABBERTON (JOHN, Author of " Helen's Babies "), NOVELS BY.
Post 8vo, illustrated boards **2s.** each; cloth limp, **2s. 6d.** each.
BRUETON'S BAYOU. | COUNTRY LUCK.

HAIR, THE : Its Treatment in Health, Weakness, and Disease. Translated from the German of Dr. J. PINCUS. Crown 8vo, **1s.**; cloth, **1s. 6d.**

HAKE (DR. THOMAS GORDON), POEMS BY. Cr. 8vo, cl. ex., **6s.** each.
NEW SYMBOLS. | LEGENDS OF THE MORROW. | THE SERPENT PLAY.
MAIDEN ECSTASY. Small 4to, cloth extra, **8s.**

HALL.—SKETCHES OF IRISH CHARACTER. By Mrs. S. C. HALL.
With numerous Illustrations on Steel and Wood by MACLISE, GILBERT, HARVEY, and GEORGE CRUIKSHANK. Medium 8vo, cloth extra, **7s. 6d.**

HALLIDAY (ANDR.).—EVERY-DAY PAPERS. Post 8vo, bds., 2s.

HANDWRITING, THE PHILOSOPHY OF. With over 100 Facsimiles and Explanatory Text. By DON FELIX DE SALAMANCA. Post 8vo, cloth limp, **2s. 6d.**

HANKY-PANKY : Easy Tricks, White Magic, Sleight of Hand, &c.
Edited by W. H. CREMER. With 200 Illustrations. Crown 8vo, cloth extra, **4s. 6d.**

HARDY (LADY DUFFUS). — PAUL WYNTER'S SACRIFICE. 2s.

HARDY (THOMAS). — UNDER THE GREENWOOD TREE. By
THOMAS HARDY, Author of " Far from the Madding Crowd." With Portrait and 15 Illustrations. Crown 8vo, cloth extra, **3s. 6d.**; post 8vo, illustrated boards, **2s.**

HARPER.—THE BRIGHTON ROAD : Old Times and New on a Classic Highway. By CHARLES G. HARPER. With a Photogravure Frontispiece and 90 Illustrations. Demy 8vo, cloth extra, **16s.**

HARWOOD.—THE TENTH EARL. By J. BERWICK HARWOOD. Post 8vo, illustrated boards, **2s.**

HAWEIS (MRS. H. R.), WORKS BY. Square 8vo, cloth extra, **6s.** each.
THE ART OF BEAUTY. With Coloured Frontispiece and 91 Illustrations.
THE ART OF DECORATION. With Coloured Frontispiece and 74 Illustrations.
CHAUCER FOR CHILDREN. With 8 Coloured Plates and 30 Woodcuts.
THE ART OF DRESS. With 32 Illustrations. Post 8vo, **1s.**; cloth, **1s. 6d.**
CHAUCER FOR SCHOOLS. Demy 8vo, cloth limp, **2s. 6d.**

HAWEIS (Rev. H. R., M.A.). —AMERICAN HUMORISTS : WASHINGTON
IRVING, OLIVER WENDELL HOLMES, JAMES RUSSELL LOWELL, ARTEMUS WARD, MARK TWAIN, and BRET HARTE. Third Edition. Crown 8vo, cloth extra, **6s.**

HAWLEY SMART.—WITHOUT LOVE OR LICENCE : A Novel. By
HAWLEY SMART. Crown 8vo, cloth extra, **3s. 6d.**; post 8vo, illustrated boards, **2s.**

HAWTHORNE. —OUR OLD HOME. By NATHANIEL HAWTHORNE.
Annotated with Passages from the Author's Note-book, and Illustrated with 31 Photogravures. Two Vols., crown 8vo, buckram, gilt top, **15s.**

HAWTHORNE (JULIAN), NOVELS BY.
Crown 8vo, cloth extra, **3s. 6d.** each; post 8vo, illustrated boards, **2s.** each.
GARTH. | ELLICE QUENTIN. | BEATRIX RANDOLPH. | DUST.
SEBASTIAN STROME. | DAVID POINDEXTER.
FORTUNE'S FOOL. | THE SPECTRE OF THE CAMERA.
Post 8vo, illustrated boards, **2s.** each.
MISS CADOGNA. | LOVE—OR A NAME.
MRS. GAINSBOROUGH'S DIAMONDS. Fcap. 8vo, illustrated cover, **1s.**

HEATH.—MY GARDEN WILD, AND WHAT I GREW THERE.
By FRANCIS GEORGE HEATH. Crown 8vo, cloth extra, gilt edges, **6s.**

HELPS (SIR ARTHUR), WORKS BY. Post 8vo, cloth limp, **2s. 6d.** each.
ANIMALS AND THEIR MASTERS. | SOCIAL PRESSURE.
IVAN DE BIRON : A Novel. Cr. 8vo, cl. extra, **3s. 6d.**; post 8vo, illust. bds., **2s.**

HENDERSON.—AGATHA PAGE : A Novel. By ISAAC HENDERSON.
Crown 8vo, cloth extra, **3s. 6d.**

HENTY.—RUJUB, THE JUGGLER. By G. A. HENTY. Three Vols.

HERMAN.—A LEADING LADY. By HENRY HERMAN, joint-Author of " The Bishops' Bible." Post 8vo, illustrated boards, **2s.**; cloth extra, **2s. 6d.**

**HERRICK'S (ROBERT) HESPERIDES, NOBLE NUMBERS, AND COMPLETE COLLECTED POEMS.** With Memorial-Introduction and Notes by the Rev. A. B. GROSART, D.D.; Steel Portrait, &c. Three Vols., crown 8vo, cl. bds., **18s.**

**HERTZKA.—FREELAND :** A Social Anticipation. By Dr. THEODOR HERTZKA. Translated by ARTHUR RANSOM. Crown 8vo, cloth extra, **6s.**

**HESSE-WARTEGG.—TUNIS :** The Land and the People. By Chevalier ERNST VON HESSE-WARTEGG. With 22 Illustrations. Cr. 8vo, cloth extra, **3s. 6d.**

**HILL.—TREASON-FELONY :** A Novel. By JOHN HILL. Two Vols.

**HINDLEY (CHARLES), WORKS BY.**
**TAVERN ANECDOTES AND SAYINGS :** Including Reminiscences connected with Coffee Houses, Clubs, &c. With Illustrations. Crown 8vo, cloth, **3s. 6d.**
**THE LIFE AND ADVENTURES OF A CHEAP JACK.** Cr. 8vo, cloth ex., **3s. 6d.**

**HOEY.—THE LOVER'S CREED.** By Mrs. CASHEL HOEY. Post 8vo, **2s.**

**HOLLINGSHEAD (JOHN).—NIAGARA SPRAY.** Crown 8vo, **1s.**

**HOLMES.—THE SCIENCE OF VOICE PRODUCTION AND VOICE PRESERVATION.** By GORDON HOLMES, M.D. Crown 8vo, **1s.**; cloth, **1s. 6d.**

**HOLMES (OLIVER WENDELL), WORKS BY.**
**THE AUTOCRAT OF THE BREAKFAST-TABLE.** Illustrated by J. GORDON THOMSON. Post 8vo, cloth limp, **2s. 6d.**—Another Edition, in smaller type, with an Introduction by G. A. SALA. Post 8vo, cloth limp, **2s.**
**THE AUTOCRAT OF THE BREAKFAST-TABLE and THE PROFESSOR AT THE BREAKFAST-TABLE.** In One Vol. Post 8vo, half-bound, **2s.**

**HOOD'S (THOMAS) CHOICE WORKS,** in Prose and Verse. With Life of the Author, Portrait, and 200 Illustrations. Crown 8vo, cloth extra, **7s. 6d.**
**HOOD'S WHIMS AND ODDITIES.** With 85 Illustrations. Post 8vo, printed on laid paper and half-bound, **2s.**

**HOOD (TOM).—FROM NOWHERE TO THE NORTH POLE :** A Noah's Arkæological Narrative. By TOM HOOD. With 25 Illustrations by W. BRUNTON and E. C. BARNES. Square 8vo, cloth extra, gilt edges, **6s.**

**HOOK'S (THEODORE) CHOICE HUMOROUS WORKS ;** including his Ludicrous Adventures, Bons Mots, Puns, and Hoaxes. With Life of the Author, Portraits, Facsimiles, and Illustrations. Crown 8vo, cloth extra, **7s. 6d.**

**HOOPER.—THE HOUSE OF RABY :** A Novel. By Mrs. GEORGE HOOPER. Post 8vo, illustrated boards, **2s.**

**HOPKINS.—"'TWIXT LOVE AND DUTY :"** A Novel. By TIGHE HOPKINS. Post 8vo, illustrated boards, **2s.**

**HORNE. —ORION :** An Epic Poem. By RICHARD HENGIST HORNE. With Photographic Portrait by SUMMERS. Tenth Edition. Cr. 8vo, cloth extra, **7s.**

**HORSE (THE) AND HIS RIDER :** An Anecdotic Medley. By "THOR-MANBY." Crown 8vo, cloth extra, **6s.**

**HUNGERFORD (MRS.),** Author of "Molly Bawn," **NOVELS BY.** Post 8vo, illustrated boards, **2s.** each; cloth limp, **2s. 6d.** each.
**A MAIDEN ALL FORLORN. | IN DURANCE VILE. | A MENTAL STRUGGLE. MARVEL. | A MODERN CIRCE.**
**LADY VERNER'S FLIGHT.** Two Vols., crown 8vo.

**HUNT.—ESSAYS BY LEIGH HUNT :** A TALE FOR A CHIMNEY CORNER, &c. Edited by EDMUND OLLIER. Post 8vo, printed on laid paper and half-bd., **2s.**

**HUNT (MRS. ALFRED), NOVELS BY.**
Crown 8vo, cloth extra, **3s. 6d.** each; post 8vo, illustrated boards, **2s.** each.
**THE LEADEN CASKET. | SELF-CONDEMNED. | THAT OTHER PERSON.**
**THORNICROFT'S MODEL.** Post 8vo, illustrated boards, **2s.**
**MRS. JULIET.** Three Vols., crown 8vo.

**HUTCHISON.—HINTS ON COLT-BREAKING.** By W. M. HUTCHISON. With 25 Illustrations. Crown 8vo, cloth extra, **3s. 6d.**

**HYDROPHOBIA :** An Account of M. PASTEUR'S System ; Technique of his Method, and Statistics. By RENAUD SUZOR, M.B. Crown 8vo, cloth extra, **6s.**

**IDLER (THE) :** A Monthly Magazine. Edited by JEROME K. JEROME and ROBERT E. BARR. Profusely Illustrated. Sixpence Monthly.—Vols. I. and II. now ready, cloth extra, **5s.** each ; Cases for Binding, **1s. 6d.**

**INGELOW (JEAN).—FATED TO BE FREE.** Post 8vo, illustrated bds., 2s.

**INDOOR PAUPERS.** By ONE OF THEM. Crown 8vo, 1s.; cloth, 1s. 6d.

**INNKEEPER'S HANDBOOK (THE) AND LICENSED VICTUALLER'S MANUAL.** By J. TREVOR-DAVIES. Crown 8vo, 1s.; cloth, 1s. 6d.

**IRISH WIT AND HUMOUR, SONGS OF.** Collected and Edited by A. PERCEVAL GRAVES. Post 8vo, cloth limp, 2s. 6d.

**JAMES.—A ROMANCE OF THE QUEEN'S HOUNDS.** By CHARLES JAMES. Post 8vo, picture cover, 1s.; cloth limp, 1s. 6d.

**JANVIER.—PRACTICAL KERAMICS FOR STUDENTS.** By CATHERINE A. JANVIER. Crown 8vo, cloth extra, 6s.

**JAY (HARRIETT), NOVELS BY.** Post 8vo, illustrated boards, 2s. each.
THE DARK COLLEEN. | THE QUEEN OF CONNAUGHT.

**JEFFERIES (RICHARD), WORKS BY.** Post 8vo, cloth limp, 2s. 6d. each.
NATURE NEAR LONDON. | THE LIFE OF THE FIELDS. | THE OPEN AIR.
*** Also the HAND-MADE PAPER EDITION, crown 8vo, buckram, gilt top, 6s. each.
THE EULOGY OF RICHARD JEFFERIES. By WALTER BESANT. Second Edition. With a Photograph Portrait. Crown 8vo, cloth extra, 6s.

**JENNINGS (H. J.), WORKS BY.**
CURIOSITIES OF CRITICISM. Post 8vo, cloth limp, 2s. 6d.
LORD TENNYSON: A Biographical Sketch. With a Photograph. Cr. 8vo, cl., 6s.

**JEROME.—STAGELAND.** By JEROME K. JEROME. With 64 Illustrations by J. BERNARD PARTRIDGE. Square 8vo, picture cover, 1s.; cloth limp, 2s.

**JERROLD.—THE BARBER'S CHAIR; & THE HEDGEHOG LETTERS.** By DOUGLAS JERROLD. Post 8vo, printed on laid paper and half-bound, 2s.

**JERROLD (TOM), WORKS BY.** Post 8vo, 1s. each; cloth limp, 1s. 6d. each.
THE GARDEN THAT PAID THE RENT.
HOUSEHOLD HORTICULTURE: A Gossip about Flowers. Illustrated.
OUR KITCHEN GARDEN: The Plants, and How we Cook Them. Cr. 8vo, cl., 1s. 6d.

**JESSE.—SCENES AND OCCUPATIONS OF A COUNTRY LIFE.** By EDWARD JESSE. Post 8vo, cloth limp, 2s.

**JONES (WILLIAM, F.S.A.), WORKS BY.** Cr. 8vo, cl. extra, 7s. 6d. each.
FINGER-RING LORE: Historical, Legendary, and Anecdotal. With nearly 300 Illustrations. Second Edition, Revised and Enlarged.
CREDULITIES, PAST AND PRESENT. Including the Sea and Seamen, Miners, Talismans, Word and Letter Divination, Exorcising and Blessing of Animals, Birds, Eggs, Luck, &c. With an Etched Frontispiece.
CROWNS AND CORONATIONS: A History of Regalia. With 100 Illustrations.

**JONSON'S (BEN) WORKS.** With Notes Critical and Explanatory, and a Biographical Memoir by WILLIAM GIFFORD. Edited by Colonel CUNNINGHAM. Three Vols., crown 8vo, cloth extra, 6s. each.

**JOSEPHUS, THE COMPLETE WORKS OF.** Translated by WHISTON. Containing "The Antiquities of the Jews" and "The Wars of the Jews." With 52 Illustrations and Maps. Two Vols., demy 8vo, half-bound, 12s. 6d.

**KEMPT.—PENCIL AND PALETTE:** Chapters on Art and Artists. By ROBERT KEMPT. Post 8vo, cloth limp, 2s. 6d.

**KERSHAW. — COLONIAL FACTS AND FICTIONS:** Humorous Sketches. By MARK KERSHAW. Post 8vo, illustrated boards, 2s.; cloth, 2s. 6d.

**KEYSER. — CUT BY THE MESS:** A Novel. By ARTHUR KEYSER. Crown 8vo, picture cover, 1s.; cloth limp, 1s. 6d.

**KING (R. ASHE), NOVELS BY.** Cr. 8vo, cl., 3s. 6d. ea.; post 8vo, bds., 2s. ea.
A DRAWN GAME. | "THE WEARING OF THE GREEN."
Post 8vo, illustrated boards, 2s. each.
PASSION'S SLAVE. | BELL BARRY.

**KNIGHTS (THE) OF THE LION:** A Romance of the Thirteenth Century. Edited, with an Introduction, by the MARQUESS of LORNE, K.T. Cr. 8vo, cl. ex., 6s.

**KNIGHT.—THE PATIENT'S VADE MECUM:** How to Get Most Benefit from Medical Advice. By WILLIAM KNIGHT, M.R.C.S., and EDWARD KNIGHT, L.R.C.P. Crown 8vo, 1s.; cloth limp, 1s. 6d.

**LAMB'S (CHARLES) COMPLETE WORKS,** in Prose and Verse, including "Poetry for Children" and "Prince Dorus." Edited, with Notes and Introduction, by R. H. SHEPHERD. With Two Portraits and Facsimile of a page of the "Essay on Roast Pig." Crown 8vo, half-bound, 7s. 6d.

    **THE ESSAYS OF ELIA.** Post 8vo, printed on laid paper and half-bound, 2s.

    **LITTLE ESSAYS:** Sketches and Characters by CHARLES LAMB, selected from his Letters by PERCY FITZGERALD. Post 8vo, cloth limp, 2s. 6d.

    **THE DRAMATIC ESSAYS OF CHARLES LAMB.** With Introduction and Notes by BRANDER MATTHEWS, and Steel-plate Portrait. Fcap. 8vo, hf.-bd., 2s. 6d.

**LANDOR.—CITATION AND EXAMINATION OF WILLIAM SHAKS-PEARE,** &c., before Sir THOMAS LUCY, touching Deer-stealing, 19th September, 1582. To which is added, **A CONFERENCE OF MASTER EDMUND SPENSER** with the Earl of Essex, touching the State of Ireland, 1595. By WALTER SAVAGE LANDOR. Fcap. 8vo, half-Roxburghe, 2s. 6d.

**LANE.—THE THOUSAND AND ONE NIGHTS,** commonly called in England THE ARABIAN NIGHTS' ENTERTAINMENTS. Translated from the Arabic, with Notes, by EDWARD WILLIAM LANE. Illustrated by many hundred Engravings from Designs by HARVEY. Edited by EDWARD STANLEY POOLE. With a Preface by STANLEY LANE-POOLE. Three Vols., demy 8vo, cloth extra, 7s. 6d. each.

**LARWOOD (JACOB), WORKS BY.**

    **THE STORY OF THE LONDON PARKS.** With Illusts. Cr. 8vo, cl. extra, 3s. 6d.

    **ANECDOTES OF THE CLERGY:** The Antiquities, Humours, and Eccentricities of the Cloth. Post 8vo, printed on laid paper and half-bound, 2s.

Post 8vo, cloth limp, 2s. 6d. each.

| | |
|---|---|
| **FORENSIC ANECDOTES.** | **THEATRICAL ANECDOTES.** |

**LEIGH (HENRY S.), WORKS BY.**

    **CAROLS OF COCKAYNE.** Printed on hand-made paper, bound in buckram, 5s.

    **JEUX D'ESPRIT.** Edited by HENRY S. LEIGH. Post 8vo, cloth limp, 2s. 6d.

**LEYS (JOHN).—THE LINDSAYS:** A Romance. Post 8vo, illust. bds., 2s.

**LIFE IN LONDON;** or, The History of JERRY HAWTHORN and COR-INTHIAN TOM. With CRUIKSHANK's Coloured Illustrations. Crown 8vo, cloth extra, 7s. 6d.    *[New Edition preparing.*

**LINTON (E. LYNN), WORKS BY.** Post 8vo, cloth limp, 2s. 6d. each.

| | |
|---|---|
| **WITCH STORIES.** | **OURSELVES:** ESSAYS ON WOMEN. |

Crown 8vo, cloth extra, 3s. 6d. each; post 8vo, illustrated boards, 2s. each.

| | |
|---|---|
| **SOWING THE WIND.** | **UNDER WHICH LORD?** |
| **PATRICIA KEMBALL.** | **"MY LOVE!"**    \|     **IONE.** |
| **ATONEMENT OF LEAM DUNDAS.** | **PASTON CAREW, Millionaire & Miser.** |
| **THE WORLD WELL LOST.** | |

Post 8vo, illustrated boards, 2s. each.

| | |
|---|---|
| **THE REBEL OF THE FAMILY.** | **WITH A SILKEN THREAD.** |

    **FREESHOOTING:** Extracts from the Works of Mrs. LYNN LINTON. Post 8vo, cloth, 2s. 6d.

**LONGFELLOW'S POETICAL WORKS.** With numerous Illustrations on Steel and Wood. Crown 8vo, cloth extra, 7s. 6d.

**LUCY.—GIDEON FLEYCE:** A Novel. By HENRY W. LUCY. Crown 8vo, cloth extra, 3s. 6d.; post 8vo, illustrated boards, 2s.

**LUSIAD (THE) OF CAMOENS.** Translated into English Spenserian Verse by ROBERT FFRENCH DUFF. With 14 Plates. Demy 8vo, cloth boards, 18s.

**MACALPINE (AVERY), NOVELS BY.**

    **TERESA ITASCA.** Crown 8vo, cloth extra, 1s.

    **BROKEN WINGS.** With 6 Illusts. by W. J. HENNESSY. Crown 8vo, cloth extra, 6s.

**MACCOLL (HUGH), NOVELS BY.**

    **MR. STRANGER'S SEALED PACKET.** Crown 8vo, cloth extra, 5s.; post 8vo, illustrated boards, 2s.

    **EDNOR WHITLOCK.** Crown 8vo, cloth extra, 6s.

**MACDONELL.—QUAKER COUSINS:** A Novel. By AGNES MACDONELL. Crown 8vo, cloth extra, 3s. 6d.; post 8vo, illustrated boards, 2s.

## McCARTHY (JUSTIN, M.P.), WORKS BY.

**A HISTORY OF OUR OWN TIMES,** from the Accession of Queen Victoria to the General Election of 1880. Four Vols. demy 8vo, cloth extra, **12s.** each.—Also a POPULAR EDITION, in Four Vols., crown 8vo, cloth extra, **6s.** each.—And a JUBILEE EDITION, with an Appendix of Events to the end of 1886, in Two Vols., large crown 8vo, cloth extra, **7s. 6d.** each.

**A SHORT HISTORY OF OUR OWN TIMES.** One Vol., crown 8vo, cloth extra, **6s.** —Also a CHEAP POPULAR EDITION, post 8vo, cloth limp, **2s. 6d.**

**A HISTORY OF THE FOUR GEORGES.** Four Vols. demy 8vo, cloth extra, **12s.** each. [Vols. I. & II. *ready.*

Cr. 8vo, cl. extra, **3s. 6d.** each; post 8vo, illust. bds., **2s.** each; cl. limp, **2s. 6d.** each.

| | |
|---|---|
| THE WATERDALE NEIGHBOURS. | MISS MISANTHROPE. |
| MY ENEMY'S DAUGHTER. | DONNA QUIXOTE. |
| A FAIR SAXON. | THE COMET OF A SEASON. |
| LINLEY ROCHFORD. | MAID OF ATHENS. |
| DEAR LADY DISDAIN. | CAMIOLA: A Girl with a Fortune. |

**THE DICTATOR.** Three Vols., crown 8vo. [*Shortly*

**"THE RIGHT HONOURABLE."** By JUSTIN McCARTHY, M.P., and Mrs. CAMPBELL-PRAED. Fourth Edition. Crown 8vo, cloth extra, **6s.**

## McCARTHY (JUSTIN H.), WORKS BY.

**THE FRENCH REVOLUTION.** Four Vols., 8vo, **12s.** each. [Vols. I. & II. *ready.*

**AN OUTLINE OF THE HISTORY OF IRELAND.** Crown 8vo, **1s.**; cloth, **1s. 6d.**

**IRELAND SINCE THE UNION:** Irish History, 1798-1886. Crown 8vo, cloth, **6s.**

**HAFIZ IN LONDON:** Poems. Small 8vo, gold cloth, **3s. 6d.**

**HARLEQUINADE:** Poems. Small 4to, Japanese vellum, **8s.**

**OUR SENSATION NOVEL.** Crown 8vo, picture cover, **1s.**; cloth limp, **1s. 6d.**

**DOOM!** An Atlantic Episode. Crown 8vo, picture cover, **1s.**

**DOLLY:** A Sketch. Crown 8vo, picture cover, **1s.**; cloth limp, **1s. 6d.**

**LILY LASS:** A Romance. Crown 8vo, picture cover, **1s.**; cloth limp, **1s. 6d.**

**THE THOUSAND AND ONE DAYS:** Persian Tales. Edited by JUSTIN H. McCARTHY. With 2 Photogravures by STANLEY L. WOOD. Two Vols., crown 8vo, half-bound, **12s.**

## MACDONALD (GEORGE, LL.D.), WORKS BY.

**WORKS OF FANCY AND IMAGINATION.** Ten Vols., cl. extra, gilt edges, in cloth case, **21s.** Or the Vols. may be had separately, in grolier cl., at **2s. 6d.** each.

Vol. I. WITHIN AND WITHOUT.—THE HIDDEN LIFE.
,, II. THE DISCIPLE.—THE GOSPEL WOMEN.—BOOK OF SONNETS.—ORGAN SONGS.
,, III. VIOLIN SONGS.—SONGS OF THE DAYS AND NIGHTS.—A BOOK OF DREAMS.— ROADSIDE POEMS.—POEMS FOR CHILDREN.
,, IV. PARABLES.—BALLADS.—SCOTCH SONGS.
,, V. & VI. PHANTASTES: A Faerie Romance. | Vol. VII. THE PORTENT.
,, VIII. THE LIGHT PRINCESS.—THE GIANT'S HEART.—SHADOWS.
,, IX. CROSS PURPOSES.—THE GOLDEN KEY.—THE CARASOYN.—LITTLE DAYLIGHT
,, X. THE CRUEL PAINTER.—THE WOW o' RIVVEN.—THE CASTLE.—THE BROKEN SWORDS.—THE GRAY WOLF.—UNCLE CORNELIUS.

**POETICAL WORKS OF GEORGE MACDONALD.** Collected and arranged by the Author. 2 vols., crown 8vo, buckram, **12s.**

**A THREEFOLD CORD.** Edited by GEORGE MACDONALD. Post 8vo, cloth, **5s.**

**HEATHER AND SNOW:** A Novel. 2 vols., crown 8vo. [*Shortly*.

## MACGREGOR. — PASTIMES AND PLAYERS: Notes on Popular

Games. By ROBERT MACGREGOR. Post 8vo, cloth limp, **2s. 6d.**

## MACKAY.—INTERLUDES AND UNDERTONES; or, Music at Twilight.

By CHARLES MACKAY, LL.D. Crown 8vo, cloth extra, **6s.**

## MACLISE PORTRAIT GALLERY (THE) OF ILLUSTRIOUS LITER-

ARY CHARACTERS: 85 PORTRAITS; with Memoirs — Biographical, Critical, Bibliographical, and Anecdotal—illustrative of the Literature of the former half of the Present Century, by WILLIAM BATES, B.A. Crown 8vo, cloth extra, **7s. 6d.**

## MACQUOID (MRS.), WORKS BY. Square 8vo, cloth extra, 7s. 6d. each.

**IN THE ARDENNES.** With 50 Illustrations by THOMAS R. MACQUOID.

**PICTURES AND LEGENDS FROM NORMANDY AND BRITTANY.** With 34 Illustrations by THOMAS R. MACQUOID.

**THROUGH NORMANDY.** With 92 Illustrations by T. R. MACQUOID, and a Map.

**THROUGH BRITTANY.** With 35 Illustrations by T. R. MACQUOID, and a Map.

**ABOUT YORKSHIRE.** With 67 Illustrations by T. R. MACQUOID.

Post 8vo, illustrated boards, **2s.** each.

**THE EVIL EYE,** and other Stories. | **LOST ROSE.**

**MAGIC LANTERN, THE,** and its Management: including full Practical Directions for producing the Limelight, making Oxygen Gas, and preparing Lantern Slides. By T. C. HEPWORTH. With 10 Illustrations. Cr. 8vo, 1s.; cloth, 1s. 6d.

**MAGICIAN'S OWN BOOK, THE:** Performances with Cups and Balls, Eggs, Hats, Handkerchiefs, &c. All from actual Experience. Edited by W. H. CREMER. With 200 Illustrations. Crown 8vo, cloth extra, 4s. 6d.

**MAGNA CHARTA:** An Exact Facsimile of the Original in the British Museum, 3 feet by 2 feet, with Arms and Seals emblazoned in Gold and Colours, 5s.

**MALLOCK (W. H.), WORKS BY.**
THE NEW REPUBLIC. Post 8vo, picture cover, 2s.; cloth limp, 2s. 6d.
THE NEW PAUL & VIRGINIA: Positivism on an Island. Post 8vo, cloth, 2s. 6d.
POEMS. Small 4to, parchment, 8s.
IS LIFE WORTH LIVING? Crown 8vo, cloth extra, 6s.
A ROMANCE OF THE NINETEENTH CENTURY. Crown 8vo, cloth, 6s.

**MALLORY'S (SIR THOMAS) MORT D'ARTHUR:** The Stories of King Arthur and of the Knights of the Round Table. (A Selection.) Edited by B. MONTGOMERIE RANKING. Post 8vo, cloth limp, 2s.

**MARK TWAIN, WORKS BY.** Crown 8vo, cloth extra, 7s. 6d. each.
THE CHOICE WORKS OF MARK TWAIN. Revised and Corrected throughout by the Author. With Life, Portrait, and numerous Illustrations.
ROUGHING IT, and INNOCENTS AT HOME. With 200 Illusts. by F. A. FRASER.
MARK TWAIN'S LIBRARY OF HUMOUR. With 197 Illustrations.
Crown 8vo, cloth extra (illustrated), 7s. 6d. each; post 8vo, illust. boards, 2s. each.
THE INNOCENTS ABROAD; or, New Pilgrim's Progress. With 234 Illustrations. (The Two-Shilling Edition is entitled MARK TWAIN'S PLEASURE TRIP.)
THE GILDED AGE. By MARK TWAIN and C. D. WARNER. With 212 Illustrations.
THE ADVENTURES OF TOM SAWYER. With 111 Illustrations.
A TRAMP ABROAD. With 314 Illustrations.
THE PRINCE AND THE PAUPER. With 190 Illustrations.
LIFE ON THE MISSISSIPPI. With 300 Illustrations.
ADVENTURES OF HUCKLEBERRY FINN. With 174 Illusts. by E. W. KEMBLE.
A YANKEE AT THE COURT OF KING ARTHUR. With 220 Illusts. by BEARD.
MARK TWAIN'S SKETCHES. Post 8vo, illustrated boards, 2s.
THE STOLEN WHITE ELEPHANT, &c. Cr. 8vo, cl., 6s.; post 8vo, illust. bds., 2s.
THE AMERICAN CLAIMANT. With 81 Illustrations by HAL HURST and DAN BEARD. Crown 8vo, cloth extra, 3s. 6d.

**MARLOWE'S WORKS.** Including his Translations. Edited, with Notes and Introductions, by Col. CUNNINGHAM. Crown 8vo, cloth extra, 6s.

**MARRYAT (FLORENCE), NOVELS BY.** Post 8vo, illust. boards, 2s. each.
A HARVEST OF WILD OATS. | FIGHTING THE AIR.
OPEN! SESAME! | WRITTEN IN FIRE.

**MASSINGER'S PLAYS.** From the Text of WILLIAM GIFFORD. Edited by Col. CUNNINGHAM. Crown 8vo, cloth extra, 6s.

**MASTERMAN.—HALF-A-DOZEN DAUGHTERS:** A Novel. By J. MASTERMAN. Post 8vo, illustrated boards, 2s.

**MATTHEWS.—A SECRET OF THE SEA,** &c. By BRANDER MATTHEWS. Post 8vo, illustrated boards, 2s.; cloth limp, 2s. 6d.

**MAYHEW.—LONDON CHARACTERS AND THE HUMOROUS SIDE** OF LONDON LIFE. By HENRY MAYHEW. With Illusts. Crown 8vo, cloth, 3s. 6d.

**MENKEN.—INFELICIA:** Poems by ADAH ISAACS MENKEN. With Illustrations by F. E. LUMMIS and F. O. C. DARLEY. Small 4to, cloth extra, 7s. 6d.

**MERRICK.—THE MAN WHO WAS GOOD.** By LEONARD MERRICK, Author of "Violet Moses," &c. Post 8vo, illustrated boards, 2s.

**MEXICAN MUSTANG (ON A),** through Texas to the Rio Grande. By A. E. SWEET and J. ARMOY KNOX. With 265 Illusts. Cr. 8vo, cloth extra, 7s. 6d.

**MIDDLEMASS (JEAN), NOVELS BY.** Post 8vo, illust. boards, 2s. each.
TOUCH AND GO. | MR. DORILLION.

**MILLER.—PHYSIOLOGY FOR THE YOUNG;** or, The House of Life: Human Physiology, with its application to the Preservation of Health. By Mrs. F. FENWICK MILLER. With numerous Illustrations. Post 8vo, cloth limp, 2s. 6d.

**MILTON (J. L.), WORKS BY.**  Post 8vo, 1s. each ; cloth, 1s. 6d. each.
THE HYGIENE OF THE SKIN.  With Directions for Diet, Soaps, Baths, &c.
THE BATH IN DISEASES OF THE SKIN.
THE LAWS OF LIFE, AND THEIR RELATION TO DISEASES OF THE SKIN.
THE SUCCESSFUL TREATMENT OF LEPROSY.  Demy 8vo, 1s.

**MINTO (WM.)—WAS SHE GOOD OR BAD?**  Cr. 8vo, 1s. ; cloth, 1s. 6d.

**MOLESWORTH (MRS.), NOVELS BY.**
HATHERCOURT RECTORY.  Post 8vo, illustrated boards, 2s.
THAT GIRL IN BLACK.  Crown 8vo, cloth, 1s. 6d.

**MOORE (THOMAS), WORKS BY.**
THE EPICUREAN; and ALCIPHRON.  Post 8vo, half-bound, 2s.
PROSE AND VERSE, Humorous, Satirical, and Sentimental, by Thomas Moore;
    with Suppressed Passages from the Memoirs of Lord Byron.  Edited by R.
    Herne Shepherd.  With Portrait.  Crown 8vo, cloth extra, 7s. 6d.

**MUDDOCK (J. E.), STORIES BY.**
STORIES WEIRD AND WONDERFUL.  Post 8vo, illust. boards, 2s. ; cloth, 2s. 6d.
THE DEAD MAN'S SECRET; or, The Valley of Gold.  With Frontispiece by
    F. Barnard.  Crown 8vo, cloth extra, 5s. ; post 8vo, illustrated boards, 2s.
FROM THE BOSOM OF THE DEEP.  Post 8vo, illustrated boards, 2s.
MAID MARIAN AND ROBIN HOOD: A Romance of Old Sherwood Forest.  With
    12 Illustrations by Stanley L. Wood.  Crown 8vo, cloth extra, 5s.

**MURRAY (D. CHRISTIE), NOVELS BY.**
Crown 8vo, cloth extra, 3s. 6d. each ; post 8vo, illustrated boards, 2s. each.

| | | |
|---|---|---|
| A LIFE'S ATONEMENT. | HEARTS. | BY THE GATE OF THE SEA. |
| JOSEPH'S COAT. | WAY OF THE WORLD | A BIT OF HUMAN NATURE. |
| COALS OF FIRE. | A MODEL FATHER. | FIRST PERSON SINGULAR. |
| VAL STRANGE. | OLD BLAZER'S HERO. | CYNIC FORTUNE. |

BOB MARTIN'S LITTLE GIRL.  Crown 8vo, cloth extra, 3s. 6d.
TIME'S REVENGES.  Three Vols., crown 8vo.

**MURRAY (D. CHRISTIE) & HENRY HERMAN, WORKS BY.**
ONE TRAVELLER RETURNS.  Cr. 8vo, cl. extra, 6s.; post 8vo, illust. bds., 2s.
    Crown 8vo, cloth extra, 3s. 6d. each; post 8vo, illustrated boards, 2s. each.
PAUL JONES'S ALIAS.  With 13 Illustrations.  |  THE BISHOPS' BIBLE.

**MURRAY (HENRY), NOVELS BY.**
A GAME OF BLUFF.  Post 8vo, illustrated boards, 2s.; cloth, 2s. 6d.
A SONG OF SIXPENCE.  Post 8vo, cloth extra, 2s. 6d.

**NEWBOLT.—TAKEN FROM THE ENEMY.**  By Henry Newbolt.
Fcap. 8vo, cloth boards, 1s. 6d.

**NISBET (HUME), BOOKS BY.**
"BAIL UP!"  Crown 8vo, cloth extra, 3s. 6d.; post 8vo, illustrated boards, 2s.
DR. BERNARD ST. VINCENT.  Post 8vo, illustrated boards, 2s.
LESSONS IN ART.  With 21 Illustrations.  Crown 8vo, cloth extra, 2s. 6d.
WHERE ART BEGINS.  With 27 Illusts. Square 8vo, cloth extra, 7s. 6d.

**NOVELISTS.—HALF-HOURS WITH THE BEST NOVELISTS OF**
THE CENTURY.  Edit. by H. T. Mackenzie Bell.  Cr. 8vo, cl., 3s. 6d.  [Preparing.

**O'HANLON (ALICE), NOVELS BY.**  Post 8vo, illustrated boards, 2s. each.
THE UNFORESEEN.  |  CHANCE? OR FATE?

**OHNET (GEORGES), NOVELS BY.**
DOCTOR RAMEAU.  9 Illusts. by E. Bayard.  Cr. 8vo, cl., 6s.; post 8vo, bds., 2s.
A LAST LOVE.  Crown 8vo, cloth, 5s.; post 8vo, boards, 2s.
A WEIRD GIFT.  Crown 8vo, cloth, 3s. 6d.; post 8vo, boards. 2s.

**OLIPHANT (MRS.), NOVELS BY.**  Post 8vo, illustrated boards, 2s. each.
THE PRIMROSE PATH.  |  THE GREATEST HEIRESS IN ENGLAND
WHITELADIES.  With Illustrations by Arthur Hopkins and Henry Woods,
    A.R.A.  Crown 8vo, cloth extra, 3s. 6d.; post 8vo, illustrated boards, 2s.

**O'REILLY (HARRINGTON).—FIFTY YEARS ON THE TRAIL:** Adventures of John Y. Nelson.  100 Illusts. by P. Frenzeny.  Crown 8vo, 3s. 6d.

**O'REILLY (MRS.).—PHŒBE'S FORTUNES.**  Post 8vo, illust. bds., 2s.

**O'SHAUGHNESSY (ARTHUR), POEMS BY.**
LAYS OF FRANCE.  Crown 8vo, cloth extra, 10s. 6d.
MUSIC & MOONLIGHT, Fp. 8vo, 7s. 6d. | SONGS OF A WORKER. Fp. 8vo, 7s. 6d.

## OUIDA, NOVELS BY.
Cr. 8vo, cl., **3s. 6d.** each; post 8vo, llust. bds., **2s.** each.

HELD IN BONDAGE.
TRICOTRIN.
STRATHMORE.
CHANDOS.
CECIL CASTLEMAINE'S GAGE.
IDALIA.
UNDER TWO FLAGS.
PUCK.
FOLLE-FARINE.
A DOG OF FLANDERS.
PASCAREL.
TWO LITTLE WOODEN SHOES.
SIGNA.
IN A WINTER CITY.
ARIADNE.
FRIENDSHIP.
MOTHS.
PIPISTRELLO.
A VILLAGE COMMUNE.
IN MAREMMA.
BIMBI. | SYRLIN.
WANDA.
FRESCOES. | OTHMAR.
PRINCESS NAPRAXINE.
GUILDEROY. | RUFFINO.

BIMBI. Presentation Edition, with Nine Illustrations by EDMUND H. GARRETT. Square 8vo, cloth, **5s.**

SANTA BARBARA, &c. Square 8vo, cloth, **6s.**; crown 8vo, cloth, **3s. 6d.**

WISDOM, WIT, AND PATHOS, selected from the Works of OUIDA by F. SYDNEY MORRIS. Post 8vo, cloth extra, **5s.** CHEAP EDITION, illustrated boards, **2s.**

## PAGE (H. A.), WORKS BY.
THOREAU: His Life and Aims. With Portrait. Post 8vo, cloth limp, **2s. 6d.**
ANIMAL ANECDOTES. Arranged on a New Principle. Crown 8vo, cloth extra, **5s.**

## PARLIAMENTARY ELECTIONS AND ELECTIONEERING, A HISTORY OF, from the Stuarts to Queen Victoria. By JOSEPH GREGO. A New Edition, with 93 Illustrations. Demy 8vo, cloth extra, **7s. 6d.**

## PASCAL'S PROVINCIAL LETTERS. A New Translation, with Historical Introduction and Notes by T. M'CRIE, D.D. Post 8vo, cloth limp, **2s.**

## PAUL.—GENTLE AND SIMPLE. By MARGARET A. PAUL. With Frontispiece by HELEN PATERSON. Crown 8vo, cloth, **3s. 6d.**; post 8vo, illust. boards. **2s.**

## PAYN (JAMES), NOVELS BY.
Crown 8vo, cloth extra, **3s. 6d.** each; post 8vo, illustrated boards, **2s.** each.

LOST SIR MASSINGBERD.
WALTER'S WORD.
LESS BLACK THAN WE'RE PAINTED.
BY PROXY.
HIGH SPIRITS.
UNDER ONE ROOF.
A CONFIDENTIAL AGENT.
A GRAPE FROM A THORN.
FROM EXILE.
THE CANON'S WARD.
THE TALK OF THE TOWN.
HOLIDAY TASKS.
GLOW-WORM TALES.
THE MYSTERY OF MIRBRIDGE.
THE WORD AND THE WILL.

Post 8vo, illustrated boards, **2s.** each.

HUMOROUS STORIES.
THE FOSTER BROTHERS.
THE FAMILY SCAPEGRACE.
MARRIED BENEATH HIM.
BENTINCK'S TUTOR.
A PERFECT TREASURE.
A COUNTY FAMILY.
LIKE FATHER, LIKE SON.
A WOMAN'S VENGEANCE.
CARLYON'S YEAR. | CECIL'S TRYST.
MURPHY'S MASTER.
AT HER MERCY.
THE CLYFFARDS OF CLYFFE.
FOUND DEAD.
GWENDOLINE'S HARVEST.
A MARINE RESIDENCE.
MIRK ABBEY.|SOME PRIVATE VIEWS.
NOT WOOED, BUT WON.
TWO HUNDRED POUNDS REWARD.
THE BEST OF HUSBANDS.
HALVES. | THE BURNT MILLION.
FALLEN FORTUNES.
WHAT HE COST HER.
KIT: A MEMORY.|FOR CASH ONLY.
A PRINCE OF THE BLOOD.
SUNNY STORIES.

IN PERIL AND PRIVATION: Stories of MARINE ADVENTURE. With 17 Illustrations. Crown 8vo, cloth extra, **3s. 6d.**

NOTES FROM THE "NEWS." Crown 8vo, portrait cover, **1s.**; cloth, **1s. 6d.**

## PENNELL (H. CHOLMONDELEY), WORKS BY. Post 8vo, cl., **2s. 6d.** each.
PUCK ON PEGASUS. With Illustrations.
PEGASUS RE-SADDLED. With Ten full-page Illustrations by G. DU MAURIER.
THE MUSES OF MAYFAIR. Vers de Société. Selected by H. C. PENNELL.

## PHELPS (E. STUART), WORKS BY. Post 8vo, **1s.** each; cloth, **1s. 6d.** each.
BEYOND THE GATES. By the Author of "The Gates Ajar."
AN OLD MAID'S PARADISE.
BURGLARS IN PARADISE.

JACK THE FISHERMAN. Illustrated by C. W. REED. Cr. 8vo, **1s.**; cloth, **1s. 6d.**

## PIRKIS (C. L.), NOVELS BY.
TROOPING WITH CROWS. Fcap. 8vo, picture cover, **1s.**
LADY LOVELACE. Post 8vo, illustrated boards, **2s.**

**PLANCHE (J. R.), WORKS BY.**
THE PURSUIVANT OF ARMS. With Six Plates, and 209 Illusts. Cr. 8vo, cl. 7s. 6d.
SONGS AND POEMS, 1819-1879. Introduction by Mrs. MACKARNESS. Cr. 8vo, cl., 6s.

**PLUTARCH'S LIVES OF ILLUSTRIOUS MEN.** Translated from the
Greek, with Notes Critical and Historical, and a Life of Plutarch, by JOHN and
WILLIAM LANGHORNE. With Portraits. Two Vols., demy 8vo, half-bound, 10s. 6d.

**POE'S (EDGAR ALLAN) CHOICE WORKS,** in Prose and Poetry. Introduction by CHAS. BAUDELAIRE, Portrait, and Facsimiles. Cr. 8vo, cloth, 7s. 6d.
THE MYSTERY OF MARIE ROGET, &c. Post 8vo, illustrated boards, 2s.

**POPE'S POETICAL WORKS.** Post 8vo, cloth limp, 2s.

**PRAED (MRS. CAMPBELL), NOVELS BY.** Post 8vo, illust. bds., 2s. ea.
THE ROMANCE OF A STATION. | THE SOUL OF COUNTESS ADRIAN.
"THE RIGHT HONOURABLE." By Mrs. CAMPBELL PRAED and JUSTIN MCCARTHY
M.P. Crown 8vo, cloth extra, 6s.

**PRICE (E. C.), NOVELS BY.**
Crown 8vo, cloth extra, 3s. 6d. each; post 8vo, illustrated boards, 2s. each.
VALENTINA. | THE FOREIGNERS. | MRS. LANCASTER'S RIVAL.
GERALD. Post 8vo, illustrated boards. 2s.

**PRINCESS OLGA.—RADNA;** or, The Great Conspiracy of 1881. By
the Princess OLGA. Crown 8vo, cloth extra, 6s.

**PROCTOR (RICHARD A., B.A.), WORKS BY.**
FLOWERS OF THE SKY. With 55 Illusts. Small crown 8vo, cloth extra, 3s. 6d.
EASY STAR LESSONS. With Star Maps for Every Night in the Year. Cr. 8vo, 6s.
FAMILIAR SCIENCE STUDIES. Crown 8vo, cloth extra, 6s.
SATURN AND ITS SYSTEM. With 13 Steel Plates. Demy 8vo, cloth ex., 10s. 6d.
MYSTERIES OF TIME AND SPACE. With Illustrations. Cr. 8vo, cloth extra, 6s.
THE UNIVERSE OF SUNS. With numerous Illustrations. Cr. 8vo, cloth ex., 6s.
WAGES AND WANTS OF SCIENCE WORKERS. Crown 8vo, 1s. 6d.

**PRYCE.—MISS MAXWELL'S AFFECTIONS.** By RICHARD PRYCE.
Frontispiece by HAL LUDLOW. Cr. 8vo, cl., 3s. 6d.; post 8vo, illust. boards., 2s.

**RAMBOSSON.—POPULAR ASTRONOMY.** By J. RAMBOSSON, Laureate
of the Institute of France. With numerous Illusts. Crown 8vo, cloth extra, 7s. 6d.

**RANDOLPH.—AUNT ABIGAIL DYKES:** A Novel. By Lt.-Colonel
GEORGE RANDOLPH, U.S.A. Crown 8vo, cloth extra, 7s. 6d.

**READE (CHARLES), NOVELS BY.**
Crown 8vo, cloth extra, illustrated, 3s. 6d. each; post 8vo, illust. bds., 2s. each.
PEG WOFFINGTON. Illustrated by S. L. FILDES, R.A.—Also a POCKET EDITION,
set in New Type, in Elzevir style, fcap. 8vo, half-leather, 2s. 6d.
CHRISTIE JOHNSTONE. Illustrated by WILLIAM SMALL.—Also a POCKET EDITION,
set in New Type, in Elzevir style, fcap. 8vo, half-leather, 2s. 6d.
IT IS NEVER TOO LATE TO MEND. Illustrated by G. J. PINWELL.
COURSE OF TRUE LOVE NEVER DID RUN SMOOTH. Illust. HELEN PATERSON.
THE AUTOBIOGRAPHY OF A THIEF, &c. Illustrated by MATT STRETCH.
LOVE ME LITTLE, LOVE ME LONG. Illustrated by M. ELLEN EDWARDS.
THE DOUBLE MARRIAGE. Illusts. by Sir JOHN GILBERT, R.A., and C. KEENE.
THE CLOISTER AND THE HEARTH. Illustrated by CHARLES KEENE.
HARD CASH. Illustrated by F. W. LAWSON.
GRIFFITH GAUNT. Illustrated by S. L. FILDES, R.A., and WILLIAM SMALL.
FOUL PLAY. Illustrated by GEORGE DU MAURIER.
PUT YOURSELF IN HIS PLACE. Illustrated by ROBERT BARNES.
A TERRIBLE TEMPTATION. Illustrated by EDWARD HUGHES and A. W. COOPER.
A SIMPLETON. Illustrated by KATE CRAUFURD.
THE WANDERING HEIR. Illust. by H. PATERSON, S. L. FILDES, C. GREEN, &c.
A WOMAN-HATER. Illustrated by THOMAS COULDERY.
SINGLEHEART AND DOUBLEFACE. Illustrated by P. MACNAB.
GOOD STORIES OF MEN AND OTHER ANIMALS. Illust. by E. A. ABBEY, &c.
THE JILT, and other Stories. Illustrated by JOSEPH NASH.
A PERILOUS SECRET. Illustrated by FRED. BARNARD.
READIANA. With a Steel-plate Portrait of CHARLES READE.
BIBLE CHARACTERS: Studies of David, Paul, &c. Fcap. 8vo, leatherette, 1s.
THE CLOISTER AND THE HEARTH. With an Introduction by WALTER BESANT.
Elzevir Edition. 4 vols., post 8vo, each with Front., cl. ex., gilt top, 14s. the set.

SELECTIONS FROM THE WORKS OF CHARLES READE. Cr. 8vo, buckram, 6s.

**RIDDELL (MRS. J. H.), NOVELS BY.**
Crown 8vo, cloth extra, **3s. 6d.** each; post 8vo, illustrated boards, **2s.** each.
THE PRINCE OF WALES'S GARDEN PARTY. | WEIRD STORIES.
Post 8vo, illustrated boards, **2s.** each.
THE UNINHABITED HOUSE. | HER MOTHER'S DARLING.
MYSTERY IN PALACE GARDENS. | THE NUN'S CURSE.
FAIRY WATER. | IDLE TALES.

**RIMMER (ALFRED), WORKS BY.** Square 8vo, cloth gilt, **7s. 6d.** each.
OUR OLD COUNTRY TOWNS. With 55 Illustrations.
RAMBLES ROUND ETON AND HARROW. With 50 Illustrations.
ABOUT ENGLAND WITH DICKENS. With 58 Illusts. by C. A. VANDERHOOF, &c.

**RIVES (Amélie).—BARBARA DERING.** By AMÉLIE RIVES, Author
of "The Quick or the Dead?" Crown 8vo, cloth extra, **3s. 6d.**

**ROBINSON CRUSOE.** By DANIEL DEFOE. (MAJOR'S EDITION.) With
37 Illustrations by GEORGE CRUIKSHANK. Post 8vo, half-bound, **2s.**

**ROBINSON (F. W.), NOVELS BY.**
WOMEN ARE STRANGE. Post 8vo, illustrated boards, **2s.**
THE HANDS OF JUSTICE. Cr. 8vo, cloth ex., **3s. 6d.**; post 8vo, illust. bds., **2s.**

**ROBINSON (PHIL), WORKS BY.** Crown 8vo, cloth extra, **6s.** each.
THE POETS' BIRDS. | THE POETS' BEASTS.
THE POETS AND NATURE: REPTILES, FISHES, AND INSECTS.

**ROCHEFOUCAULD'S MAXIMS AND MORAL REFLECTIONS.** With
Notes, and an Introductory Essay by SAINTE-BEUVE. Post 8vo, cloth limp, **2s.**

**ROLL OF BATTLE ABBEY, THE:** A List of the Principal Warriors
who came from Normandy with William the Conqueror, and Settled in this Country,
A.D. 1066-7. With Arms emblazoned in Gold and Colours. Handsomely printed, **5s.**

**ROWLEY (HON. HUGH), WORKS BY.** Post 8vo, cloth, **2s. 6d.** each.
PUNIANA: RIDDLES AND JOKES. With numerous Illustrations.
MORE PUNIANA. Profusely Illustrated.

**RUNCIMAN (JAMES), STORIES BY.** Post 8vo, bds., **2s.** ea.; cl., **2s. 6d.** ea.
SKIPPERS AND SHELLBACKS. | GRACE BALMAIGN'S SWEETHEART.
SCHOOLS AND SCHOLARS.

**RUSSELL (W. CLARK), BOOKS AND NOVELS BY:**
Cr. 8vo, cloth extra, **6s.** each; post 8vo, illust. boards, **2s.** each; cloth limp, **2s. 6d.** ea.
ROUND THE GALLEY-FIRE. | A BOOK FOR THE HAMMOCK.
IN THE MIDDLE WATCH. | MYSTERY OF THE "OCEAN STAR."
A VOYAGE TO THE CAPE. | THE ROMANCE OF JENNY HARLOWE
Cr. 8vo, cl. extra, **3s. 6d.** ea.; post 8vo, illust. boards, **2s.** ea.; cloth limp, **2s. 6d.** ea.
AN OCEAN TRAGEDY. | MY SHIPMATE LOUISE.
ALONE ON A WIDE WIDE SEA.
ON THE FO'K'SLE HEAD. Post 8vo, illust. boards, **2s.**; cloth limp, **2s. 6d.**

**SAINT AUBYN (ALAN), NOVELS BY.**
Crown 8vo, cloth extra, **3s. 6d.** each; post 8vo, illust. boards, **2s.** each.
A FELLOW OF TRINITY. Note by OLIVER WENDELL HOLMES and Frontispiece.
THE JUNIOR DEAN.
Fcap. 8vo, cloth boards, **1s. 6d.** each.
THE OLD MAID'S SWEETHEART. | MODEST LITTLE SARA.
THE MASTER OF ST. BENEDICT'S. Two Vols., crown 8vo.

**SALA (G. A.).—GASLIGHT AND DAYLIGHT.** Post 8vo, boards, 2s.

**SANSON.—SEVEN GENERATIONS OF EXECUTIONERS:** Memoirs
of the Sanson Family (1688 to 1847). Crown 8vo, cloth extra, **3s. 6d.**

**SAUNDERS (JOHN), NOVELS BY.**
Crown 8vo, cloth extra, **3s. 6d.** each; post 8vo, illustrated boards, **2s.** each.
GUY WATERMAN. | THE LION IN THE PATH. | THE TWO DREAMERS
BOUND TO THE WHEEL. Crown 8vo, cloth extra, **3s. 6d.**

**SAUNDERS (KATHARINE), NOVELS BY.**
Crown 8vo, cloth extra, **3s. 6d.** each; post 8vo, illustrated boards, **2s.** each.
MARGARET AND ELIZABETH. | HEART SALVAGE.
THE HIGH MILLS. | SEBASTIAN.
JOAN MERRYWEATHER. Post 8vo, illustrated boards, **2s.**
GIDEON'S ROCK. Crown 8vo, cloth extra, **3s. 6d.**

**SCIENCE-GOSSIP.** Edited by Dr. J. E. TAYLOR, F.L.S., &c. Devoted to Geology, Botany, Physiology, Chemistry, Zoology, Microscopy, Telescopy, Physiography, &c. **4d.** Monthly. Pts. 1 to 300, **8d.** each; Pts. 301 to date, **4d.** each. Vols. I. to XIX., **7s. 6d.** each; Vols. XX. to date, **5s.** each. Cases for Binding, **1s. 6d.**

**SCOTLAND YARD:** Experiences of 37 Years. By Chief-Inspector CAVANAGH. Post 8vo, illustrated boards, **2s.**; cloth, **2s. 6d.**

**SECRET OUT, THE:** One Thousand Tricks with Cards; with Entertaining Experiments in Drawing-room or "White Magic." By W. H. CREMER. With 300 Illustrations. Crown 8vo, cloth extra, **4s. 6d.**

**SEGUIN (L. G.), WORKS BY.**
THE COUNTRY OF THE PASSION PLAY (OBERAMMERGAU) and the Highlands of Bavaria. With Map and 37 Illustrations. Crown 8vo, cloth extra, **3s. 6d.**
WALKS IN ALGIERS. With 2 Maps and 16 Illusts. Crown 8vo, cloth extra. **6s.**

**SENIOR (WM.).—BY STREAM AND SEA.** Post 8vo, cloth, 2s. 6d.

**SHAKESPEARE FOR CHILDREN: LAMB'S TALES FROM SHAKESPEARE.** With Illustrations, coloured and plain, by J. MOYR SMITH. Cr. 4to, **6s.**

**SHARP.—CHILDREN OF TO-MORROW:** A Novel. By WILLIAM SHARP. Crown 8vo, cloth extra, **6s.**

**SHARP, LUKE (ROBERT BARR), STORIES BY.**
IN A STEAMER CHAIR. With 2 Illustrations. Crown 8vo, cloth extra, **3s. 6d.**
FROM WHOSE BOURNE? &c. With Fifty Illustrations. *[Shortly.*

**SHELLEY.—THE COMPLETE WORKS IN VERSE AND PROSE OF** PERCY BYSSHE SHELLEY. Edited, Prefaced, and Annotated by R. HERNE SHEPHERD. Five Vols., crown 8vo, cloth boards, **3s. 6d.** each.
**POETICAL WORKS,** in Three Vols.:
Vol. I. Introduction by the Editor; Posthumous Fragments of Margaret Nicholson; Shelley's Correspondence with Stockdale; The Wandering Jew; Queen Mab, with the Notes; Alastor, and other Poems; Rosalind and Helen; Prometheus Unbound; Adonais, &c.
Vol. II. Laon and Cythna; The Cenci; Julian and Maddalo; Swellfoot the Tyrant; The Witch of Atlas; Epipsychidion; Hellas.
Vol. III. Posthumous Poems; The Masque of Anarchy; and other Pieces.
**PROSE WORKS,** in Two Vols.:
Vol. I. The Two Romances of Zastrozzi and St. Irvyne; the Dublin and Marlow Pamphlets; A Refutation of Deism; Letters to Leigh Hunt, and some Minor Writings and Fragments.
Vol. II. The Essays; Letters from Abroad; Translations and Fragments, Edited by Mrs. SHELLEY. With a Bibliography of Shelley, and an Index of the Prose Works.

**SHERARD (R. H.).—ROGUES:** A Novel. Crown 8vo, **1s.**; cloth, **1s. 6d.**

**SHERIDAN (GENERAL). — PERSONAL MEMOIRS OF GENERAL** P. H. SHERIDAN. With Portraits and Facsimiles. Two Vols., demy 8vo, cloth, **24s.**

**SHERIDAN'S (RICHARD BRINSLEY) COMPLETE WORKS.** With Life and Anecdotes. Including his Dramatic Writings, his Works in Prose and Poetry, Translations, Speeches and Jokes. 10 Illusts. Cr. 8vo, hf.-bound, **7s. 6d.**
THE RIVALS, THE SCHOOL FOR SCANDAL, and other Plays. Post 8vo, printed on laid paper and half-bound, **2s.**
SHERIDAN'S COMEDIES: THE RIVALS and THE SCHOOL FOR SCANDAL. Edited, with an Introduction and Notes to each Play, and a Biographical Sketch, by BRANDER MATTHEWS. With Illustrations. Demy 8vo, half-parchment, **12s. 6d.**

**SIDNEY'S (SIR PHILIP) COMPLETE POETICAL WORKS,** including all those in "Arcadia." With Portrait, Memorial-Introduction, Notes, &c. by the Rev. A. B. GROSART, D.D. Three Vols., crown 8vo, cloth boards, **18s.**

**SIGNBOARDS:** Their History. With Anecdotes of Famous Taverns and Remarkable Characters. By JACOB LARWOOD and JOHN CAMDEN HOTTEN. With Coloured Frontispiece and 94 Illustrations. Crown 8vo, cloth extra, **7s. 6d.**

**SIMS (GEORGE R.), WORKS BY.**
Post 8vo, illustrated boards, **2s.** each; cloth limp, **2s. 6d.** each.
| | |
|---|---|
| ROGUES AND VAGABONDS. | MARY JANE MARRIED. |
| THE RING O' BELLS. | TALES OF TO-DAY. |
| MARY JANE'S MEMOIRS. | DRAMAS OF LIFE. With 60 Illustrations. |

TINKLETOP'S CRIME. With a Frontispiece by MAURICE GREIFFENHAGEN.
ZEPH: A Circus Story, &c.

Crown 8vo, picture cover, **1s.** each; cloth, **1s. 6d.** each.
HOW THE POOR LIVE; and HORRIBLE LONDON.
THE DAGONET RECITER AND READER: being Readings and Recitations in Prose and Verse, selected from his own Works by GEORGE R. SIMS.
THE CASE OF GEORGE CANDLEMAS. | DAGONET DITTIES.

**SISTER DORA:** A Biography. By MARGARET LONSDALE. With Four Illustrations. Demy 8vo, picture cover, **4d.**; cloth, **6d.**

**SKETCHLEY.—A MATCH IN THE DARK.** By ARTHUR SKETCHLEY. Post 8vo, illustrated boards, **2s.**

**SLANG DICTIONARY (THE):** Etymological, Historical, and Anecdotal. Crown 8vo, cloth extra, **6s. 6d.**

**SMITH (J. MOYR), WORKS BY.**
**THE PRINCE OF ARGOLIS.** With 130 Illusts. Post 8vo, cloth extra, **3s. 6d.**
**TALES OF OLD THULE.** With numerous Illustrations. Crown 8vo, cloth gilt, **6s.**
**THE WOOING OF THE WATER WITCH.** Illustrated. Post 8vo, cloth, **6s.**

**SOCIETY IN LONDON.** By A FOREIGN RESIDENT. Crown 8vo, **1s.**; cloth, **1s. 6d.**

**SOCIETY IN PARIS:** The Upper Ten Thousand. A Series of Letters from Count PAUL VASILI to a Young French Diplomat. Crown 8vo, cloth, **6s.**

**SOMERSET. — SONGS OF ADIEU.** By Lord HENRY SOMERSET. Small 4to, Japanese vellum, **6s.**

**SPALDING.—ELIZABETHAN DEMONOLOGY:** An Essay on the Belief in the Existence of Devils. By T. A. SPALDING, LL.B. Crown 8vo, cloth extra, **5s.**

**SPEIGHT (T. W.), NOVELS BY.**
Post 8vo, illustrated boards, **2s.** each.

| | |
|---|---|
| **THE MYSTERIES OF HERON DYKE.** | **HOODWINKED; and THE SANDY-** |
| **BY DEVIOUS WAYS, &c.** | **CROFT MYSTERY.** |
| **THE GOLDEN HOOP.** | **BACK TO LIFE.** |

Post 8vo, cloth limp, **1s. 6d.** each.

| | |
|---|---|
| **A BARREN TITLE.** | **WIFE OR NO WIFE?** |

**THE SANDYCROFT MYSTERY.** Crown 8vo, picture cover, **1s.**

**SPENSER FOR CHILDREN.** By M. H. TOWRY. With Illustrations by WALTER J. MORGAN. Crown 4to, cloth gilt, **6s.**

**STARRY HEAVENS (THE):** A POETICAL BIRTHDAY BOOK. Royal 16mo, cloth extra, **2s. 6d.**

**STAUNTON.—THE LAWS AND PRACTICE OF CHESS.** With an Analysis of the Openings. By HOWARD STAUNTON. Edited by ROBERT B. WORMALD. Crown 8vo, cloth extra, **5s.**

**STEDMAN (E. C.), WORKS BY.**
**VICTORIAN POETS.** Thirteenth Edition. Crown 8vo, cloth extra, **9s.**
**THE POETS OF AMERICA.** Crown 8vo, cloth extra, **9s.**

**STERNDALE. — THE AFGHAN KNIFE:** A Novel. By ROBERT ARMITAGE STERNDALE. Cr. 8vo, cloth extra, **3s. 6d.**; post 8vo, illust. boards, **2s.**

**STEVENSON (R. LOUIS), WORKS BY.** Post 8vo, cl. limp, **2s. 6d.** each.
**TRAVELS WITH A DONKEY.** Seventh Edit. With a Frontis. by WALTER CRANE.
**AN INLAND VOYAGE.** Fourth Edition. With a Frontispiece by WALTER CRANE.

Crown 8vo, buckram, gilt top, **6s.** each.
**FAMILIAR STUDIES OF MEN AND BOOKS.** Sixth Edition.
**THE SILVERADO SQUATTERS.** With a Frontispiece. Third Edition.
**THE MERRY MEN.** Third Edition. | **UNDERWOODS:** Poems. Fifth Edition.
**MEMORIES AND PORTRAITS.** Third Edition.
**VIRGINIBUS PUERISQUE,** and other Papers. Seventh Edition. | **BALLADS.**
**ACROSS THE PLAINS,** with other Memories and Essays.

**NEW ARABIAN NIGHTS.** Eleventh Edition. Crown 8vo, buckram, gilt top, **6s.**; post 8vo, illustrated boards, **2s.**
**THE SUICIDE CLUB; and THE RAJAH'S DIAMOND.** (From NEW ARABIAN NIGHTS.) With Six Illustrations by J. BERNARD PARTRIDGE. Crown 8vo, cloth extra, **5s.**
**PRINCE OTTO.** Sixth Edition. Post 8vo, illustrated boards, **2s.**
**FATHER DAMIEN:** An Open Letter to the Rev. Dr. Hyde. Second Edition. Crown 8vo, hand-made and brown paper, **1s.**

**STODDARD. — SUMMER CRUISING IN THE SOUTH SEAS.** By C. WARREN STODDARD. Illustrated by WALLIS MACKAY. Cr. 8vo, cl. extra, **3s. 6d.**

**STORIES FROM FOREIGN NOVELISTS.** With Notices by HELEN and ALICE ZIMMERN. Crown 8vo, cloth extra, **3s. 6d.**; post 8vo, illustrated boards, **2s.**

**STRANGE MANUSCRIPT (A) FOUND IN A COPPER CYLINDER.**
With 19 Illustrations by GILBERT GAUL.   Third Edition.  Crown 8vo, cloth extra, **5s.**

**STRANGE SECRETS.** Told by CONAN DOYLE, PERCY FITZGERALD, FLOR-
ENCE MARRYAT, &c.  Cr. 8vo, cl. ex., Eight Illusts., **6s.**; post 8vo, illust. bds., **2s.**

**STRUTT'S SPORTS AND PASTIMES OF THE PEOPLE OF**
ENGLAND; including the Rural and Domestic Recreations, May Games, Mum-
meries, Shows, &c., from the Earliest Period to the Present Time.   Edited by
WILLIAM HONE.   With 140 Illustrations.   Crown 8vo, cloth extra, **7s. 6d.**

**SUBURBAN HOMES (THE) OF LONDON :** A Residential Guide.   With
a Map, and Notes on Rental, Rates, and Accommodation.  Crown 8vo, cloth, **7s. 6d.**

**SWIFT'S (DEAN) CHOICE WORKS,** in Prose and Verse.   With Memoir,
Portrait, and Facsimiles of the Maps in "Gulliver's Travels."  Cr. 8vo. cl., **7s. 6d.**
**GULLIVER'S TRAVELS, and A TALE OF A TUB.**   Post 8vo, half-bound, **2s.**
**A MONOGRAPH ON SWIFT.**  By J. CHURTON COLLINS.  Cr. 8vo, cloth, **8s.** [Shortly.

**SWINBURNE (ALGERNON C.), WORKS BY.**

**SELECTIONS FROM POETICAL WORKS**
OF A. C. SWINBURNE.  Fcap. 8vo, **6s.**
**ATALANTA IN CALYDON.**  Crown 8vo,
**6s.**
**CHASTELARD :** A Tragedy.  Cr. 8vo, **7s.**
**POEMS AND BALLADS.**  FIRST SERIES.
Crown 8vo or fcap. 8vo, **9s.**
**POEMS AND BALLADS.**  SECOND SERIES.
Crown 8vo or fcap. 8vo, **9s.**
**POEMS AND BALLADS.**  THIRD SERIES.
Crown 8vo, **7s.**
**SONGS BEFORE SUNRISE.**  Crown 8vo,
**10s. 6d.**
**BOTHWELL :** A Tragedy.   Crown 8vo,
**12s. 6d.**
**SONGS OF TWO NATIONS.**  Cr. 8vo, **6s.**
**GEORGE CHAPMAN.**  (See Vol. II. of G.
CHAPMAN'S Works.)  Crown 8vo, **6s.**

**ESSAYS AND STUDIES.**  Cr. 8vo, **12s.**
**ERECHTHEUS :** A Tragedy.  Cr. 8vo, **6s.**
**SONGS OF THE SPRINGTIDES.**  Crown
8vo, **6s.**
**STUDIES IN SONG.**  Crown 8vo, **7s.**
**MARY STUART :** A Tragedy.  Cr. 8vo, **8s.**
**TRISTRAM OF LYONESSE.**  Cr. 8vo, **9s.**
**A CENTURY OF ROUNDELS.**  Sm. 4to, **8s.**
**A MIDSUMMER HOLIDAY.**  Cr. 8vo, **7s.**
**MARINO FALIERO :** A Tragedy.   Crown
8vo, **6s.**
**A STUDY OF VICTOR HUGO.**  Cr. 8vo, **6s.**
**MISCELLANIES.**  Crown 8vo, **12s.**
**LOCRINE :** A Tragedy.  Cr. 8vo, **6s.**
**A STUDY OF BEN JONSON.**  Cr. 8vo, **7s.**
**THE SISTERS :** A Tragedy.  Cr. 8vo, **6s.**

**SYMONDS.—WINE, WOMEN, AND SONG :** Mediæval Latin Students'
Songs. With Essay and Trans. by J. ADDINGTON SYMONDS.  Fcap. 8vo, parchment, **6s.**

**SYNTAX'S (DR.) THREE TOURS :** In Search of the Picturesque, in
Search of Consolation, and in Search of a Wife. With ROWLANDSON'S Coloured Illustrations, and Life of the Author by J. C. HOTTEN.   Crown 8vo, cloth extra, **7s. 6d.**

**TAINE'S HISTORY OF ENGLISH LITERATURE.**   Translated by
HENRY VAN LAUN.  Four Vols., small demy 8vo, cl. bds., **30s.**—POPULAR EDITION,
Two Vols., large crown 8vo, cloth extra, **15s.**

**TAYLOR'S (BAYARD) DIVERSIONS OF THE ECHO CLUB :** Bur-
lesques of Modern Writers.  Post 8vo, cloth limp, **2s.**

**TAYLOR (DR. J. E., F.L.S.), WORKS BY.**  Cr. 8vo, cl. ex., **7s. 6d.** each.
**THE SAGACITY AND MORALITY OF PLANTS :** A Sketch of the Life and Conduct
of the Vegetable Kingdom.   With a Coloured Frontispiece and 100 Illustrations.
**OUR COMMON BRITISH FOSSILS,** and Where to Find Them.  331 Illustrations.
**THE PLAYTIME NATURALIST.**  With 366 Illustrations.  Crown 8vo, cloth, **5s.**

**TAYLOR'S (TOM) HISTORICAL DRAMAS.** Containing "Clancarty,"
"Jeanne Darc," "'Twixt Axe and Crown," "The Fool's Revenge," "Arkwright's
Wife," "Anne Boleyn," "Plot and Passion."  Crown 8vo, cloth extra, **7s. 6d.**
*** The Plays may also be had separately, at **1s.** each.

**TENNYSON (LORD) :** A Biographical Sketch.   By H. J. JENNINGS.
With a Photograph-Portrait.  Crown 8vo, cloth extra, **6s.**—Cheap Edition, post 8vo,
portrait cover, **1s.**; cloth, **1s. 6d.**

**THACKERAYANA :** Notes and Anecdotes.   Illustrated by Hundreds of
Sketches by WILLIAM MAKEPEACE THACKERAY.  Crown 8vo, cloth extra, **7s. 6d.**

**THAMES.—A NEW PICTORIAL HISTORY OF THE THAMES.**
By A. S. KRAUSSE.  With 340 Illustrations  Post 8vo, **1s.**; cloth, **1s. 6d.**

**THOMAS (BERTHA), NOVELS BY.**  Cr. 8vo, cl., **3s. 6d.** ea.; post 8vo, **2s.** ea.
**THE VIOLIN-PLAYER.**                  |  **PROUD MAISIE.**
**CRESSIDA.**  Post 8vo, illustrated boards, **2s.**

**THOMSON'S SEASONS, and CASTLE OF INDOLENCE.** With Introduction by ALLAN CUNNINGHAM, and 48 Illustrations.  Post 8vo, half-bound, 2s.

**THORNBURY (WALTER), WORKS BY.** Cr. 8vo, cl. extra, 7s. 6d. each.
**THE LIFE AND CORRESPONDENCE OF J. M. W. TURNER.** Founded upon Letters and Papers furnished by his Friends.  With Illustrations in Colours.
**HAUNTED LONDON.** Edit. by E. WALFORD, M.A. Illusts. by F. W. FAIRHOLT, F.S.A.
Post 8vo, illustrated boards, 2s. each.
**OLD STORIES RE-TOLD.** | **TALES FOR THE MARINES.**

**TIMBS (JOHN), WORKS BY.** Crown 8vo, cloth extra, 7s. 6d. each.
**THE HISTORY OF CLUBS AND CLUB LIFE IN LONDON:** Anecdotes of its Famous Coffee-houses, Hostelries, and Taverns.  With 42 Illustrations.
**ENGLISH ECCENTRICS AND ECCENTRICITIES:** Stories of Delusions, Impostures, Sporting Scenes, Eccentric Artists, Theatrical Folk, &c.  48 Illustrations.

**TROLLOPE (ANTHONY), NOVELS BY.**
Crown 8vo, cloth extra, 3s. 6d. each; post 8vo, illustrated boards, 2s. each.
**THE WAY WE LIVE NOW.** | **MARION FAY.**
**KEPT IN THE DARK.** | **MR. SCARBOROUGH'S FAMILY.**
**FRAU FROHMANN.** | **THE LAND-LEAGUERS.**
Post 8vo, illustrated boards, 2s. each.
**GOLDEN LION OF GRANPERE.** | **JOHN CALDIGATE.** | **AMERICAN SENATOR.**

**TROLLOPE (FRANCES E.), NOVELS BY.**
Crown 8vo, cloth extra, 3s. 6d. each; post 8vo, illustrated boards, 2s. each.
**LIKE SHIPS UPON THE SEA.** | **MABEL'S PROGRESS.** | **ANNE FURNESS.**

**TROLLOPE (T. A.).—DIAMOND CUT DIAMOND.** Post 8vo, illust. bds., 2s.

**TROWBRIDGE.—FARNELL'S FOLLY:** A Novel.  By J. T. TROWBRIDGE.  Post 8vo, illustrated boards, 2s.

**TYTLER (C. C. FRASER-).—MISTRESS JUDITH:** A Novel.  By C. C. FRASER-TYTLER.  Crown 8vo, cloth extra, 3s. 6d.; post 8vo, illust. boards, 2s.

**TYTLER (SARAH), NOVELS BY.**
Crown 8vo, cloth extra, 3s. 6d. each; post 8vo, illustrated boards, 2s. each.
**THE BRIDE'S PASS.** | **BURIED DIAMONDS.**
**LADY BELL.** | **THE BLACKHALL GHOSTS.**
Post 8vo, illustrated boards, 2s. each.
**WHAT SHE CAME THROUGH.** | **BEAUTY AND THE BEAST.**
**CITOYENNE JACQUELINE.** | **DISAPPEARED.**
**SAINT MUNGO'S CITY.** | **THE HUGUENOT FAMILY.**
**NOBLESSE OBLIGE.**

**VILLARI.—A DOUBLE BOND.** By LINDA VILLARI.  Fcap. 8vo, picture cover, 1s.

**WALT WHITMAN, POEMS BY.** Edited, with Introduction, by WILLIAM M. ROSSETTI.  With Portrait.  Cr. 8vo, hand-made paper and buckram, 6s.

**WALTON AND COTTON'S COMPLETE ANGLER;** or, The Contemplative Man's Recreation, by IZAAK WALTON; and Instructions how to Angle for a Trout or Grayling in a clear Stream, by CHARLES COTTON.  With Memoirs and Notes by Sir HARRIS NICOLAS, and 61 Illustrations.  Crown 8vo, cloth antique, 7s. 6d.

**WARD (HERBERT), WORKS BY.**
**FIVE YEARS WITH THE CONGO CANNIBALS.** With 92 Illustrations by the Author, VICTOR PERARD, and W. B. DAVIS.  Third ed.  Roy. 8vo, cloth ex., 14s.
**MY LIFE WITH STANLEY'S REAR GUARD.** With a Map by F. S. WELLER, F.R.G.S.  Post 8vo, 1s.; cloth, 1s. 6d.

**WARNER.—A ROUNDABOUT JOURNEY.** By CHARLES DUDLEY WARNER.  Crown 8vo, cloth extra, 6s.

**WARRANT TO EXECUTE CHARLES I.** A Facsimile, with the 59 Signatures and Seals.  Printed on paper 22 in. by 14 in.  2s.
**WARRANT TO EXECUTE MARY QUEEN OF SCOTS.** A Facsimile, including Queen Elizabeth's Signature and the Great Seal.  2s.

**WASSERMANN (LILLIAS), NOVELS BY.**
**THE DAFFODILS.** Crown 8vo, 1s.; cloth, 1s. 6d.
**THE MARQUIS OF CARABAS.** By AARON WATSON and LILLIAS WASSERMANN.  3 vols., crown 8vo,

**WALFORD (EDWARD, M.A.), WORKS BY.**
 WALFORD'S COUNTY FAMILIES OF THE UNITED KINGDOM (1893). Containing the Descent, Birth, Marriage, Education, &c., of 12,000 Heads of Families, their Heirs, Offices, Addresses, Clubs, &c. Royal 8vo, cloth gilt, 50s.
 WALFORD'S WINDSOR PEERAGE, BARONETAGE, AND KNIGHTAGE (1893). Crown 8vo, cloth extra, 12s. 6d.
 WALFORD'S SHILLING PEERAGE (1893). Containing a List of the House of Lords, Scotch and Irish Peers, &c. 32mo, cloth, 1s.
 WALFORD'S SHILLING BARONETAGE (1893). Containing a List of the Baronets of the United Kingdom, Biographical Notices, Addresses, &c. 32mo, cloth, 1s.
 WALFORD'S SHILLING KNIGHTAGE (1893). Containing a List of the Knights of the United Kingdom, Biographical Notices, Addresses, &c. 32mo, cloth, 1s.
 WALFORD'S SHILLING HOUSE OF COMMONS (1893). Containing a List of all Members of the New Parliament, their Addresses, Clubs, &c. 32mo, cloth, 1s.
 WALFORD'S COMPLETE PEERAGE, BARONETAGE, KNIGHTAGE, AND HOUSE OF COMMONS (1893). Royal 32mo, cloth extra, gilt edges, 5s.
 TALES OF OUR GREAT FAMILIES. Crown 8vo, cloth extra, 3s. 6d.

**WEATHER, HOW TO FORETELL THE, WITH POCKET SPEC-**
 TROSCOPE. By F. W. Cory. With 10 Illustrations. Cr. 8vo, 1s.; cloth, 1s. 6d.

**WESTALL (William).—TRUST-MONEY.** Three Vols., crown 8vo.

**WHIST.—HOW TO PLAY SOLO WHIST.** By Abraham S. Wilks and Charles F. Pardon. New Edition. Post 8vo, cloth limp, 2s.

**WHITE.—THE NATURAL HISTORY OF SELBORNE.** By Gilbert White, M.A. Post 8vo, printed on laid paper and half-bound, 2s.

**WILLIAMS (W. MATTIEU, F.R.A.S.), WORKS BY.**
 SCIENCE IN SHORT CHAPTERS. Crown 8vo, cloth extra, 7s. 6d.
 A SIMPLE TREATISE ON HEAT. With Illusts. Cr. 8vo, cloth limp, 2s. 6d.
 THE CHEMISTRY OF COOKERY. Crown 8vo, cloth extra, 6s.
 THE CHEMISTRY OF IRON AND STEEL MAKING. Crown 8vo, cloth extra, 9s.

**WILLIAMSON (MRS. F. H.).—A CHILD WIDOW.** Post 8vo, bds., 2s.

**WILSON (DR. ANDREW, F.R.S.E.), WORKS BY.**
 CHAPTERS ON EVOLUTION. With 259 Illustrations. Cr. 8vo, cloth extra, 7s. 6d.
 LEAVES FROM A NATURALIST'S NOTE-BOOK. Post 8vo, cloth limp, 2s. 6d.
 LEISURE-TIME STUDIES. With Illustrations. Crown 8vo, cloth extra, 6s.
 STUDIES IN LIFE AND SENSE. With numerous Illusts. Cr. 8vo, cl. ex., 6s.
 COMMON ACCIDENTS: HOW TO TREAT THEM. Illusts. Cr. 8vo, 1s.; cl., 1s. 6d.
 GLIMPSES OF NATURE. With 35 Illustrations. Crown 8vo, cloth extra, 3s. 6d.

**WINTER (J. S.), STORIES BY.** Post 8vo, illustrated boards, 2s. each; cloth limp, 2s. 6d. each.
 CAVALRY LIFE.                     | REGIMENTAL LEGENDS.
 A SOLDIER'S CHILDREN. With 34 Illustrations by E. G. Thomson and E. Stuart Hardy. Crown 8vo, cloth extra, 3s. 6d.

**WISSMANN.—MY SECOND JOURNEY THROUGH EQUATORIAL**
 AFRICA. By Hermann von Wissmann. With 92 Illusts. Demy 8vo, 16s.

**WOOD.—SABINA: A Novel.** By Lady Wood. Post 8vo, boards, 2s.

**WOOD (H. F.), DETECTIVE STORIES BY.** Cr. 8vo, 6s. ea.; post 8vo, bds. 2s.
 PASSENGER FROM SCOTLAND YARD. | ENGLISHMAN OF THE RUE CAIN.

**WOOLLEY.—RACHEL ARMSTRONG;** or, Love and Theology. By Celia Parker Woolley. Post 8vo, illustrated boards, 2s.; cloth, 2s. 6d.

**WRIGHT (THOMAS), WORKS BY.** Crown 8vo, cloth extra, 7s. 6d. each.
 CARICATURE HISTORY OF THE GEORGES. With 400 Caricatures, Squibs, &c.
 HISTORY OF CARICATURE AND OF THE GROTESQUE IN ART, LITERA-TURE, SCULPTURE, AND PAINTING. Illustrated by F. W. Fairholt, F.S.A.

**WYNMAN.—MY FLIRTATIONS.** By Margaret Wynman. With 13 Illustrations by J. Bernard Partridge. Crown 8vo, cloth extra, 3s. 6d.

**YATES (EDMUND), NOVELS BY.** Post 8vo, illustrated boards, 2s. each.
 LAND AT LAST.      |      THE FORLORN HOPE.  | CASTAWAY.

**ZOLA (EMILE), NOVELS BY.** Crown 8vo, cloth extra, 3s. 6d. each.
 THE DOWNFALL. Translated by E. A. Vizetelly. Third Edition.
 THE DREAM. Translated by Eliza Chase. With 8 Illustrations by Jeanniot.

## LISTS OF BOOKS CLASSIFIED IN SERIES.

*.* *For fuller cataloguing, see alphabetical arrangement, pp. 1-25.*

### THE MAYFAIR LIBRARY. Post 8vo, cloth limp, **2s. 6d.** per Volume.

A Journey Round My Room. By XAVIER DE MAISTRE.
Quips and Quiddities. By W. D. ADAMS.
The Agony Column of "The Times."
Melancholy Anatomised: Abridgment of "Burton's Anatomy of Melancholy."
The Speeches of Charles Dickens.
Poetical Ingenuities. By W. T. DOBSON.
The Cupboard Papers. By FIN-BEC.
W. S. Gilbert's Plays. FIRST SERIES.
W. S. Gilbert's Plays. SECOND SERIES.
Songs of Irish Wit and Humour.
Animals and Masters. By Sir A. HELPS.
Social Pressure. By Sir A. HELPS.
Curiosities of Criticism. H. J. JENNINGS.
Holmes's Autocrat of Breakfast-Table.
Pencil and Palette. By R. KEMPT.
Little Essays: from LAMB's Letters.

Forensic Anecdotes. By JACOB LARWOOD.
Theatrical Anecdotes. JACOB LARWOOD.
Jeux d'Esprit. Edited by HENRY S. LEIGH.
Witch Stories. By E. LYNN LINTON.
Ourselves. By E. LYNN LINTON.
Pastimes & Players. By R. MACGREGOR.
New Paul and Virginia. W. H. MALLOCK.
New Republic. By W. H. MALLOCK.
Puck on Pegasus. By H. C. PENNELL.
Pegasus Re-Saddled. By H. C. PENNELL.
Muses of Mayfair. Ed. H. C. PENNELL.
Thoreau: His Life & Aims. By H. A. PAGE.
Puniana. By Hon. HUGH ROWLEY.
More Puniana. By Hon. HUGH ROWLEY.
The Philosophy of Handwriting.
By Stream and Sea. By WM. SENIOR.
Leaves from a Naturalist's Note-Book. By Dr. ANDREW WILSON.

### THE GOLDEN LIBRARY. Post 8vo, cloth limp, **2s.** per Volume.

Bayard Taylor's Diversions of the Echo Club.
Bennett's Ballad History of England.
Bennett's Songs for Sailors.
Godwin's Lives of the Necromancers.
Pope's Poetical Works.
Holmes's Autocrat of Breakfast Table.

Jesse's Scenes of Country Life.
Leigh Hunt's Tale for a Chimney Corner.
Mallory's Mort d'Arthur: Selections.
Pascal's Provincial Letters.
Rochefoucauld's Maxims & Reflections.

### THE WANDERER'S LIBRARY. Crown 8vo, cloth extra, **3s. 6d.** each.

Wanderings in Patagonia. By JULIUS BEERBOHM. Illustrated.
Camp Notes. By FREDERICK BOYLE.
Savage Life. By FREDERICK BOYLE.
Merrie England in the Olden Time. By G. DANIEL. Illustrated by CRUIKSHANK.
Circus Life. By THOMAS FROST.
Lives of the Conjurers. THOMAS FROST.
The Old Showmen and the Old London Fairs. By THOMAS FROST.
Low-Life Deeps. By JAMES GREENWOOD.

Wilds of London. JAMES GREENWOOD.
Tunis. Chev. HESSE-WARTEGG. 22 Illusts.
Life and Adventures of a Cheap Jack.
World Behind the Scenes. P. FITZGERALD.
Tavern Anecdotes and Sayings.
The Genial Showman. By E. P. HINGSTON
Story of London Parks. JACOB LARWOOD.
London Characters. By HENRY MAYHEW.
Seven Generations of Executioners.
Summer Cruising in the South Seas. By C. WARREN STODDARD. Illustrated.

### POPULAR SHILLING BOOKS.

Harry Fludyer at Cambridge.
Jeff Briggs's Love Story. BRET HARTE.
Twins of Table Mountain. BRET HARTE.
Snow-bound at Eagle's. By BRET HARTE.
A Day's Tour. By PERCY FITZGERALD.
Esther's Glove. By R. E. FRANCILLON.
Sentenced! By SOMERVILLE GIBNEY.
The Professor's Wife. By L. GRAHAM.
Mrs. Gainsborough's Diamonds. By JULIAN HAWTHORNE.
Niagara Spray. By J. HOLLINGSHEAD.
A Romance of the Queen's Hounds. By CHARLES JAMES.
Garden that Paid Rent. TOM JERROLD.
Cut by the Mess. By ARTHUR KEYSER.
Teresa Itasca. By A. MACALPINE.
Our Sensation Novel. J. H. MCCARTHY.
Doom! By JUSTIN H. MCCARTHY.
Dolly. By JUSTIN H. MCCARTHY.

Lily Lass. JUSTIN H. MCCARTHY.
Was She Good or Bad? By W. MINTO.
Notes from the "News." By JAS. PAYN.
Beyond the Gates. By E. S. PHELPS.
Old Maid's Paradise. By E. S. PHELPS.
Burglars in Paradise. By E. S. PHELPS.
Jack the Fisherman. By E. S. PHELPS.
Trooping with Crows. By C. L. PIRKIS.
Bible Characters. By CHARLES READE.
Rogues. By R. H. SHERARD.
The Dagonet Reciter. By G. R. SIMS.
How the Poor Live. By G. R. SIMS.
Case of George Candlemas. G. R. SIMS.
Sandycroft Mystery. T. W. SPEIGHT.
Hoodwinked. By T. W. SPEIGHT.
Father Damien. By R. L. STEVENSON.
A Double Bond. By LINDA VILLARI.
My Life with Stanley's Rear Guard. By HERBERT WARD.

### HANDY NOVELS. Fcap. 8vo, cloth boards, **1s. 6d.** each.

The Old Maid's Sweetheart. A. ST. AUBYN
Modest Little Sara. ALAN ST. AUBYN.

Taken from the Enemy. H. NEWBOLT.
A Lost Soul. By W. L. ALDEN.

The Seven Sleepers of Ephesus. By M. E. COLERIDGE.

## MY LIBRARY.

Choice Works, printed on laid paper, bound half-Roxburghe, **2s. 6d.** each.

Four Frenchwomen. By AUSTIN DOBSON.

Citation and Examination of William Shakspeare. By W. S. LANDOR.

Tho Journal of Maurice de Guerin.

Christie Johnstone. By CHARLES READE. With a Photogravure Frontispiece.

Peg Woffington. By CHARLES READE.

The Dramatic Essays of Charles Lamb.

## THE POCKET LIBRARY. Post 8vo, printed on laid paper and hf.-bd., **2s.** each.

The Essays of Elia. By CHARLES LAMB.

Robinson Crusoe. Edited by JOHN MAJOR. With 37 Illusts. by GEORGE CRUIKSHANK.

Whims and Oddities. By THOMAS HOOD. With 85 Illustrations.

The Barber's Chair, and The Hedgehog Letters. By DOUGLAS JERROLD.

Gastronomy. By BRILLAT-SAVARIN.

The Epicurean, &c. By THOMAS MOORE.

Leigh Hunt's Essays. Ed. E. OLLIER.

White's Natural History of Selborne.

Gulliver's Travels, and The Tale of a Tub. By Dean SWIFT.

The Rivals, School for Scandal, and other Plays by RICHARD BRINSLEY SHERIDAN.

Anecdotes of the Clergy. J. LARWOOD.

Thomson's Seasons. Illustrated.

The Autocrat of the Breakfast-Table and The Professor at the Breakfast-Table. By OLIVER WENDELL HOLMES.

# THE PICCADILLY NOVELS.

LIBRARY EDITIONS OF NOVELS, many Illustrated, crown 8vo, cloth extra, **3s. 6d.** each.

### By F. M. ALLEN.
Green as Grass.

### By GRANT ALLEN.
Philistia.　　The Tents of Shem.
Babylon.　　For Maimie's Sake.
Strange Stories.　　The Devil's Die.
Beckoning Hand.　　This Mortal Coil.
In all Shades.　　The Great Taboo.
Dumaresq's Daughter. | Blood Royal.
The Duchess of Powysland.

### By EDWIN L. ARNOLD.
Phra the Phoenician.

### By ALAN ST. AUBYN.
A Fellow of Trinity.

### By Rev. S. BARING GOULD.
Red Spider.　　| Eve.

### By W. BESANT & J. RICE.
My Little Girl.　　By Celia's Arbour.
Case of Mr. Lucraft.　　Monks of Thelema.
This Son of Vulcan.　　The Seamy Side.
Golden Butterfly.　　Ten Years' Tenant.
Ready-Money Mortiboy.
With Harp and Crown.
'Twas in Trafalgar's Bay.
The Chaplain of the Fleet.

### By WALTER BESANT.
All Sorts and Conditions of Men.
The Captains' Room. | Herr Paulus.
All in a Garden Fair
The World Went Very Well Then.
For Faith and Freedom.
Dorothy Forster.　　The Holy Rose.
Uncle Jack.　　Armorel of Lyon-
Children of Gibeon.　　esse.
Bell of St. Paul's.　　St. Katherine's by
To Call Her Mine.　　the Tower.

### By ROBERT BUCHANAN.
The Shadow of the Sword. | Matt.
A Child of Nature. | Heir of Linne.
The Martyrdom of Madeline.
God and the Man. | The New Abelard.
Love Me for Ever. | Foxglove Manor.
Annan Water. | Master of the Mine.

### By HALL CAINE.
The Shadow of a Crime.
A Son of Hagar. | The Deemster.

### MORT. & FRANCES COLLINS.
Transmigration.
From Midnight to Midnight.
Blacksmith and Scholar.
Village Comedy. | You Play Me False.

### By WILKIE COLLINS.
Armadale.　　The Frozen Deep.
After Dark.　　The Two Destinies.
No Name.　　Law and the Lady.
Antonina. | Basil.　　Haunted Hotel.
Hide and Seek.　　The Fallen Leaves.
The Dead Secret.　　Jezebel's Daughter.
Queen of Hearts.　　The Black Robe.
My Miscellanies.　　Heart and Science.
Woman in White.　　"I Say No."
The Moonstone.　　Little Novels.
Man and Wife.　　The Evil Genius.
Poor Miss Finch.　　The Legacy of Cain.
Miss or Mrs?　　A Rogue's Life.
New Magdalen.　　Blind Love.

### By DUTTON COOK.
Paul Foster's Daughter.

### By MATT CRIM.
Adventures of a Fair Rebel.

### By B. M. CROKER.
Diana Barrington. | Pretty Miss Neville.
Proper Pride. | A Bird of Passage.

### By WILLIAM CYPLES.
Hearts of Gold.

### By ALPHONSE DAUDET.
The Evangelist; or, Port Salvation.

### By ERASMUS DAWSON.
The Fountain of Youth.

### By JAMES DE MILLE.
A Castle in Spain.

### By J. LEITH DERWENT.
Our Lady of Tears. | Circe's Lovers.

### By DICK DONOVAN.
Tracked to Doom.

### By Mrs. ANNIE EDWARDES.
Archie Lovell.

### By G. MANVILLE FENN.
The New Mistress.

### By PERCY FITZGERALD.
Fatal Zero.

### By R. E. FRANCILLON.
Queen Cophetua. | A Real Queen.
One by One. | King or Knave

### Pref. by Sir BARTLE FRERE.
Pandurang Hari.

**THE PICCADILLY (3/6) NOVELS—*continued.***

**By EDWARD GARRETT.**
The Capel Girls.

**By CHARLES GIBBON.**
Robin Gray. | The Golden Shaft.
Loving a Dream. | Of High Degree.
The Flower of the Forest.

**By E. GLANVILLE.**
The Lost Heiress. | The Fossicker.

**By CECIL GRIFFITH.**
Corinthia Marazion.

**By THOMAS HARDY.**
Under the Greenwood Tree.

**By BRET HARTE.**
A Waif of the Plains.
A Ward of the Golden Gate.
A Sappho of Green Springs.
Colonel Starbottle's Client.
Susy. | Sally Dows.

**By JULIAN HAWTHORNE.**
Garth. | Dust.
Ellice Quentin. | Fortune's Fool.
Sebastian Strome. | Beatrix Randolph.
David Poindexter's Disappearance.
The Spectre of the Camera.

**By Sir A. HELPS.**
Ivan de Biron.

**By ISAAC HENDERSON.**
Agatha Page.

**By Mrs. ALFRED HUNT.**
The Leaden Casket. | Self-Condemned.
That other Person.

**By R. ASHE KING.**
A Drawn Game.
"The Wearing of the Green."

**By E. LYNN LINTON.**
Patricia Kemball. | Ione.
Under which Lord? | Paston Carew.
"My Love!" | Sowing the Wind.
The Atonement of Leam Dundas.
The World Well Lost.

**By HENRY W. LUCY.**
Gideon Fleyce.

**By JUSTIN McCARTHY.**
A Fair Saxon. | Donna Quixote.
Linley Rochford. | Maid of Athens.
Miss Misanthrope. | Camiola.
The Waterdale Neighbours.
My Enemy's Daughter.
Dear Lady Disdain.
The Comet of a Season.

**By AGNES MACDONELL.**
Quaker Cousins.

**By D. CHRISTIE MURRAY.**
Life's Atonement. | Val Strange.
Joseph's Coat. | Hearts.
Coals of Fire. | A Model Father.
Old Blazer's Hero.
By the Gate of the Sea.
A Bit of Human Nature.
First Person Singular. | Cynic Fortune.
The Way of the World.

**By MURRAY & HERMAN.**
The Bishops' Bible.
Paul Jones's Alias.

**By HUME NISBET.**
"Bail Up!"

**By GEORGES OHNET.**
A Weird Gift.

**By Mrs. OLIPHANT.**
Whiteladies.

**THE PICCADILLY (3/6) NOVELS—*continued.***

**By OUIDA.**
Held in Bondage. | Two Little Wooden
Strathmore. | Shoes.
Chandos. | In a Winter City.
Under Two Flags. | Ariadne.
Idalia. | Friendship.
CecilCastlemaine's | Moths. | Ruffino.
Gage. | Pipistrello.
Tricotrin. | Puck. | AVillageCommune
Folle Farine. | Bimbi. | Wanda.
A Dog of Flanders. | Frescoes. | Othmar.
Pascarel. | Signa. | In Maremma.
Princess Naprax- | Syrlin. | Guilderoy.
ine. | Santa Barbara.

**By MARGARET A. PAUL.**
Gentle and Simple.

**By JAMES PAYN.**
Lost Sir Massingberd.
Less Black than We're Painted.
A Confidential Agent.
A Grape from a Thorn.
In Peril and Privation.
The Mystery of Mirbridge.
The Canon's Ward.
Walter's Word. | Talk of the Town
By Proxy. | Holiday Tasks.
High Spirits. | The Burnt Million.
Under One Roof. | The Word and the
From Exile. | Will.
Glow-worm Tales. | Sunny Stories.

**By E. C. PRICE.**
Valentina. | The Foreigners.
Mrs. Lancaster's Rival.

**By RICHARD PRYCE.**
Miss Maxwell's Affections.

**By CHARLES READE.**
It is Never Too Late to Mend.
The Double Marriage.
Love Me Little, Love Me Long.
The Cloister and the Hearth.
The Course of True Love.
The Autobiography of a Thief.
Put Yourself in his Place.
A Terrible Temptation.
Singleheart and Doubleface.
Good Stories of Men and other Animals.
Hard Cash. | Wandering Heir.
Peg Woffington. | A Woman-Hater.
ChristieJohnstone. | A Simpleton.
Griffith Gaunt. | Readiana.
Foul Play. | The Jilt.
A Perilous Secret.

**By Mrs. J. H. RIDDELL.**
The Prince of Wales's Garden Party.
Weird Stories.

**By F. W. ROBINSON.**
Women are Strange.
The Hands of Justice.

**By W. CLARK RUSSELL.**
An Ocean Tragedy.
My Shipmate Louise.
Alone on a Wide Wide Sea.

**By JOHN SAUNDERS.**
Guy Waterman. | Two Dreamers.
Bound to the Wheel.
The Lion in the Path.

**By KATHARINE SAUNDERS**
Margaret and Elizabeth.
Gideon's Rock. | Heart Salvage.
The High Mills. | Sebastian.

THE PICCADILLY (3/6) NOVELS—*continued.*
### By LUKE SHARP.
In a Steamer Chair.
### By HAWLEY SMART.
Without Love or Licence.
### By R. A. STERNDALE.
The Afghan Knife.
### By BERTHA THOMAS.
Proud Maisie. | The Violin-player.
### By FRANCES E. TROLLOPE.
Like Ships upon the Sea.
Anne Furness. | Mabel's Progress.
### By IVAN TURGENIEFF, &c.
Stories from Foreign Novelists.

THE PICCADILLY (3/6) NOVELS—*continued.*
### By ANTHONY TROLLOPE.
Frau Frohmann. | Kept in the Dark.
Marion Fay. | Land-Leaguers.
The Way We Live Now.
Mr. Scarborough's Family.
### By C. C. FRASER-TYTLER.
Mistress Judith.
### By SARAH TYTLER.
The Bride's Pass. | Lady Bell.
Buried Diamonds.
The Blackhall Ghosts.
### By MARK TWAIN.
The American Claimant.
### By J. S. WINTER.
A Soldier's Children.

# CHEAP EDITIONS OF POPULAR NOVELS.
Post 8vo, illustrated boards, 2s. each.

### By ARTEMUS WARD.
Artemus Ward Complete.
### By EDMOND ABOUT.
The Fellah.
### By HAMILTON AIDE.
Carr of Carrlyon. | Confidences.
### By MARY ALBERT.
Brooke Finchley's Daughter.
### By Mrs. ALEXANDER.
Maid, Wife, or Widow? | Valerie' Fate.
### By GRANT ALLEN.
Strange Stories. | The Devil's Die.
Philistia. | This Mortal Coil.
Babylon. | In all Shades.
The Beckoning Hand.
For Maimie's Sake. | Tents of Shem.
Great Taboo. | Dumaresq's Daughter.
### By E. LESTER ARNOLD.
Phra the Phœnician.
### By ALAN ST. AUBYN.
A Fellow of Trinity. | The Junior Dean.
### By Rev. S. BARING GOULD.
Red Spider. | Eve.
### By FRANK BARRETT.
Fettered for Life.
Between Life and Death.
The Sin of Olga Zassoulich.
Folly Morrison. | Honest Davie.
Lieut. Barnabas. | A Prodigal's Progress.
Found Guilty. | A Recoiling Vengeance.
For Love and Honour.
John Ford; and His Helpmate.
Little Lady Linton.
### By W. BESANT & J. RICE.
This Son of Vulcan. | By Celia's Arbour.
My Little Girl. | Monks of Thelema.
Case of Mr. Lucraft. | The Seamy Side.
Golden Butterfly. | Ten Years' Tenant.
Ready-Money Mortiboy.
With Harp and Crown.
'Twas in Trafalgar's Bay.
The Chaplain of the Fleet.
### By SHELSLEY BEAUCHAMP.
Grantley Grange.
### By AMBROSE BIERCE.
In the Midst of Life.
### By FREDERICK BOYLE.
Camp Notes. | Savage Life.
Chronicles of No-man's Land.

### By WALTER BESANT.
Dorothy Forster. | Uncle Jack.
Children of Gibeon. | Herr Paulus.
All Sorts and Conditions of Men.
The Captains' Room.
All in a Garden Fair.
The World Went Very Well Then.
For Faith and Freedom.
To Call Her Mine.
The Bell of St. Paul's. | The Holy Rose.
Armorel of Lyonesse.
St. Katherine's by the Tower.
### By BRET HARTE.
Californian Stories. | Gabriel Conroy.
An Heiress of Red Dog. | Flip.
The Luck of Roaring Camp. | Maruja.
A Phyllis of the Sierras.
### By HAROLD BRYDGES.
Uncle Sam at Home.
### By ROBERT BUCHANAN.
The Shadow of the Sword. | The Martyrdom of Madeline.
A Child of Nature. | Annan Water.
God and the Man. | The New Abelard.
Love Me for Ever. | Matt.
Foxglove Manor. | The Heir of Linne.
The Master of the Mine.
### By HALL CAINE.
The Shadow of a Crime.
A Son of Hagar. | The Deemster.
### By Commander CAMERON.
The Cruise of the "Black Prince."
### By Mrs. LOVETT CAMERON.
Deceivers Ever. | Juliet's Guardian.
### By AUSTIN CLARE.
For the Love of a Lass.
### By Mrs. ARCHER CLIVE.
Paul Ferroll.
Why Paul Ferroll Killed his Wife.
### By MACLAREN COBBAN.
The Cure of Souls.
### By C. ALLSTON COLLINS.
The Bar Sinister.
### MORT. & FRANCES COLLINS.
Sweet Anne Page. | Transmigration.
From Midnight to Midnight.
Fight with Fortune. | Village Comedy.
Sweet and Twenty. | You Play me False.
Blacksmith and Scholar. | Frances.

Two-Shilling Novels—*continued.*

**By WILKIE COLLINS.**

| | |
|---|---|
| Armadale. | My Miscellanies. |
| After Dark. | Woman in White. |
| No Name. | The Moonstone. |
| Antonina. \| Basil. | Man and Wife. |
| Hide and Seek. | Poor Miss Finch. |
| The Dead Secret. | The Fallen Leaves. |
| Queen of Hearts. | Jezebel's Daughter |
| Miss or Mrs? | The Black Robe. |
| New Magdalen. | Heart and Science. |
| The Frozen Deep. | "I Say No." |
| Law and the Lady. | The Evil Genius. |
| The Two Destinies. | Little Novels. |
| Haunted Hotel. | Legacy of Cain. |
| A Rogue's Life. | Blind Love. |

**By M. J. COLQUHOUN.**

Every Inch a Soldier.

**By DUTTON COOK.**

| | |
|---|---|
| Leo. | Paul Foster's Daughter. |

**By C. EGBERT CRADDOCK.**

Prophet of the Great Smoky Mountains.

**By MATT CRIM.**

Adventures of a Fair Rebel.

**By B. M. CROKER.**

| | |
|---|---|
| Pretty Miss Neville. | Bird of Passage. |
| Diana Barrington. | Proper Pride. |

**By WILLIAM CYPLES.**

Hearts of Gold.

**By ALPHONSE DAUDET.**

The Evangelist; or, Port Salvation.

**By ERASMUS DAWSON.**

The Fountain of Youth.

**By JAMES DE MILLE.**

A Castle in Spain.

**By J. LEITH DERWENT.**

| | |
|---|---|
| Our Lady of Tears. | Circe's Lovers. |

**By CHARLES DICKENS.**

| | |
|---|---|
| Sketches by Boz. | Oliver Twist. |
| Pickwick Papers. | Nicholas Nickleby. |

**By DICK DONOVAN.**

| | |
|---|---|
| The Man-Hunter. | Caught at Last! |
| Tracked and Taken. | Wanted! |

Who Poisoned Hetty Duncan?
The Man from Manchester.
A Detective's Triumphs.
In the Grip of the Law.
From Information Received.
Tracked to Doom.

**By Mrs. ANNIE EDWARDES.**

| | |
|---|---|
| A Point of Honour. | Archie Lovell. |

**By M. BETHAM-EDWARDS.**

| | |
|---|---|
| Felicia. | Kitty. |

**By EDWARD EGGLESTON.**

Roxy.

**By G. MANVILLE FENN.**

The New Mistress.

**By PERCY FITZGERALD.**

| | |
|---|---|
| Bella Donna. | Polly. |
| Never Forgotten. | Fatal Zero. |

The Second Mrs. Tillotson.
Seventy-five Brooke Street.
The Lady of Brantome.

**By PERCY FITZGERALD**
**and others.**

Strange Secrets.

**ALBANY DE FONBLANQUE.**

Filthy Lucre.

**By R. E. FRANCILLON.**

| | |
|---|---|
| Olympia. | Queen Cophetua. |
| One by One. | King or Knave? |
| A Real Queen. | Romances of Law. |

Two-Shilling Novels—*continued.*

**By HAROLD FREDERICK.**

Seth's Brother's Wife.
The Lawton Girl.

**Pref. by Sir BARTLE FRERE.**

Pandurang Hari.

**By HAIN FRISWELL.**

One of Two.

**By EDWARD GARRETT.**

The Capel Girls.

**By CHARLES GIBBON.**

| | |
|---|---|
| Robin Gray. | In Honour Bound. |
| Fancy Free. | Flower of Forest. |
| For Lack of Gold. | Braes of Yarrow. |
| What will the | The Golden Shaft. |
|   World Say? | Of High Degree. |
| In Love and War. | Mead and Stream. |
| For the King. | Loving a Dream. |
| In Pastures Green. | A Hard Knot. |
| Queen of Meadow. | Heart's Delight. |
| A Heart's Problem. | Blood-Money. |
| The Dead Heart. | |

**By WILLIAM GILBERT.**

| | |
|---|---|
| Dr. Austin's Guests. | James Duke. |

The Wizard of the Mountain.

**By ERNEST GLANVILLE.**

| | |
|---|---|
| The Lost Heiress. | The Fossicker. |

**By HENRY GREVILLE.**

| | |
|---|---|
| A Noble Woman. | Nikanor. |

**By JOHN HABBERTON.**

| | |
|---|---|
| Brueton's Bayou. | Country Luck. |

**By ANDREW HALLIDAY.**

Every-Day Papers.

**By Lady DUFFUS HARDY.**

Paul Wynter's Sacrifice.

**By THOMAS HARDY.**

Under the Greenwood Tree.

**By J. BERWICK HARWOOD.**

The Tenth Earl.

**By JULIAN HAWTHORNE.**

| | |
|---|---|
| Garth. | Sebastian Strome. |
| Ellice Quentin. | Dust. |
| Fortune's Fool. | Beatrix Randolph. |
| Miss Cadogna. | Love—or a Name. |

David Poindexter's Disappearance.
The Spectre of the Camera.

**By Sir ARTHUR HELPS.**

Ivan de Biron.

**By HENRY HERMAN.**

A Leading Lady.

**By Mrs. CASHEL HOEY.**

The Lover's Creed.

**By Mrs. GEORGE HOOPER.**

The House of Raby.

**By TIGHE HOPKINS.**

'Twixt Love and Duty.

**By Mrs. HUNGERFORD.**

A Maiden all Forlorn.

| | |
|---|---|
| In Durance Vile. | A Mental Struggle |
| Marvel. | A Modern Circe. |

**By Mrs. ALFRED HUNT.**

| | |
|---|---|
| Thornicroft's Model. | Self-Condemned. |
| That Other Person. | Leaden Casket. |

**By JEAN INGELOW.**

Fated to be Free.

**By HARRIETT JAY**

The Dark Colleen.
The Queen of Connaught.

**By MARK KERSHAW.**

Colonial Facts and Fictions.